MW01278335

Microsoft Dynamics AX 2009 Administration

A practical and efficient approach to planning, installing, and configuring your Dynamics AX 2009 environment

Marco Carvalho

[PACKT] enterprise
PUBLISHING
professional expertise distilled

BIRMINGHAM - MUMBAI

Microsoft Dynamics AX 2009 Administration

Copyright © 2011 Packt Publishing

All rights reserved. No part of this book may be reproduced, stored in a retrieval system, or transmitted in any form or by any means, without the prior written permission of the publisher, except in the case of brief quotations embedded in critical articles or reviews.

Every effort has been made in the preparation of this book to ensure the accuracy of the information presented. However, the information contained in this book is sold without warranty, either expressed or implied. Neither the author, nor Packt Publishing, and its dealers and distributors will be held liable for any damages caused or alleged to be caused directly or indirectly by this book.

Packt Publishing has endeavored to provide trademark information about all of the companies and products mentioned in this book by the appropriate use of capitals. However, Packt Publishing cannot guarantee the accuracy of this information.

First published: January 2011

Production Reference: 2170111

Published by Packt Publishing Ltd.
32 Lincoln Road
Olton
Birmingham, B27 6PA, UK.

ISBN 978-1-847197-84-9

www.packtpub.com

Cover Image by Vinayak Chittar (vinayak.chittar@gmail.com)

Credits

Author
Marco Carvalho

Reviewers
Harish Mohan
Mohammed Rasheed
Dick Wenning

Acquisition Editor
Kerry George

Development Editor
Kerry George

Technical Editors
Arun Nadar
Bianca Sequeira

Copy Editor
Laxmi Subramanian

Indexers
Monica Ajmera Mehta
Rekha Nair

Editorial Team Leader
Aditya Belpathak

Project Team Leader
Lata Basantani

Project Coordinator
Leena Purkait

Proofreader
Aaron Nash

Production Coordinator
Alwin Roy

Cover Work
Alwin Roy

About the Author

Marco Carvalho has over 13 years' experience in the software development and IT industry. He started working with Dynamics AX in 2003 and has since been exclusively developing and implementing solutions for Dynamics AX. Among many other things, he has pioneered along with Microsoft and various ISVs the integration of Dynamics AX with proprietary and third party systems. He has also developed unique solutions that integrate Dynamics AX with Mobile and other .NET technologies. He enjoys educating organizations and training developers on Dynamics AX. He has also held senior and management level positions as well as manage his own Microsoft partner company.

During his free time, he enjoys producing music, walking in nature, spending time with close friends and families and reading about quantum physics and ancient history.

As with any other book, the job of the author is only a portion of the entire creation of a book, and I personally would like to extend my gratitude to my editors, projects managers, proof readers and very experienced reviewers for making this book a reality. I would like to thank my family who have been positive and unconditional supporters. I would also like to thank my daughter, who is one of the greatest teachers in my life. I would also like to thank my clients and colleagues with whom I have worked through the years that have provided opportunities for me to expand my knowledge and shape my career.

About the Reviewers

Harish Mohanbabu has over 12 years of consulting experience in a variety of roles including developer, lead developer, design authority, and technical architect in Dynamics AX and Microsoft technologies. He was nominated as a Microsoft MVP in recognition of his contribution to the Dynamics AX community. He is also the technical editor of two books on Dynamics AX, including PacktPub's 'Microsoft Dynamics AX 2009 Programming: Getting started'. Harish lives in Hertfordshire, England with his wife, Chelvy and their two children, Swetha and Rahul. He can be contacted via his web sites, `www.harishm.com`, `www.harish-m.livejournal.com` and you can follow his tweets on `www.twitter.com/HarishM`.

Mohammed Rasheed is a Solutions Architect at Junction Solutions UK (`www.Junctionsolutions.co.uk`) where he is responsible for the delivery of integrations and customizations on Dynamics AX. Junction Solutions are the most exciting Microsoft Dynamics AX Partner for retail, with over 40 successful implementations across the world and a retail solution that has been certified by Microsoft for quality. Junction Solutions' innovative multi-channel retail software was built on Dynamics AX to resolve the unique challenges of 21st century retailers, who trade across many channels including stores, web online, mail order, franchise, wholesale, and direct sales. Junction Solutions bring these channels together and provide modern retailers with a holistic view of their business, enabling them to develop new revenue opportunities, drive better customer service, and deliver improved profitability.

Junction Solutions was also named The Microsoft Dynamics Retail Partner of the Year in the 2010 Microsoft Partner Awards. Mohammed has a double masters in Dynamics AX with over 8 certifications on Dynamics AX. Though his strengths are rooted in x++ development, he is a highly regarded Generalist and has solid knowledge of both functional and technical aspects of Dynamics AX. His passion for development is evident in the fact that he takes pleasure from refactoring and optimizing x++ code.

Mohammed lives with his family in Chester(UK)and blogs on his website: `www.dynamic-ax.co.uk`.

Dick Wenning studied Computer Science in the Netherlands. After completing his education he has developed software for the medical and telecom industries, and local government.

Dick started working in 2001 for Navision Netherlands, where he was giving technical training and managing escalations at partner support. He became a member of the localisation team of Dynamics AX when Navision became part of Microsoft.

His career continued for a short period at Watermark and for the last few years Dick has been working for Crimsonwing Promentum, where he's part of a skilled team responsible for ramping up Partners on Dynamics AX. Dick specialized himself in performance and integration with Dynamics AX and he's frequently asked to consult partners and also Microsoft in Europe.

In his spare time, Dick is running his blog `axstart.spaces.live.com` and is a frequent speaker at technical seminars in Western Europe; this commitment has been recognized and rewarded by Microsoft with the MVP award. Dick is also a Microsoft Certified Trainer (MCT) for Dynamics AX development and installation.

Beside these activities on AX, Dick is married with Inge and has two kids, Marleen and Ruben. Dick is also a regular chess and tennis player, and you can challenge him on `playchess.com`.

www.PacktPub.com

Support files, eBooks, discount offers and more

You might want to visit www.PacktPub.com for support files and downloads related to your book.

Did you know that Packt offers eBook versions of every book published, with PDF and ePub files available? You can upgrade to the eBook version at www.PacktPub.com and as a print book customer, you are entitled to a discount on the eBook copy. Get in touch with us at service@packtpub.com for more details.

At www.PacktPub.com, you can also read a collection of free technical articles, sign up for a range of free newsletters and receive exclusive discounts and offers on Packt books and eBooks.

http://PacktLib.PacktPub.com

Do you need instant solutions to your IT questions? PacktLib is Packt's online digital book library. Here, you can access, read and search across Packt's entire library of books.

Why Subscribe?

- Fully searchable across every book published by Packt
- Copy & paste, print and bookmark content
- On demand and accessible via web browser

Free Access for Packt account holders

If you have an account with Packt at www.PacktPub.com, you can use this to access PacktLib today and view nine entirely free books. Simply use your login credentials for immediate access.

Instant Updates on New Packt Books

Get notified! Find out when new books are published by following @PacktEnterprise on Twitter, or the *Packt Enterprise* Facebook page.

Table of Contents

Preface

Microsoft Dynamics AX 2009 is an advanced Enterprise Resource Planning system, essentially a comprehensive business management solution, designed for midsize and large organizations. Dynamics AX provides a centralized source for business data and enables you to consolidate and standardize your business processes, helping to improve productivity and provide visibility across your organization, for a variety of business needs.

This book will enable you to successfully set up and configure Dynamics AX 2009 into your business with clear, practical, step-by-step demonstrations. You will learn how to plan and implement Dynamics AX 2009 efficiently, how to manage the Enterprise Portal, Role Centers, Kerberos Authentication, Workflow, Application Integration Framework (AIF), and much more.

This practical tutorial shows you how to set up and configure Dynamics AX 2009 into your business and then how to improve and maintain its performance. Each chapter of the book explores the different aspects of administrating and configuring Dynamics AX 2009 to fit any company's needs.

The book begins by introducing you to the important process of planning and implementing Dynamics AX 2009, providing the basic components to get you started with your Dynamics AX environment.

It then deep dives into the installation of the multi-component server of Dynamics AX and how to get it up and running efficiently, specifically the Base Server Components, Enterprise Portal, Role Centers, Kerberos Authentication, Workflow, and the Application Integration Framework (AIF).

Other content includes the actual usage of Microsoft Dynamics AX 2009, the process of importing data into your Dynamics AX 2009 instance, common user administration functions, and Alerts and Notifications.

Finally, the book will consider how to enhance your Dynamics AX environment after it has been installed and it is being utilized from tuning your system to work more efficiently to backing up and maintaining Dynamics AX to make sure you are prepared for worst-case scenarios, enabling you to keep Dynamics AX 2009 functioning at its best.

By following the clear and practical steps found in the book, you will successfully master how to administer and configure Dynamics AX 2009 into your company.

Who this book is for

If you are a network administrator or IT personnel charged with setting up and configuring Dynamics AX 2009 into your company, then this book is for you. A basic knowledge of Dynamics AX 2009 and general Windows Server Administration is required and familiarity with maintaining a SQL Server database server. Additionally, if you are a VAR tasked with implementing Dynamics AX into companies, then this book will provide you with a good overview and detail of the whole Dynamics AX 2009 system.

What this book covers

Chapter 1, System Planning and Hardware Sizing will help you understand the current hardware, software, and network infrastructure in which you will be implementing Microsoft Dynamics AX.

Chapter 2, Setup and Configuration of the Base Server Components will help you fully understand the base Dynamics AX 2009 components and their features to get your Dynamics AX environment up and running effectively.

Chapter 3, Setup and Configuration of the Enterprise Portal will show you how to implement the Enterprise Portal, a web-based solution to access data from Dynamics AX and perform many functions such as Purchase Requisitions, Sales Orders, Customer lookups, CRM, and much more!

Chapter 4, Setup and Configuration of the Role Centers will teach you how to set up and configure the business intelligence and advanced reporting capabilities of your data by using the Role Centers in Dynamics AX.

Chapter 5, Setting Up Kerberos Authentication will enhance the security of multiple services by ensuring that the Kerberos Authentication protocol is implemented into your Dynamics AX environment.

Chapter 6, Setup and Configuration of the Workflow talks about the process of setting up and configuring workflow to fit the needs of a company that requires various workflow capabilities.

Chapter 7, Setup and Configuration of Application Integration Framework looks at how to use the Application Integration Framework to exchange data either synchronously or asynchronously between one system and another.

Chapter 8, Data Migration helps you to manage, migrate, and convert your data in Dynamics AX.

Chapter 9, Security and User Administration looks at how to get a hold of the common user administration functions that are built into Dynamics AX, including setting up domains, importing users, permissions, profiles, company accounts, and much more!

Chapter 10, Alerts and Notifications shows you how to make critical, on-time business decisions by fully understanding the Alerts and Notifications features that notify you when specific criteria has been met with your data.

Chapter 11, Tuning Your Setup explains how to tweak and enhance Dynamics AX and its components for optimal performance.

Chapter 12, Backup and Maintenance teaches you how to maintain the data integrity of Dynamics AX data and develop backup and recovery processes.

Appendix A, contains additional topics on Dynamics AX administration and configuration.

Appendix B, contains additional settings, configuration options, and troubleshooting techniques.

What you need for this book

The following are the minimum requirements:

OS: Windows Server 2003 (2008 preferred)

Database: SQL Server 2005 (2008 Preferred) plus: Analysis Services, Reporting Services and Integration Services

Other: Visual Studio 2008, .NET 2.0, latest .NET 3.x version, and latest Internet Explorer 8.x

SharePoint: WSS 3.0 or SharePoint 2007

Dynamics AX 200-9 with SP1

Conventions

In this book, you will find a number of styles of text that distinguish between different kinds of information. Here are some examples of these styles, and an explanation of their meaning.

New terms and **important words** are shown in bold. Words that you see on the screen, in menus or dialog boxes for example, appear in the text like this: "The **View history** form and **Windows Event Log** will assist in determining the source of any errors ".

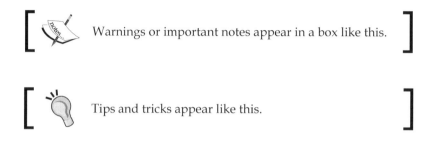

Warnings or important notes appear in a box like this.

Tips and tricks appear like this.

Reader feedback

Feedback from our readers is always welcome. Let us know what you think about this book—what you liked or may have disliked. Reader feedback is important for us to develop titles that you really get the most out of.

To send us general feedback, simply send an e-mail to feedback@packtpub.com, and mention the book title via the subject of your message.

If there is a book that you need and would like to see us publish, please send us a note in the **SUGGEST A TITLE** form on www.packtpub.com or e-mail suggest@packtpub.com.

If there is a topic that you have expertise in and you are interested in either writing or contributing to a book, see our author guide on www.packtpub.com/authors.

Customer support

Now that you are the proud owner of a Packt book, we have a number of things to help you to get the most from your purchase.

> **Downloading the example code for this book**
>
> You can download the example code files for all Packt books you have purchased from your account at http://www.PacktPub.com. If you purchased this book elsewhere, you can visit http://www.PacktPub.com/support and register to have the files e-mailed directly to you.

Errata

Although we have taken every care to ensure the accuracy of our content, mistakes do happen. If you find a mistake in one of our books—maybe a mistake in the text or the code—we would be grateful if you would report this to us. By doing so, you can save other readers from frustration and help us improve subsequent versions of this book. If you find any errata, please report them by visiting http://www.packtpub.com/support, selecting your book, clicking on the **errata submission form** link, and entering the details of your errata. Once your errata are verified, your submission will be accepted and the errata will be uploaded on our website, or added to any list of existing errata, under the Errata section of that title. Any existing errata can be viewed by selecting your title from http://www.packtpub.com/support.

Piracy

Piracy of copyright material on the Internet is an ongoing problem across all media. At Packt, we take the protection of our copyright and licenses very seriously. If you come across any illegal copies of our works, in any form, on the Internet, please provide us with the location address or website name immediately so that we can pursue a remedy.

Please contact us at copyright@packtpub.com with a link to the suspected pirated material.

We appreciate your help in protecting our authors, and our ability to bring you valuable content.

Questions

You can contact us at questions@packtpub.com if you are having a problem with any aspect of the book, and we will do our best to address it.

1
System Planning and Hardware Sizing

Before you plan your Dynamics AX implementation, it is vital that you understand the current hardware, network, and software infrastructure in which you will be implementing Microsoft Dynamics AX. It is also equally important to gather information about a company's business requirements, functions, and departments that will be utilizing Dynamics AX 2009. At times, there may be a need to implement new hardware, network, or software resources to fulfill the needs and requirements of Dynamics AX. Therefore, gathering as much information as possible on hardware, network, and software is essential to the success of the functionality and performance of Dynamics AX.

In this chapter, we will cover:

- Typical phases of a Dynamics AX implementation
- How to create a robust environment in which Dynamics AX 2009 can be installed and utilized
- How to size hardware, networking, and software resources that will support the Dynamics AX 2009 system

Phases of a Dynamics AX implementation

In order for Dynamics AX to function at its best, hardware and network infrastructure has a large effect on the level of performance a company will experience. Luckily, there are requirements to ensure that Dynamics AX will function at its best. You can also expand on these requirements to provide even better performance. For example, you can certainly expand and implement a better infrastructure (scaling out) that supports more network bandwidth or implement more data capacity or processing power as well (scaling up).

The requirements of the network and hardware are determined by the number of concurrent users and transactions as well as the other services whose demands will take up network resources alongside Dynamics AX.

Since Dynamics AX is a modular server system, requirements are also based on which of these systems will need to be utilized and to what degree. For example, for the Enterprise Portal, you will need to decide if it will be accessible using an Intranet on a **Local Area Network (LAN)** or using the Internet on a **Wide Area Network (WAN)**.

In this case, your hardware, software, and even network requirements will have to compensate to handle the bandwidth, security, and load. Another example may be that your implementation may be running many batch jobs in which they handle large sums of data. For that reason, you may consider implementing extra **Application Object Servers (AOS)** to compensate for the batch loads and demands.

You may also want to be prepared for emergency scenarios or for compensating additional demands that occur from company expansions.

Microsoft Dynamics Sure Step implementation methodology (`http://www.microsoft.com/dynamics/support/implementation/success.aspx`) is an excellent collection of guidelines for successful implementations, especially for Dynamics AX. The following table is adapted from the Sure Step methodology and provides an overview of processes during an implementation:

Modeling phase

Phase	Tasks during phase
Diagnostics	• Evaluate a customer's business processes and infrastructure
	• Prepare a proposal
Analysis	• Analyze the current business model
	• Produce a gap/fit analysis
	• Create the requirements documentation
Design	• Create documents:
	◦ Feature design
	◦ Data migration design
	◦ Test criteria
	◦ Technical design

Development, testing, and training

Phase	Tasks during phase
Development	• Set up the production environment • Configure the system • Migrate data • Test the system • Train the end-users • Bring the system live

Production (Go live)

Phase	Tasks during phase
Deployment and Operation	• Resolve pending issues • Finalize the user documentation and knowledge transfer • Conduct a post-mortem of the project • Provide on-going support These are on-going activities that continue after the project is closed and throughout any future involvement with the client

Planning phase

Phase	Tasks during phase
Optimization	• Analyze the system to determine how it can be optimized for best performance based on the customer's needs • Perform the optimization • Carry out testing The purpose of this phase is to help the customer optimize the benefit they get from the business solution.
Upgrade	• Review the customer's business processes • Align the business processes with new functionality • Put the systems in place to support the upgrade

Delegation phase

Before beginning a Dynamics AX implementation, it is important that roles are determined and delegated. This ensures a steady process throughout the implementation and lessens the possibility of any bottlenecks occurring. The following table shows a theoretical sequence of the initial phase of an implementation:

Sequence or Priority	Responsible party (Company, Implementer, or Both)	Action item	Description
1	Both	Choose required features that a company will need to perform business functions.	Specific licenses will need to be purchased to enable certain functions in Dynamics AX to be useable. Also, third party modules may need to be utilized.
2	Company	Gather current network, hardware, and software capabilities.	Review installed software such as operating systems, hardware such as processing speed, available RAM and HDD space. Also review current bandwidth capacity and current network load.
3	Implementer	Gather user, usage, and topology requirements. Estimate projected growth rate.	Number of total users in the company, number of concurrent users, and number of transactions per minute. Topology requirements, such as Intranet or Extranet (VPN).
4	Company	Install any new hardware, software and/or configure the network to fit the previously mentioned requirements.	Examples of modifications at this phase are to set up the Windows Domain Controller to support Kerberos authentication.
5	Company	Set up user accounts.	Create users that will need to have specific privileges from the implementation company to perform installation, setup, and the configuration of Microsoft Dynamics AX 2009.

Sequence or Priority	Responsible party (Company, Implementer, or Both)	Action item	Description
6	Implementer	Create implementation directories.	Specific directories for Dynamics AX configuration files, user documentation, installation and utilities, or any other miscellaneous yet relevant files for the implementation.
7	Implementer	Install required software for Dynamics AX 2009.	Install required software that the Dynamics AX 2009 installation program needs in order to install and run base and server components. For example, Internet Information Services (IIS) and Windows SharePoint Services will need to be installed and set up for the Enterprise Portal to be installed.
8	Implementer	Create and set up development environment.	In conjunction with the previous step, there should be a server dedicated to development. The development environment will contain everything that the production environment has; however, the base and server components can run on the same system. Sometimes, the test environment can also reside on the development server.
9	Implementer	Create and set up test and staging environment.	Similar to the previously mentioned; however, these environments will resemble the production more so. Typically, the staging environment is practically identical to the production environment.
10	Implementer	Create and set up production environment.	The production environment should be considered an "island" from the other environments and should be treated as sacred.
11	Implementer	Import users.	Import company users into required environments.

A well-coordinated team with specific tasks is an integral part of a successful implementation. Without such a team, unforeseen failures and setbacks may occur. Each role is required due to the responsibilities incurred during an implementation lifecycle. The following roles will need to be occupied by qualified professionals:

- A Project Manager is a person who will oversee the implementation process. Such an individual may encompass some skill sets of each preceding role. Ultimately, the job of the project manager is to orchestrate each individual during the process of an implementation and also communicate with the business to create functional and technical requirements.

- An Architecture specialist is one who can determine methods to balance performance and scalability with manageability, interoperability, security, and maintainability.

- A Developer is responsible for tailoring Dynamics AX 2009 to a company's specific needs by providing custom development and integration.

- A Tester is an individual with functional knowledge of developed modifications and functionality of Dynamics AX.

- The role of a Trainer can be fulfilled by a Tester who will be in charge of specifically training individuals on how to use the systems for business functions.

- A System Administrator would typically already be working at a position in the company that requires familiarity with network topology and server hardware. The primary goal of this individual, especially during the implementation phase, would be to monitor and ensure that all resources are operating sufficiently, enabling them to provide optimal performance and meet service level agreements.

At times, responsibilities fluctuate, consolidate, and deviate from the initial roles. The previously mentioned list provides mere guidelines to understand the typical responsibilities required for an implementation. Keep in mind, the larger the implementation, the greater the responsibilities, as the number of roles required will increase proportionally.

Setting up an environment for Dynamics AX 2009 follows similar guidelines to other Microsoft infrastructure methodologies. A list of possible implementation methodologies are as follows:

- **Infrastructure Planning and Design (IPD)**
- **Windows Server System Reference Architecture (WSSRA)**

- **Infrastructure Optimization Model**
- **Microsoft Operations Framework**

Hardware planning

Having hardware performing at its best is crucial for the performance of Dynamics AX 2009. Therefore, planning hardware setup and infrastructure is essential to the overall implementation and post implementation of Dynamics AX. There is a level of performance that is proportional to the level of utilization. The goals of achieving performance requirements are to minimize response time, maximize throughput, and balance resource utilization and workload. This is also a function of capacity management, which is the process of planning, analyzing, sizing, and optimizing capacity to fulfill demands in the least timely and lowest cost approach. The following table is a list of items that need to be collected and quantified in order to create an optimal Dynamics AX 2009 environment:

Requirement	Description
Number of companies	Some implementations may contain one or more companies.
Number of users	Maximum number of concurrent users as well as company size. Keep in mind that the number of concurrent users will increase as a company grows.
Number of departments	It is important to know the number of departments present within a company. In Dynamics AX, departments can be partitioned into a company account. It is also important to determine the following: • Department requirements • Department business processes • Number of department personnel • Permission requirements and restrictions
Number of transactions	Determine the number of transactions that are occurring during on and off peak hours. Resources need to be leveraged to handle the loads. Keep in mind that different times during the year may also put variable strain on the system. • Note: One purchase order with 50 line items is considered as 50 plus the order itself, number of transactions.

Requirement	Description
Required features	Will EDI, business analysis, web, or mobile access be required? These are just a few examples of features you must consider.
	Consider that, when users access role centers, behind the scenes, they will be accessing SQL Server Analysis Services. Depending on your data and role centers, these can be intensive calculations and may require extra processing power to compensate.
	Another scenario would be an EDI scenario. If part of your information is being received from an outside vendor and orders are also being created to another outside vendor, consider that there may be a need for a specialized setup to efficiently work with the two endpoints.
External user access	Determine whether users will be accessing Dynamics AX using the Internet or extranet. What features, permissions, and resources do these users require? What are the peak and off-peak hours for users, as well as the number of transactions within those periods?
Internal user access	Similar to External user access, however for the intranet.
Estimated growth rate	To determine this, take the current growth rate in the last two to five years and distribute it over the next several years. The following mathematical formula can be used to calculate the rate:

$$PR = \frac{(V_{Present} - V_{Past})}{V_{Past}} \times 100$$

For example, if "Carvalho Company" had 50 employees five years ago and now has 200, the calculation would be as follows:

(200 – 50)/50 = 3 * 100 = 300%

Therefore, one should determine the potential of another 300 percent growth rate since the company had grown 300 percent in the past five years. Besides, with all the money the company would be saving by implementing Dynamics AX, they could focus more on strategy and hire more employees!

Requirement	Description
Availability (uptime)	Although the availability of an ERP system should be 100 percent throughout the day and year, you must determine the appropriate uptime requirements. For example, there are times for regular maintenance and upgrades where systems must be brought offline.
Number of sites	Many companies have various locations. Although Dynamics AX does not need to be implemented in each location, it is certainly the goal.

Based on the information here, you should now have a better idea about completing a company's requirements. For example, depending on the number of users, clustering or load balancing may be necessary for the AOS.

Virtualization

Microsoft Dynamics AX can function in a virtualized environment and does not require any specific setup since virtual environments, by nature, simulate a physical environment. Therefore, in many cases, your company will benefit greatly by deploying Dynamics AX 2009 on a virtualized infrastructure. There are many added benefits if you choose to follow this route such as cost, speed of client deployment, and modifying resources in real-time, to name a few. There are many vendors that provide virtualization solutions, including Microsoft. Price, features, and ease of use all play a role in deciding which solution is better. Consult the virtual solution vendor for more detailed information on server virtualization products.

 When choosing a virtualization solution, consider the impact on the Dynamics AX 2009 support agreement.

Database sizing

Database sizing is potentially the most critical step in performance for a Dynamics AX 2009 implementation. Each database server has its own specifications for hardware. However, the general ideas are the same. We will primarily be focusing on Microsoft SQL Server. The following table contains resources that are useful references when setting up a database for Dynamics AX:

Description	URL
Microsoft SQL Server TechNet site	`http://msdn.microsoft.com/en-us/library/bb545450.aspx`
Microsoft SQL Server 2008 and Microsoft SQL Server 2008 R2 Books Online	SQL Server 2008: `http://technet.microsoft.com/en-us/library/bb418439(SQL.10).aspx` SQL Server 2008 R2: `http://technet.microsoft.com/en-us/library/bb418432(SQL.10).aspx`
Microsoft SQL Server Storage Top 10 Best Practices	`http://www.microsoft.com/technet/prodtechnol/sql/bestpractice/storage-top-10.mspx`
Data Warehousing Best Practices in SQL Server	`http://technet.microsoft.com/en-us/library/cc719165(v=SQL.100).aspx`
Scaling Up Your Data Warehouse with SQL Server	`http://technet.microsoft.com/en-us/library/cc719182(v=SQL.100).aspx`
SQL Server Database requirements	`http://technet.microsoft.com/en-us/library/bb500469.aspx`
Microsoft Dynamics AX Performance Team Blog	`http://blogs.msdn.com/axperf/archive/2008/03/10/welcome-database-configuration-checklist-part-1.aspx`
Microsoft Dynamics AX 2009 Planning Database Configuration	`http://www.microsoft.com/downloads/details.aspx?displaylang=en&FamilyID=ab4cd401-b366-4c1c-9a73-88c945ae8191`

As with any company, the level of database space, redundancy, and efficiency is dependent on the number of transactions that the database will have to handle. Therefore, the larger the business, the more is the need for a robust and redundant data store. These constraints will also be important when determining the best database configuration.

As far as the hardware configuration for a database goes, there are many robust options available such as RAID and SAN storage. The database server may contain all the business data and SharePoint content data as well as run SQL Analysis Services for business intelligence. If using RAID, the configuration should be RAID 0+1 (01) or RAID 1+0 (10), in case of the unlikely event of data loss or corruption.

It is certainly possible to have all the databases for the development and test environments on such a server. However, the production environment should have its own database server. For example, a multiple processor core system with 8 GB to 16 GB of RAM per database with at least 2 TB of storage. Additionally, backups should occur as needed, otherwise, they should occur daily during off-peak hours.

For minimum database server requirements, please refer to the following table:

OS	CPU speed (GHz)	Single Core CPUs	Dual Core CPUs	RAM (GB)	HDD (GB)	Network (GB)
Windows Server 2008/2008 R2 Enterprise Edition (x64)	2.00+	2+	1+	8-16 or more	500 or more on RAID configuration	1

 These are manual requirements. Since computer hardware evolves exponentially, these recommendations may not be the best approach for hardware setup as time goes by.

Additionally, the larger the enterprise, the greater the need to have a SAN storage system. The following table outlines a possible hardware setup scenario:

Storage solution	Technology	Number of disks for SQL Server and Tempdb	Number of disks for SQL Server log	Total number of disks
Direct Attached Storage (DAS)	SCSI	12-16 (RAID-10)	2 (RAID-1)	14-18
Storage Area Network (SAN)	Fiber/SCSI	12-16 (RAID-10)	2 (RAID-1)	14-18
Storage Area Network (SAN)	Fiber/Fiber	12-16 (RAID-10)	2 (RAID-1)	14-18
Storage Area Network (SAN)	Fiber/SCSI	16-20 (RAID-10)	2 (RAID-1)	18-22
Storage Area Network (SAN)	Fiber/Fiber	16-20 (RAID-10)	2 (RAID-1)	18-22

SAN setup and configuration may be different among vendors. Therefore, please consult your SAN vendor for more detailed information.

Application Object Server requirements

The Application Object Server (AOS) is essentially the "heart" of Dynamics AX. This is where all the business logic, application objects, and operations are handled. Due to this, it is no surprise how important it is to make sure that the AOS operates as best as it can. Performance resources allocated to one or more AOSs must be done as follows: depending on the number of concurrent users, you may be required to implement multiple AOSs.

In order to successfully determine how many AOSs are required, the basic rule of thumb is that there should be one AOS for every 60 concurrent users (based on the recommended configuration). Therefore, if your company has 120 concurrent users, you would need to implement two AOSs and load balance them both. You can load balance either using hardware or software. Dynamics AX already includes the feature of clustering multiple AOSs. Clustering may be a more cost-effective approach to load balancing, yet may not be as powerful as hardware-based solutions. A company will need to leverage the two based on performance and cost.

Application file server requirements

The Application file server will hold all the application files, which contain all the application code, modules, and customizations for Dynamics AX. The server should have sufficient space to hold this information. Typically, for one environment, the application file folder with base modules takes about 7 GB of space. However, for backups and additional possible maintenance tasks, 100 GB is recommended. Network bandwidth, disk performance, and fault tolerance (RAID configuration) are the emphasis for this server. The server will not be performing any business calculations; however, it will be serving the AOS server application data. In a clustered or load balanced environment, the application file folder, for an environment, will be a network share. However, the shared folder cannot be set up as a **Distributed File System (DFS)**. Although it's not required to backup the application files unless the codebase is modified, backups of the application file folder should occur daily during off-peak hours to ensure an easy restore plan.

The following table describes a recommended configuration for a typical Application file server:

OS	CPU speed (GHz)	Single Core CPUs	Dual Core CPUs	RAM (GB)	Storage	Network (GB)
Windows Server 2008/2008 R2 Enterprise Edition (x64)	2.00+	2	1	4-6 (without SQL Server)	Two 100 GB HDD with RAID configuration	1

Web server requirements

A web server will serve Enterprise Portal content, Reporting Services reports, **Application Integration Framework (AIF)** web services, or Workflow. Depending on the number of concurrent users or available resources, a single web server can contain more than one Dynamics AX extended server component or a dedicated web server may be required for each extended server component. It is important to assess the requirements for accessing such services. Available network bandwidth, security, response time, and processor speed are the emphasis for a web server. This server will connect to the AOS server and serve as a frontend access to Dynamics AX instead of using the rich client. The following table describes the minimal requirements for a typical web server used for Dynamics AX extended server components:

OS	CPU speed (GHz)	Single Core CPUs	Dual Core CPUs	RAM (GB)	Storage	Network (GB)
Windows Server 2008/2008R2 Enterprise Edition (x64)	2.00+	2	1	4-6	100 GB	1

Network planning

There is a minimum requirement in order for Dynamics AX 2009 to function. That is, a data rate of no less than 100 Megabits per second (Mbps) between the client to the AOS and the AOS to the database. There must also be latency of no more than 5 milliseconds between the client to the AOS and the AOS to the database, as shown in the following table:

Requirement	Client to AOS	AOS to database
Bandwidth	100 Mbps	100 Mbps
Latency	5 ms	5 ms

The information here should fit the current majority of megabit Ethernet network infrastructure; however, it is recommended to have a more current gigabit Ethernet infrastructure.

Domain Controller setup

Dynamics AX will integrate seamlessly with Active Directory. However, in order for this to work properly, appropriate steps must be completed. You will need to consider the following domain requirements when installing Dynamics AX:

- Computers running Microsoft Dynamics AX components must have access to other computers in the same Active Directory domain, with Active Directory configured in native mode.

- In the recommended production configuration, since Microsoft Dynamics AX extended server components, such as the Enterprise Portal, Role Centers, and Reporting Extensions are installed on separate servers, Kerberos authentication is the required method of authentication. Otherwise, the Role Center web parts will fail to load.

- More information on setting up Kerberos authentication will be detailed in *Chapter 5, Setting Up Kerberos Authentication*.

- It is recommended that current users in an organization are partitioned into logical groups. This will be very helpful when importing users into Dynamics AX, and assigning group permissions and setting up alerts.

Software planning

Dynamics AX is a flexible ERP system, so there are certain features and modules that a company may need while others may not. It is important to determine what functions a company will require prior to performing any hardware or network sizing. One cannot possibly make an accurate estimate as to determine what will be required. For example, a company may require the usage of the Dynamics AX .NET Business Connector to integrate with other systems; therefore, a license will have to be acquired for the business connector. Having said that, the first steps will be to determine which functions and features a company will require. Afterwards, it will be easier to determine the server, hardware, and network resources to support the modules. Currently, there are three editions of pre-selected Dynamics AX 2009 licensing options:

1. Business Essentials
2. Advanced Management
3. Advanced Management Enterprise

A Microsoft Certified Partner would be able to assist you in choosing the appropriate software license.

Dynamics AX components will only work in a Windows environment. You can run Dynamics AX server components on either Windows Server 2003 with Service Pack 2, Windows Server 2008, or Windows Server 2008 R2. Both 32-bit and 64-bit versions are supported; however, we will be using a 64-bit version because 64-bit computing provides greater processing and memory addressing gains. Simply put, you can access and process larger sets of data in equal or greater speed than a 32-bit system.

The .NET Business Connector can be installed on either a 32-bit or 64-bit system. The Dynamics AX client, which is a 32-bit application, can be installed on Windows XP Service Pack 2, all Windows Vista versions with Service Pack 1, all Windows 7 versions, and Windows Server 2003 or 2008 systems.

 Microsoft Dynamics AX 2009 does not support the Itanium platform.

Database software

Dynamics AX 2009 can use either Microsoft SQL Server 2005 with Service Pack 2 (Standard or Enterprise editions), Microsoft SQL Server 2008 (Standard or Enterprise edition), or Oracle Database Server 10g R2 (Enterprise or Standard Windows versions only) for a database. **Online Analytical Processing (OLAP)** is not supported by the Oracle Database Server. Each database server provides its own strengths and weaknesses. For example, your organization may decide to opt for SQL Server 2005 because of its maturity level or opt for SQL Server 2008 for many new and unique features. For the purpose of this book, we will cover the setup and configuration on SQL Server 2008 and 2008 R2.

Software integration

It may be part of an implementation to integrate Dynamics AX with other systems such as Microsoft Project Server, BizTalk, Web service, or any other application or service. It should be noted that specific requirements will need to be established. Depending on the implementation of these integration points, you may have to include the load and usage into determining the level of usage of Dynamics AX.

Single server topology

A single server topology is when all Dynamics AX extended and base server components are installed on a single server. This can also be considered as a development or demo environment. A single server topology consists of all the server base and extended components on the same system. This topology should never be used for a production environment.

Small-scale topology

A small-scale server topology is when related components are on a single server because they share the same resources. For example, Dynamics AX extended server components that use **Internet Information Services (IIS)**, such as the Enterprise Portal, Reporting Extensions, Workflow, or the AIF. In such a configuration, Kerberos authentication is not required. Although a small-scale topology may be quicker and easier to implement, it lacks scalability, availability, or the best possible performance. For an example diagram of a small-scale topology implementation, refer to: `http://i.technet.microsoft.com/Dd309710.Small_scale_deployment(en-US,AX.50).gif`.

Large-scale topology

In a large-scale topology implementation, base server components, such as the AOS, database, and Application file server exist in their own server. The AOS and database can be clustered to increase scalability, resources, and availability. However, the Enterprise Portal can exist in an IIS cluster along with Workflow, AIF, and Reporting Extensions. A large-scale topology is based on a small-scale topology except it is far more scalable, reliable, and provides a greater performance capacity. This would require more time to implement and Kerberos authentication is required. However, the benefits include the best possible availability and scalability, as well as failover precautions and load balancing for optimal user and transaction performance. For an example diagram of a large-scale topology implementation refer to: `http://i.technet.microsoft.com/Dd309717.Large-scale_deployment_topology(en-US,AX.50).gif`.

Large-scale distribution topology

In a large-scale distributed topology implementation, each base and extended server component has its own dedicated server, which may or may not be clustered. A large-scale distributed topology is almost identical to the large-scale topology. However, this topology configuration provides scalability, availability, greater performance capacity, and fault tolerance. For an example diagram of a large-scale topology implementation, refer to: `http://i.technet.microsoft.com/Dd309620.Large_scale_distributed_deployment(en-US,AX.50).gif`.

Intranet and extranet topologies

Typically, most companies only access their ERP system using an intranet configuration. However, it may be required that Dynamics AX will need to be accessible outside of a company's intranet using an extranet connection. Such an example is connecting to a company's network through a remote **Virtual Private Network (VPN)** connection. This shows a possible scenario where users may want to connect to Dynamics AX resources remotely. Extra considerations will need to be made to incorporate mobile devices since, these devices are usually provided by third party vendors. Typically, mobile devices can access Dynamics AX resources in both topologies.

Permission requirements

Each component for Dynamics AX requires specific permissions. Most of these permissions are administrator level permissions. However, to make sure you audit your permissions carefully, the following table gives a list of the components and required installation rights:

Component	Permissions required to install
Application Object Server (AOS)	Member of the **securityadmin** role on Microsoft SQL Server database.
Microsoft SQL Server database	Member of the **dbcreator** role on SQL Server database. (Specific permissions will need to be set for Oracle.)
Application files	Administrator
Client	Administrator
Role Centers and Enterprise Portal framework	Administrator
Workflow	Member of the Administrators group in Microsoft Dynamics AX.
Analysis extensions	Administrator
Reporting extensions	Administrator
Reporting tools	Administrator
Enterprise Portal developer tools	Administrator
Synchronization service	Administrator
Synchronization proxy	Member of the **dbowner** database role on the SQL Server database for Microsoft Project server, and an administrator on the computer that is running Office Project Server.
AIF Web services	Administrator
BizTalk adapter	Administrator
.NET Business Connector	Administrator
Developer installation	Member of the **dbcreator** role on the SQL Server database.

During an implementation of Dynamics AX, remote access to the network will be required for outside development and testing tasks. For security reasons, it is recommended that you use a secured VPN to provide remote access to an internal company network.

Miscellaneous implementation tasks

During an implementation, there will be specific documents, configuration files, applications, and other miscellaneous files that will be required for a Dynamics AX 2009 implementation. This file store should be in an easily accessible location for people involved in an implementation. Such files can be stored on a SharePoint site or on a network drive. The following screenshot contains a sample file structure:

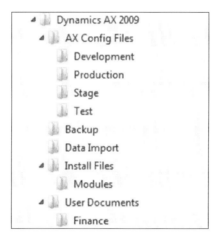

This screenshot only represents an example sample file structure, but depending on your specific implementation, more directories may be required. However, the **AX Config Files** folder is very important as this will be the file to access Dynamics AX 2009.

Before creating your environments, you will need to determine what to name your environments. Your environment names should contain enough information to know the version and instance. The following table contains sample names for the Ingnomics example company:

Environment	Name
Development	AX2009_INGNOMICS_DEV
Test	AX2009_INGNOMICS_TEST
Staging	AX2009_INGNOMICS_STAGE
Training	AX2009_INGNOMICS_TRAIN
Production	AX2009_INGNOMICS_PROD

Summary

In this chapter, we discussed the processes that you will need to follow in order to prepare your environment for implementing Dynamics AX 2009. Having a properly orchestrated preparation saves many unnecessary issues and potential setbacks that can be easily eliminated if the configuration and setup is done properly from the beginning.

In the next chapter, we will go through the setup and configuration of the Dynamics AX 2009 base server components and the running of the Dynamics AX AOS.

2
Setup and Configuration of the Base Server Components

The setup and configuration of the base server components will essentially create a functioning Dynamics AX system without Business Intelligence, Workflow, or the Enterprise Portal. Once you have installed and configured the base server components you can access the **Application Object Server (AOS)** using the Dynamics AX client.

This chapter focuses on implementing Dynamics AX on a server platform. Although the installation program provides a lot of self-governance, when it comes to installing each component, it does not do everything. At times, you will have to perform some manual tasks to get the components working the way you intend them to work. In this chapter, we will not just cover the basic installation of the base server components from the beginning to the end but also advanced procedures that cover just about any scenario sequentially. Although many components can be installed at the same time, which speeds up the installation process, it is far better to avoid this approach as you have less control over the integrity of the installation.

In this chapter, we will specifically cover:

- Installing the Dynamics AX database
- Installing the Dynamics AX Application files directory
- Installing the Application Object Server (AOS)
- Installing the Dynamics AX Client
- Completing the Dynamics AX Initialization checklist

Installing the Dynamics AX database

The very first component that must be installed is the Dynamics AX database server component. The database server component is a SQL database that will store all the Dynamics AX data for quick retrieval. To install and set up the database server component, perform the following steps:

1. Run the **Microsoft Dynamics AX Setup** installation program and select your language:

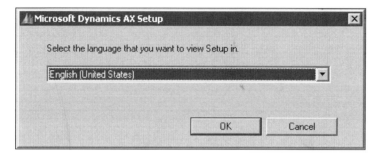

2. After clicking on the **OK** button, you will now be in the Dynamics AX installation wizard. With all the defaults set, click on the **Next** button until you arrive at the **Add or modify components** screen:

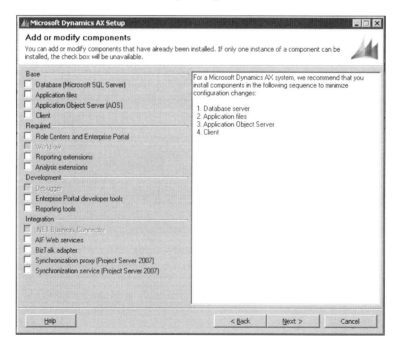

You can either create a database automatically using the installation wizard or manually. If creating a database manually, ensure that the appropriate permissions are set, as described in the following steps.

3. To start creating a database using the wizard, check the **Database (Microsoft SQL Server)** option in the **Base** section of the wizard and then click on the **Next** button.

4. The next screen **Database: Create new SQL Server database**, will enable you to perform the actual creation of the new SQL Server database. Although it's not required to have Dynamics AX working, you should name your database with the same name you intend to use for your AOS instance. In this instance, since we are creating a development environment, the database name will be **AX2009_INGNOMICS_DEV01**. It is best practice to have the same name for the database, Application Object Server, and Application file directory. It is also best practice to name the database as <AXVersion><Company>_<Instance> or <AXVersion>_<Company>_<Instance>.

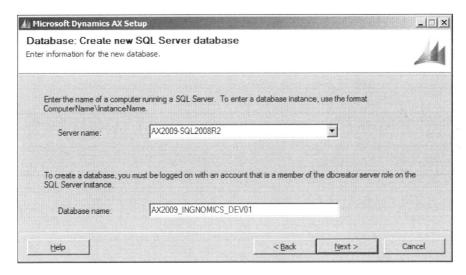

5. The final screen indicates whether the installation was performed successfully. The color of the box on the right side of the component installed can be green, orange, or red. Green indicates that the installation was successful, orange indicates that there was a warning, yet the component was installed, and red indicates that there was a fatal error and the component did not install at all. If there is either a warning or error, check the **Open the log file when Setup closes** option and click on the **Finish** button to view the reasons for the warning and errors:

Manually installing and setting up the Dynamics AX database

Manually installing and setting up the Dynamics AX database is preferred when there is a desire to understand the permissions and setup involved. For example, in instances where demo data is copied or when you copy an existing Dynamics AX database from one server to another, it is likely that the permissions may be set up differently. In this case, understanding what permissions need to be set on which object will prevent lots of unnecessary issues. From now on, understanding how the Dynamics AX database is set up is not only useful but essential as well. Once understood, you will be able to create the Dynamics AX database more quickly. This procedure covers the process of manually creating and installing the database in Microsoft SQL Server 2008 or 2008 R2. To do this, you will need to perform the following steps:

1. As an administrator, access SQL Server using SQL Server Management Studio and log in to the server that you want the database to reside in.

2. In the database engine, create a new database by right clicking on the **Databases** folder and then clicking on **New Database...**.

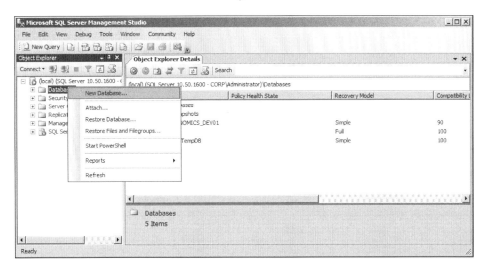

3. In the **New Database** window, provide the appropriate **Database name** and location on the disk to store the database. Once complete, click on the **OK** button to create the database.

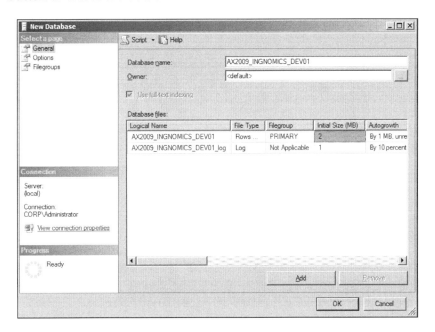

4. Once you have specified the name you want for your database, you can click on the **OK** button in the **New Database** wizard to create the database you specified. The database will now appear below the **Databases** folder, (you may need to refresh).

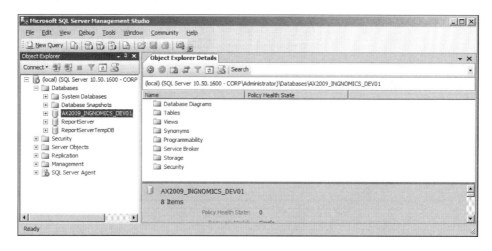

5. Now that you have created the database manually, you will need to set the permissions manually as well. First, the service account name that will be running the AOS must be added as a valid SQL login. Expand the Dynamics AX database and right-click on the **Security** folder and click on **New | User...**.

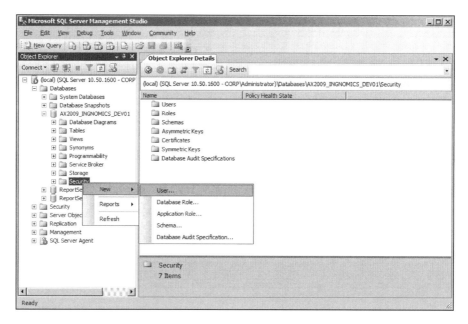

6. In the **Database User – New** window, provide the AOS service account name in the **User name** and **Login name** fields and assign the login to **db_datareader**, **db_datawriter**, and **db_ddladmin** in the **Database role membership** section.

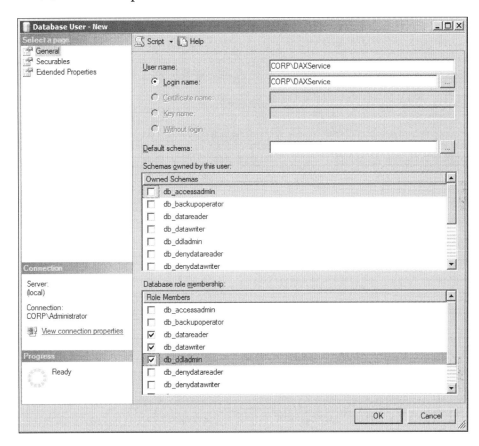

 If the NT AUTHORITY\NetworkService or LocalSerivce account are the AOS service accounts, then the account login should follow the format <AOSServer>$, where <AOSServer> is the server that the AOS is running on. For example, AX2009-AOS$ would be a valid account login to add to the database.

7. Next we need to assign the permissions on two stored procedures. To do this, go to the **Securables** page.

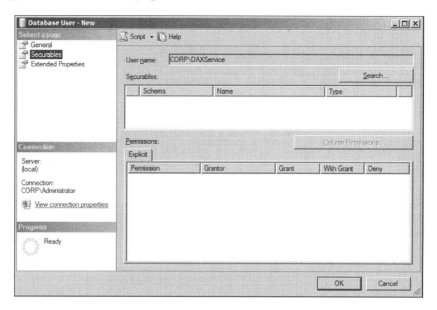

8. Click on the **Search..** button, and the **Add Objects** window will be displayed. Ensure that the **Specific objects...** radio button is marked and click on the **OK** button.

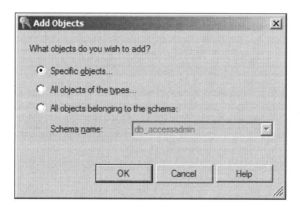

9. The **Select Objects** window will open, click on the **Object Types...** button to search for specific object types.

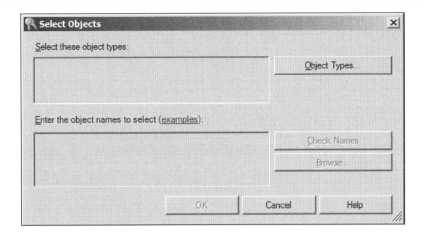

10. The **Select Object Types** window will open, mark **Stored procedures** and then click on the **OK** button. This will filter our search to only include stored procedures in the database.

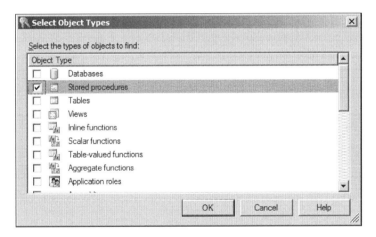

11. Now that we are back in the **Select Objects** window, click on the **Browse…** button to view the list of stored procedures in the database.

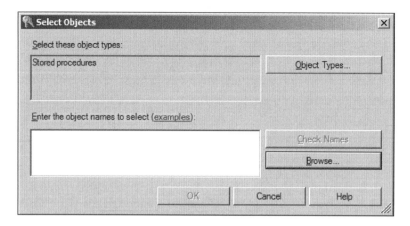

12. In the **Browse for Objects** window that pops up, mark the **CREATESERVERSESSIONS** and **CREATEUSERSESSIONS** stored procedures in order to modify permissions. When complete, click on the **OK** button.

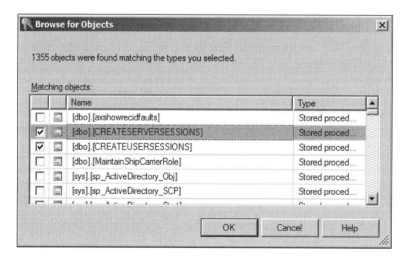

13. Verify that the **Select Objects** window has the two stored procedures listed, then click on the **OK** button to add the **Securables**.

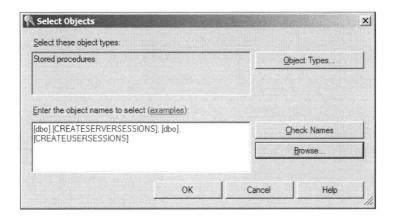

14. The **Securables** page will now have the two stored procedures listed. Grant **Execute** permissions to the account on both of the stored procedures. When complete, click on the **OK** button to finalize the permission settings on the Dynamics AX database for the account.

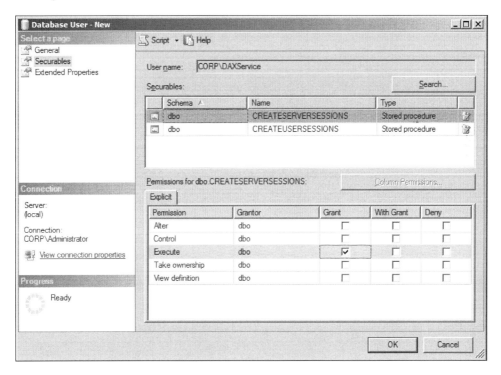

Installing the Dynamics AX Application files

The Dynamics AX AOS requires the Application files server component because that is where all the application code, label files, and system files are stored. The best practice is to install the Application file server on a dedicated server. When setting up multiple Dynamics AX environments, such as a development, test, or training system, each environment should have its own Application file folder. However, when setting up a clustered or load-balanced environment, essentially the same environment with multiple AOSs, all of them will share a single Application file folder. The following steps outline the process of installing the **Application files** base server component:

1. Run the Dynamics AX setup. In the **Add or modify components** screen, mark the **Application files** in the **Base** component and click on the **Next** button.

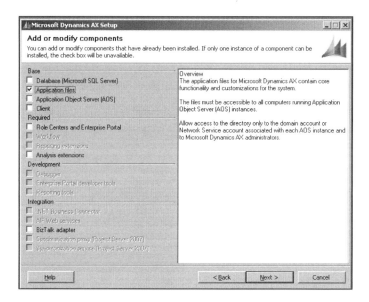

2. In the next window of the wizard, specify the appropriate folder to install the **Application files**. Verify that the location is appropriate for your setup and then click on the **Next** button.

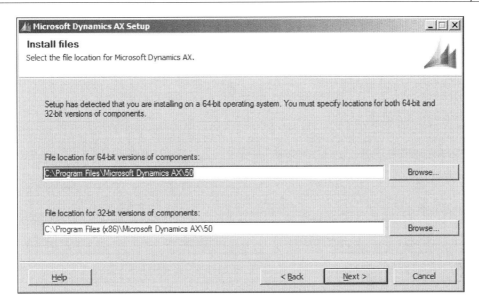

3. The next step is to specify the **Application Instance Name**. This name will also be used as the name for the Application Instance's Application file folder. The database, Application Object Server instance, and Application file folder need to have the same name.

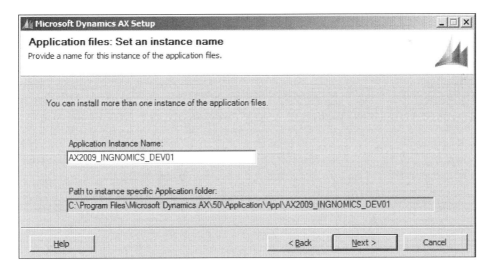

4. Click on the **Next** button and finally complete the wizard to create the Application file folder by clicking on **Finish**.

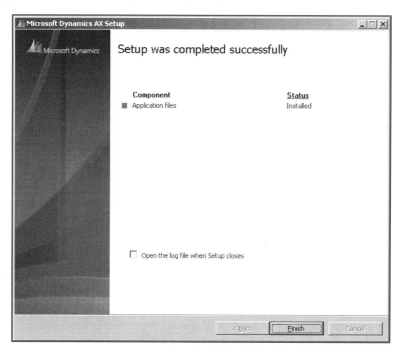

Now that the Application files have been installed, the next step is to create a network share of the Application file folder, so that the AOS server can access the Application files. Furthermore, this is also necessary to have in place when setting up multiple AOSs in a load-balanced or clustered setup as they will all access the same Application file directory. The following steps describe this process:

1. Go to the top level folder in which the Dynamics AX Application files were installed.

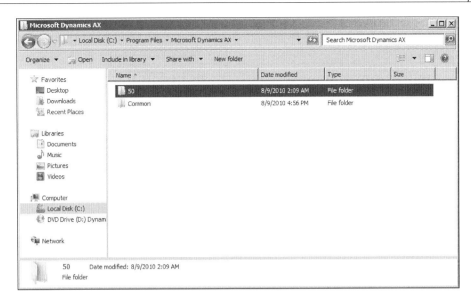

2. Right-click on the **50** folder and go to **Share with | Advanced sharing...**.

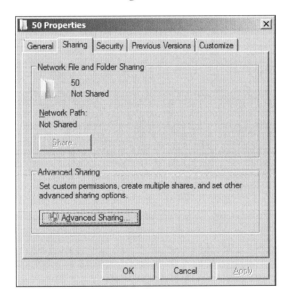

3. In the **50 Properties** form, click on the **Advanced Sharing...** button to assign sharing permissions.

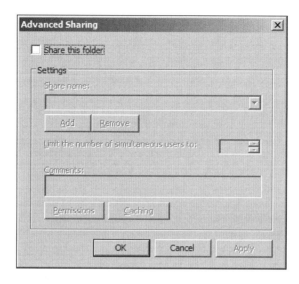

4. In the **Advanced Sharing** window, mark the **Share this folder** checkbox to enable the sharing **Settings** section. Then, click on the **Permissions** button to assign permissions to this share.

5. We will now need to add a user. Click on the **Add...** button to add a user.

6. The **Select Users, Computers, Service Accounts, or Groups** window will open.

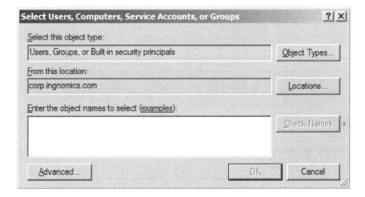

7. Type in the AOS service account name and click on the **OK** button.

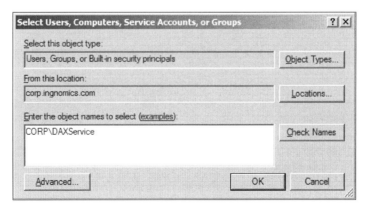

> If the AOS service account is `NT Authority\`
> `NetworkService` or `LocalService`, then provide the
> `<AOSServer>$` instead. For example, if the AOS server is
> AX2009-AOS, provide AX2009-AOS$ as the account name.

8. Now that the AOS service account has been added, assign **Full Control** permission access to the folder so that the AOS service can modify the directory. Click on the **OK** button to save the changes.

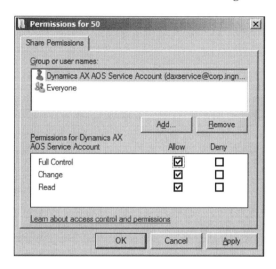

9. Now we are back in the **Advanced Sharing** window. Click on the **OK** button.

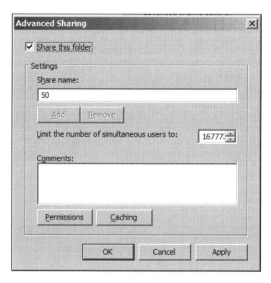

10. Now we are back in the **50 Properties** window. Click on the **Close** button to complete the sharing and permission setup.

11. Now that the folder has been shared, we need to ensure that the permission has been set to the root folder, subfolders, and files. To do this, right-click on the **50** folder and go to **Properties**.

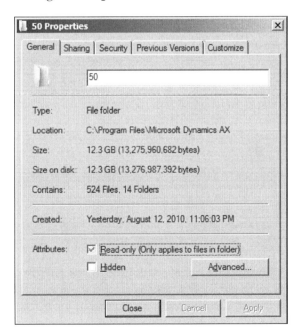

12. In the **Properties** window, click on the **Security** tab.

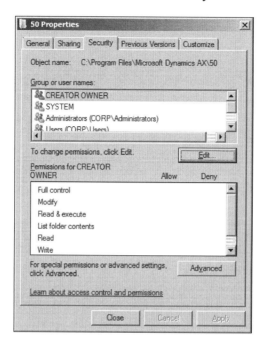

13. In the **Security** tab, click on the **Edit...** button to modify the permissions.

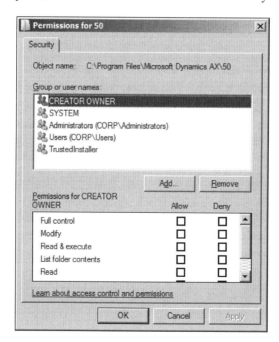

14. Click on the **Add...** button to add permissions to the Dynamics AX AOS service. Add the AOS service and click on the **OK** button.

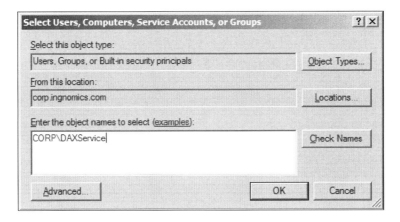

15. In the **50 Properties** window, assign **Full Control** to the **Dynamics AX AOS Service Account** and click on **OK** to apply and save the modifications.

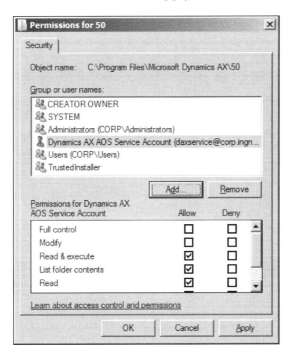

Installing the Application Object Server (AOS)

Now that the database and application files base server components have been installed and configured, the next step is to install and configure the AOS. First we will start by creating a single AOS and then progress into a more sophisticated setup and arrangement of multiple AOS servers either for a clustered or load balancing environment. The following steps describe this process:

1. Run the Dynamics AX setup program. In the **Add or modify components** screen, mark the **Application Object Server (AOS)** and click on the **Next** button to start the installation of the Dynamics AX AOS. A message may pop up notifying you that you don't have a Windows Firewall/**Internet Connection Sharing (ICS)** setup, you can override this message and continue with the installation process by clicking on the **Yes** button.

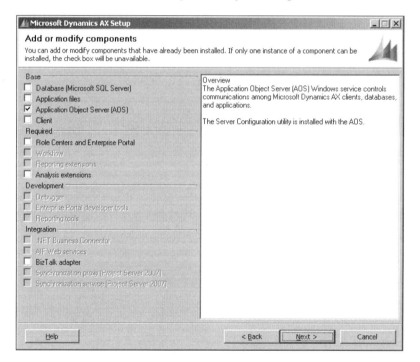

2. On the **Select database type** screen, you will be prompted to select the appropriate type of database that the AOS will be connected to, as shown in the following screenshot. There are specific calls and routines that the AOS must utilize for SQL Server and Oracle. After selecting the appropriate database brand, click on the **Next** button to progress to the next step:

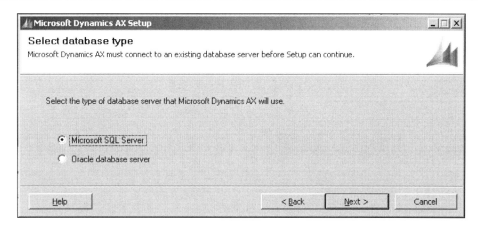

3. On the **AOS: Connect to a SQL Server Database** screen of the AOS installation wizard, you can select the appropriate SQL server hostname and instance as well as the database we created earlier, as shown in the following screenshot. Upon selecting the appropriate SQL Server, the installation program may select the database with a matching AOS name. However, if the name is different, select the correct one. When complete, click on the **Next** button to progress to the next step:

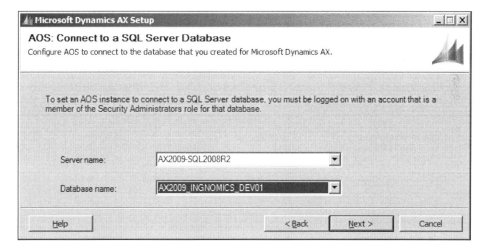

4. In this section of the AOS installation wizard, you will need to specify the folder in which you installed the Application file directories, as shown in the following screenshot. If your application files are in a separate folder than the server in which you are installing your AOS, you must specify the Network Share directory. When you have set the correct directory, proceed by clicking on the **Next >** button:

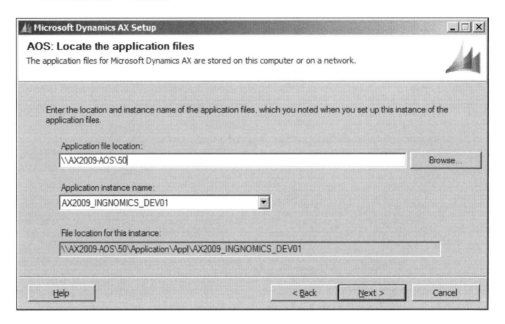

5. Once you have specified your application files directory, the next step is to set the appropriate port for the AOS to listen and communicate through. The initial and default port is 2712. However, if you already have an AOS installed on that port, the wizard will automatically detect that and select the next available port by incrementing up by 1. In this example, we already have an AOS instance installed on port 2712; therefore, the wizard has automatically set the port to **2713**, as shown in the following screenshot. When you have completed this step, click on the **Next** button to proceed forward:

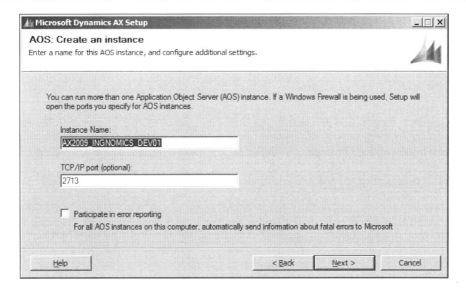

6. Next, we will provide the account that will run the AOS service. It is recommended to use a dedicated account. You can create an AOS account on your Active Directory domain controller. It must have permissions to access the SQL Server database, as described in the *Manually installing and setting up the Dynamics AX Database* section and permissions to access the Application files folder, as described in the *Installing the Dynamics AX Application files* section, found earlier in this chapter. The Network Service account is an acceptable option for the AOS service account. However, it is recommended that you use a dedicated domain account to run the AOS service. Once you have specified the AOS service account, click on the **Next** button and then click on the **Install** button to complete the installation of the AOS:

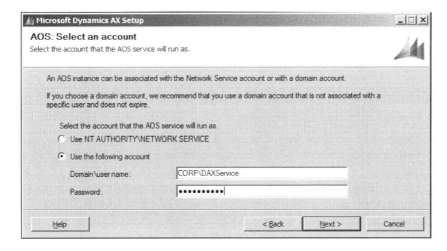

7. Once the AOS installation wizard is complete and there are no errors, we will need to confirm that the AOS service has been created. The AOS service should have started if you have marked the option to start the AOS service after the install completes option. We will then need to open the Windows Services program by going to **Start | Administrative Tools | Services**. Your AOS service name will follow the following format: `Dynamics AX Object Server 5.0$<AOS NUMBER>-<AOS NAME>`, where `<AOS NUMBER>` is the number of the AOS created, relative to the sequence it was created in and `<AOS NAME>` is the name for the AOS that was provided during the install.

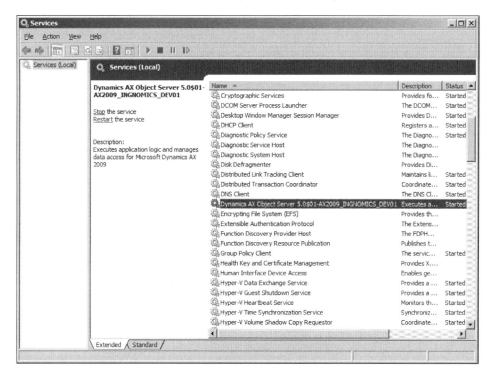

 Now is not only an appropriate but convenient time to install any Hotfixes (for example, latest hotfix rollup) and/or Service Packs (for example, SP1). This ensures that all the base server components and the client are up-to-date before use or initialization. It will also save additional steps in the future.

Installing the Dynamics AX Client

Now that the Database, Application files, Application Object Server (AOS) have been installed and the AOS service is running, the next step is to access Dynamics AX using the client. In order to do this, the Dynamics AX Client must be installed. To install the Dynamics AX Client, simply run the Dynamics AX setup program and install the Dynamics AX Client. The following steps describe the process of installing the client:

1. In the **Add or modify components** screen, mark the **Client** checkbox and click on the **Next >** button.

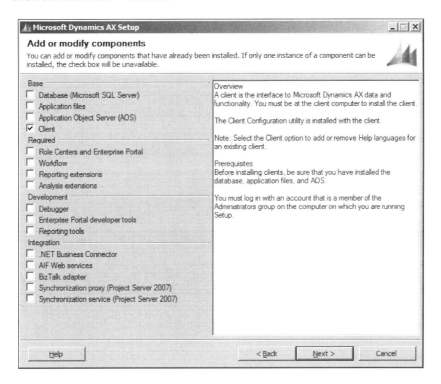

2. Select your language and then click on the **Next >** button.

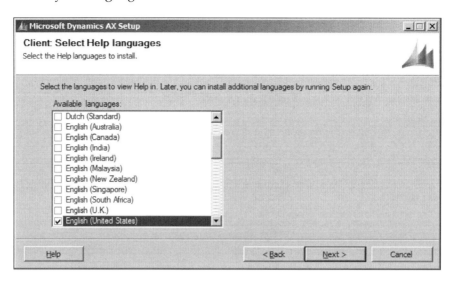

3. Click on **Install** to install the client.

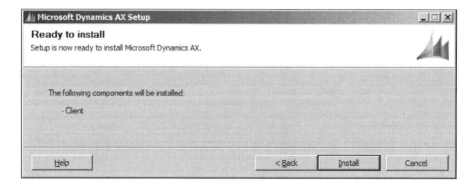

For advanced setup of the client, refer to the Accessing the Client Configuration section in *Chapter 11, Tuning Your Setup.*

Dynamics AX Initialization checklist

Now that the Database, Application files, Application Object Server (AOS), and Client have been installed and the AOS service is running, the next step is to log in to Dynamics AX. Initially, the Administrator is the only user that can access the Dynamics AX environment. Before Dynamics AXs modules and features can be used, it must be initialized. An initialization checklist automatically loads when logging into Dynamics AX for the first time or until the checklist has been completed or supclicked to be displayed. Completing the checklist is also necessary to install extended server components such as the Enterprise Portal and Reporting Extensions. The following screenshot is the checklist that will appear:

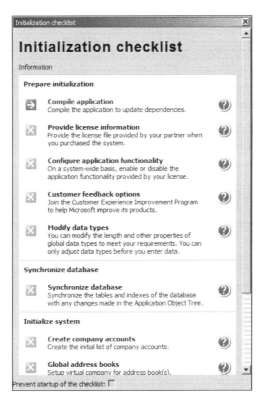

Several steps are required to be completed while others can be bypassed with default settings. The following are the settings that are required to be processed:

- Compile application
- Providing license information
- Configure application functionality
- Synchronize database

Once you have completed the checklist, mark the **Prevent startup** option of the checklist checkbox at the bottom of the checklist to prevent it from displaying again. Once complete, log out and then log back into Dynamics AX. Upon logging back into Dynamics AX, various features and modules will be available for use, depending on your licensing scheme, as displayed in the following screenshot:

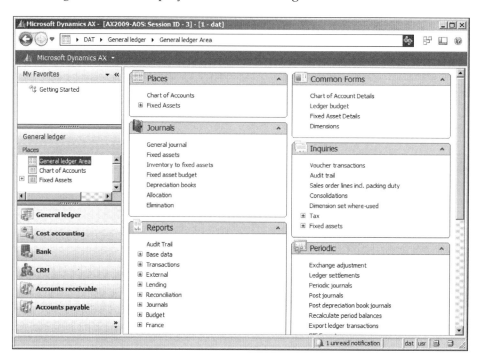

Summary

In this chapter, we discussed that having all the base server components installed and configured and the initialization checklist completed is sufficient for Dynamics AX 2009 to function.

In the next chapter, we will cover the process of installing an additional feature, the Enterprise Portal, which is essentially client access to Dynamics AX using an Internet browser and an Internet or intranet connection.

3
Setup and Configuration of the Enterprise Portal

The **Enterprise Portal** is a SharePoint site that uses the Dynamics AX .NET Business Connector to access data from Dynamics AX. You can perform many common functions such as purchase requisitions, sales orders, customer lookups, CRM, and more, as you would from within the Dynamics AX Client. Additionally, you can access SharePoint web parts from within Dynamics AX, enabling you to access cues or reports on the user's home page. The Enterprise Portal can also provide access using a Local Area Network (LAN) or a Wide Area Network (WAN) such as the internet.

The setup and configuration of the Enterprise Portal will provide end users with access to Dynamics AX from their web browser. In addition, the Enterprise Portal will need to be installed to host Role Center pages, which we will go over in *Chapter 4, Setup and configuration of the Role Centers*.

In this chapter, we will cover the process of installing and configuring the Enterprise Portal for your Dynamics AX installation. In this chapter, we will specifically cover:

- Installation and configuration of the Enterprise Portal
- Setting up an Enterprise Portal in a Load Balanced web farm
- Additional resources for the Enterprise Portal

Installation and configuration of the Enterprise Portal

Before we begin installing the Enterprise Portal, there are several prerequisites that need to be in place. The following are the prerequisite requirements needed for the Enterprise Portal to be installed and to run:

- Internet Information Services (IIS) 7

- Windows SharePoint Services 3.0 with at least SP1 or Office SharePoint Server 2007 with at least SP1

- Internet Explorer 6.0 with at least SP2

 We will cover the process of installing the Enterprise Portal on Windows SharePoint Services 3.0. However, the process is virtually identical when installing on Office SharePoint Server 2007.

Before we continue, the prerequisites must be set up and working; otherwise, we cannot successfully complete the rest of the instructions in this chapter. For example, verify that your SharePoint site is accessible. After the prerequisites are set up and configured properly, the next task is to set up and configure the Enterprise Portal site; this consists of the following steps:

1. Creating the Enterprise Portal SharePoint Application:
    ◦ Creating the Business Connector proxy user

2. Installing the Enterprise Portal.

Creating the Enterprise Portal SharePoint Application

Before we install the Enterprise Portal, we need to create a SharePoint Application to store the Enterprise Portal site. To do this, you will need to complete the following steps:

1. First, we will need to open up the **SharePoint 3.0 Central Administration** page by going to **Start | Administration | SharePoint 3.0 Central Administration**. A page similar to the one shown in the following screenshot will open up in Internet Explorer:

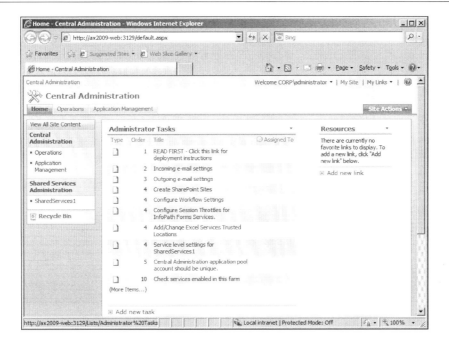

2. In order to create a new SharePoint site, we must go to the **Application Management** page. Click on **Application Management** tab in the **Central Administration** page, as shown in the following screenshot:

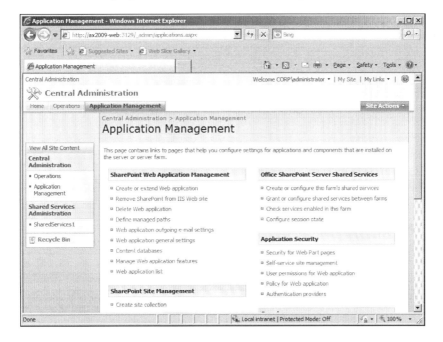

3. In the **Application Management** page, click on the **Create or extend Web application** link under the **SharePoint Web Application Management** section to start creating a new SharePoint site. Once you click on the **Create or extend Web application** link, you will initiate the site creation wizard as follows:

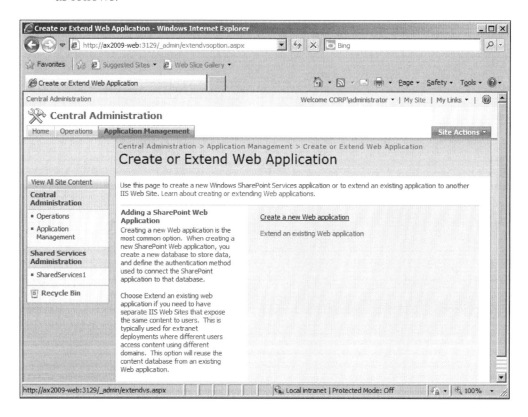

4. Since we want to create a new SharePoint site from scratch, click on the **Create a new Web application** link.

5. In the **Create New Web Application** page, you will notice many fields in which you can customize. We do not need to change everything. For the description of the SharePoint, you can prefix the site description with the name of the AOS in which the Enterprise Portal will reference. In this case, it is **AX2009_INGNOMICS_DEV01**, as shown in the following screenshot:

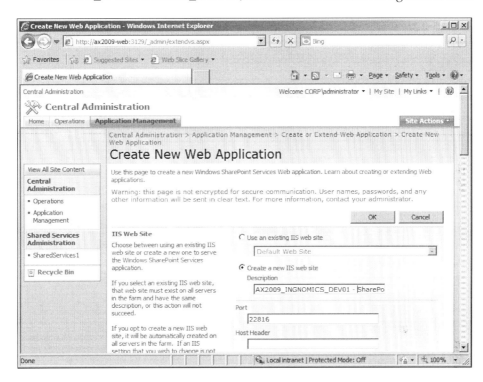

6. In a multiple server configuration, in which each Dynamics AX server component such as the database, Enterprise Portal, Reporting, and Analysis server are on different servers, we will need to use Kerberos authentication for the SharePoint site in order for the Role Centers to work properly, which we will cover in *Chapter 4, Setup and configuration of the Role Centers*. Therefore, we will need to manually enable Kerberos authentication as follows:

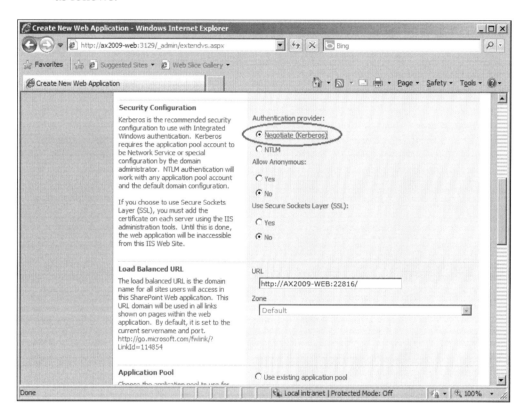

7. You will also need to set the appropriate service account to run the application pool for the new SharePoint site. Although it's not best practice to assign the **Network Services** account by default, it is acceptable here because the Dynamics AX 2009 installation wizard will change this anyway. It may be beneficial to also prefix the **Application pool name** with the name of the AOS, as shown in the following screenshot:

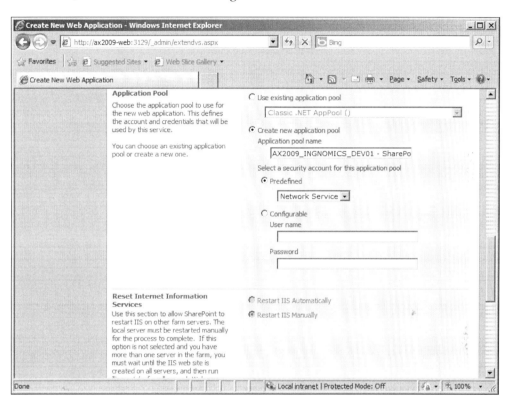

8. In the **Database Name and Authentication** section, it is acceptable to use the default specified database information. However, if your SQL database instance is on a different server, provide the appropriate location here. Additionally, it is also beneficial to change the name of the content database to the same name as the Dynamics AX instance. Specify the appropriate database instance to create the content database on. Once you have completed the previously mentioned steps, you can click on the **OK** button.

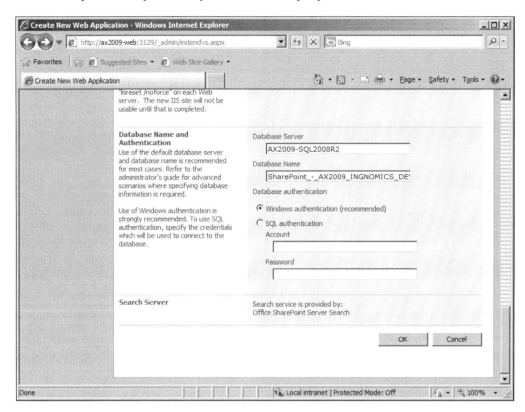

9. After the site is created successfully, you will be prompted to run `iisreset / noforce` in the command prompt.

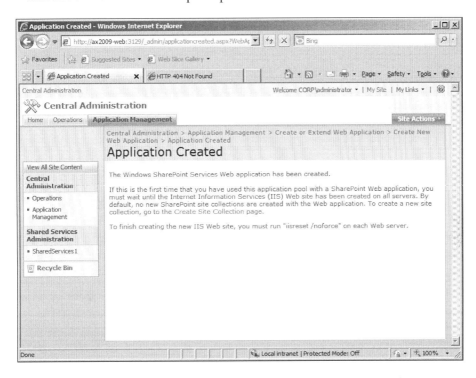

Now that you have created the SharePoint application in which the Enterprise Portal site and Role Center content files will be installed into, the next step is to continue with the additional prerequisites for installing and configuring the Enterprise Portal.

Creating the Business Connector proxy user

The Enterprise Portal requires the Business Connector to be installed. This component will automatically be installed when installing the Role Centers and Enterprise Portal because the Enterprise Portal uses the Business Connector to access Dynamics AX. However, you must create an Active Directory account in which the Business Connector will run on. The following is a list of attributes that the Business Connector domain account should have in place:

- The password must never expire
- It must not have an interactive login
- It must not be associated to any Dynamics AX users

The Business Connector is utilized by various components in Dynamics AX such as Workflow, AIF, and the development tools. The Business Connector allows applications to communicate with Dynamics AX. It may also be utilized by third-party programs that integrate with Dynamics AX.

The Enterprise Portal uses the Business Connector to connect to the AOS and retrieve data and utilize the application file code base to perform business processes. After you have created the Business Connector proxy account, the next step is to notify Dynamics AX what the proxy account is. The Enterprise Portal will use this user account when accessing the AOS. The following steps describe this process:

1. Log in to Dynamics AX.

2. Go to **Administration | Setup | Security | System service accounts**.

3. In the **System service accounts** form, provide the **Business Connector Proxy** account information and then click on the **OK** button when complete.

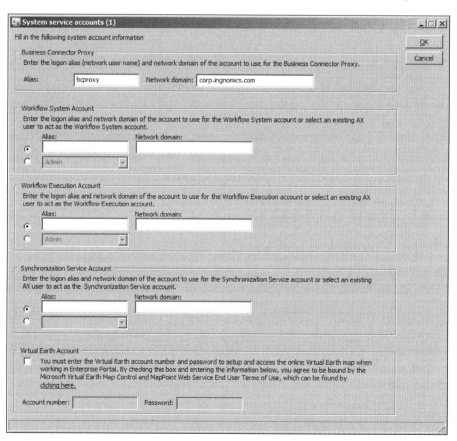

Now that the **Business Connector Proxy** user has been specified in the **System service accounts** form, the AOS can now identify the appropriate privileges on the AOS for the Enterprise Portal or any other application that use the Business Connector.

Installing the Enterprise Portal

By now the SharePoint application for hosting the Enterprise Portal site has been created in either Windows **SharePoint Services 3.0** or **SharePoint 2007**. Now, we can begin installing the Dynamics AX 2009 Enterprise Portal. The base server components of Dynamics AX such as the database, Application files, and AOS are required in order to proceed with the installation of the Enterprise Portal. Moreover, you must also have completed the installation checklist. Refer to *Chapter 2, Setup and Configuration of the Base Server Components* for the process of installing the base server components.

The following steps cover the process of installing the Enterprise Portal content into the SharePoint site that we created earlier:

1. In the **Add or modify components** window of the installation wizard, mark the **Role Centers and Enterprise Portal** checkbox and then click on the **Next >** button.

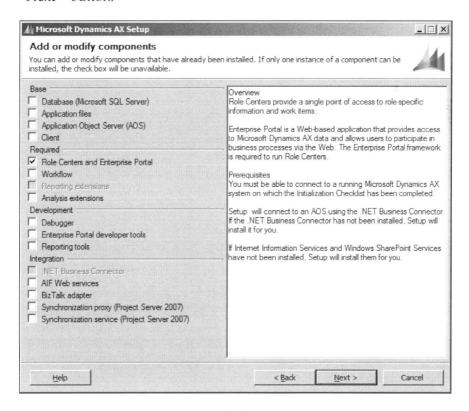

2. In the next screen, you will be prompted to enter the password for the user account associated with the Business Connector, as shown in the following screenshot. If the Business Connector was already installed or the Business Connector proxy account has already been specified in Dynamics AX in the **Administration | Setup | Security | System service accounts** form, then it will automatically be selected and cannot be changed. To change the Business Connector proxy account, simply modify the account name in the **System service accounts** form, as covered in the Creating the Business Connector Proxy User section. Once the Business Connector credential information has been provided, click on the **Next** button.

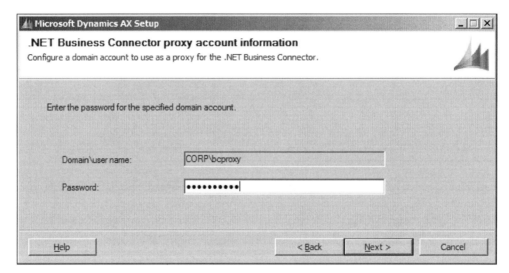

3. In the **Configure IIS** section of the wizard, select the SharePoint site that was newly created and ensure that both checkboxes are marked. The **Configure for Windows SharePoint Services** ensures that the selected **Web site** will be set up to accommodate an Enterprise Portal site. The **Create Web site** checkbox installs the entire Enterprise Portal content into the SharePoint site that was created, overwriting any existing content. When creating an Enterprise Portal site for the first time, both checkboxes must be marked. Once completed click on the **Next** button.

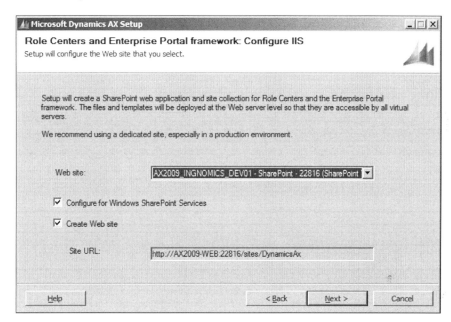

If your version of Dynamics AX does not have a license for the language EN-US, you must:

1. Install the SharePoint or MOSS version of the language pack.
2. Only mark **Configure for Windows SharePoint Services**.
3. Create the site from Dynamics AX in **Administration | Setup | Internet | Enterprise Portal | Web sites** form..

4. In the **Ready to install** section of the wizard, you will be prompted to install the Enterprise Portal. To install, click on the **Install** button.

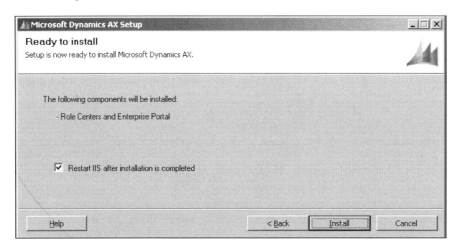

5. If there were no errors during the installation, you will see the following screen. Otherwise, you should mark the checkbox, **Open the log file when Setup closes**, for details on any errors or warnings. To complete the wizard, simply click on the **Finish** button.

In this section, we installed the Enterprise Portal. The Role Center page content was also installed along with the Enterprise Portal content. However, it will not be until the next chapter where we will actually set up and configure the Role Centers for use. Unfortunately, the Dynamics AX 2009 installation wizard for the Enterprise Portal does not provide the means to easily run multiple Enterprise Portal sites on the same SharePoint server, at the same time. To do this requires additional steps, which are outlined in the *Appendix* under the Multiple Instances of an Enterprise Portal in a Web Server section.

By default, only the Administrator can access the Enterprise Portal and its content. To provide users with access to the Enterprise Portal content requires the users to be set up with appropriate security privileges not only in Dynamics AX but also on the Enterprise Portal SharePoint site. This process is covered in *Chapter 9, Security and User Administration*.

Verifying the Enterprise Portal installation

After installing the Enterprise Portal, we should verify that it has been installed to ensure that it is accessible before proceeding to the next step. During the installation, the wizard performs various operations, from copying the Enterprise Portal content files to the specified SharePoint site, as well as setting up Dynamics AX for the Enterprise Portal. To verify that the Enterprise Portal has been installed and is running, we can simply access the Enterprise Portal site. Typically, the Enterprise Portal site is located at `http://<SharePoint EP site URL>/sites/DynamicsAx`. The following steps outline the process of verifying that the Enterprise Portal content was installed:

1. Log in to Dynamics AX and go to **Administration | Setup | Internet | Enterprise Portal | Web sites**.

2. In the **Web sites** form, there should be a record that contains the Enterprise Portal URL and additional settings.

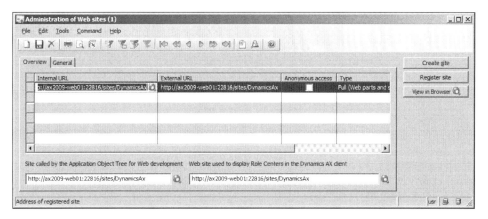

3. Select the record and click on the **View in Browser** button to open the URL in your default browser. Your web browser will load and should display the default **Role Center** page. This signifies that the Enterprise Portal has been successfully installed.

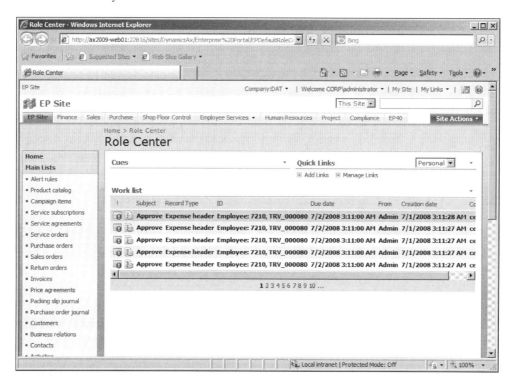

 Your view of your Enterprise Portal may differ depending on your license.

Setting up an Enterprise Portal in a Load Balanced web farm

If the Enterprise Portal is to be utilized heavily, it will be necessary to set up the Enterprise Portal in a web farm. A web farm distributes the load across multiple servers and is used in a large-scale distributed topology as described in *Chapter 1, System Planning & Hardware Sizing*. A web farm provides two key benefits:

- The ability to distribute load and balancing server resources
- The ability to provide redundant access

In the following section, we will cover the process of setting up the Enterprise Portal in a load-balanced SharePoint web farm.

Before we begin, you will need to ensure that the following is available and/or setup:

- A configured Network Load Balanced (NLB) cluster on all SharePoint servers and SharePoint databases

 For information on NLB cluster architecture, refer to the following site: `http://technet.microsoft.com/en-us/library/cc754833(WS.10).aspx`. For information on setting up an NLB cluster, refer to the following site: `http://www.jppinto.com/2009/05/install-and-configure-wlbs-nlb-on-windows-server-2008/`

- An existing SharePoint web farm:

 For more information on setting up a SharePoint web farm on an NLB cluster, refer to the following site: `http://sharepointmagazine.net/technical/administration/best-practices-of-sharepoint-farm-configuring-and-deployment-part-1-architectural-and-logical-planning`.

In the following diagram, there are five SharePoint web servers and one Windows SharePoint Service Database:

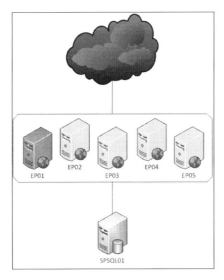

EP01 is highlighted in green to signify that it is the main SharePoint server on the web farm. The process of creating a SharePoint application is identical to creating a site on a non-SharePoint web farm implementation. Even though there will be one Enterprise Portal site, each SharePoint web server will have to have the Enterprise Portal setup.

Deploying the Enterprise Portal in a SharePoint NLB web farm

In order for users to access a load-balanced Enterprise Portal, it must be deployed to a SharePoint NLB web farm. To deploy the Enterprise Portal in a SharePoint NLB web farm, you will need to perform the following steps. The example in these steps deploys the Enterprise Portal on a web farm that consists of two SharePoint servers but the process is the same for additional SharePoint servers.

1. Create a SharePoint application as described in the *Creating the Enterprise Portal SharePoint Application* section of this chapter. Before creating the application, ensure that a host header is specified. This host header is the host address that users will access. One host will be the access point that users will access while the NLB web farm will automatically forward requests to the appropriate server. After clicking on the **OK** button to create the web application, a site will be created on each IIS server in the SharePoint web farm.

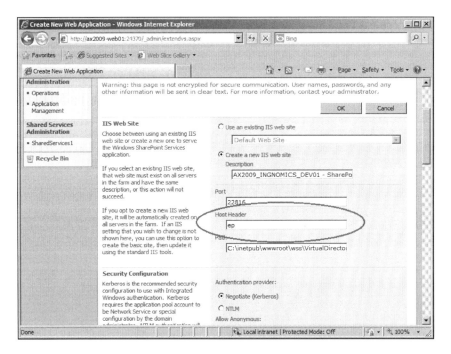

2. Now that the SharePoint application for the Enterprise Portal site has been created with a host header, the next step is to run the installation wizard on all non-primary SharePoint servers in the web farm. (Typically, the SharePoint server that was first used to set up the SharePoint web farm is the primary SharePoint server. Additional SharePoint servers added to the web farm are considered non-primary.) On the wizard step **Role Centers and Enterprise Portal framework: Configure IIS**, make sure both checkboxes are unmarked. When complete, proceed through the wizard as you would when installing on a non-SharePoint web farm.

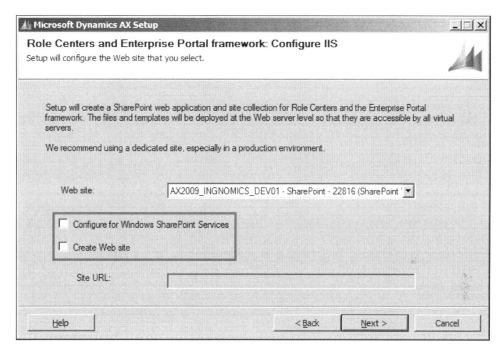

3. Now that each non-primary SharePoint server on the web farm has had the Enterprise Portal content installed, the final step is to install the Enterprise Portal on the primary SharePoint server. Simply install the Enterprise Portal content as described in the Creating the Enterprise Portal SharePoint *Application*. In the wizard step, **Role Centers and Enterprise Portal framework: Configure IIS**, ensure that both checkboxes are marked.

Here, we covered the process of installing and deploying the Enterprise Portal in an NLB SharePoint web farm. In large Enterprise Portal implementations where traffic demands are high, whether many users are external and/or internal users, a load-balanced web farm is absolutely necessary. Fortunately, the process is very straightforward.

Additional resources for the Enterprise Portal

For more information that tailors to the setup, administration, and troubleshooting of the Enterprise Portal, refer to the following table of additional resources. A subscription to Customer Source or Partner Source may be required to access the following content.

Resource description	Site
Troubleshooting Enterprise Portal installation and deployment	http://technet.microsoft.com/en-us/library/ee355087.aspx
Enterprise Portal Tips and Tricks	https://mbs.microsoft.com/partnersource/documentation/howtoarticles/ax2009_epinstall.htm
Enterprise Portal Administration	https://mbs.microsoft.com/customersource/documentation/userguides/ax2009_epadminguide.htm
Redeploying Enterprise Portal sites using the AxUpdatePortal utility	http://msdn.microsoft.com/en-us/library/dd261467.aspx

Summary

At this point, the Enterprise Portal is fully functional with out-of-the-box features of Dynamics AX 2009. However, the scope of the features available depends on your license scheme.

In the next chapter, we will be going a step further and setting up the Role Centers, the business intelligence component of Dynamics AX. Role Centers marriage SQL Server Analysis Services, SQL Server Reporting Services, and the Enterprise Portal to provide an informative yet aesthetically pleasing approach to viewing Dynamics AX data.

4

Setup and Configuration of the Role Centers

In the previous chapter, we covered the implementation of the Enterprise Portal, which provided a limited web client interface access to Dynamics AX. Dynamics AX comes with a new feature called Role Centers, which goes hand-in-hand with the Enterprise Portal. Role Centers build on top of the Enterprise Portal to provide business intelligence and advanced reporting from the data in Dynamics AX. It is a new and powerful addition to the Dynamics AX component arsenal that will evolve as proceeding versions are released.

Role Centers are essentially dashboards that provide an overview of information to an end user. They are just SharePoint web pages with web parts. This implies that you can customize Role Centers like any other SharePoint page. For example, you can add a SQL Server Reporting Services report or an Exchange calendar to a Role Center. You can even modify the structure of how the web parts are displayed if you so desire. For more information on customizing SharePoint web pages, consult the following website: `http://office.microsoft.com/en-us/sharepoint-server-help/CH010178298.aspx`.

Dynamics AX comes with approximately 31 Role Centers. These Role Centers represent many business functions or roles. For example, a specific role could be a CEO, CFO, controller, or even a warehouse manager. At the heart of Role Centers is not only the Application Object Server (AOS) but also SQL Server Analysis Services and SQL Server Reporting Services that work in unison to generate a relevant representation of business data for analysis. Afterwards, all the data is organized into a SharePoint page for representation in the Enterprise Portal, which is also the default view when a user logs into Dynamics AX using the client or Enterprise Portal. From there, the user can quickly see the information that matters.

In this chapter, we will cover the following:

- Installation and setup of Role Centers
- Installation and setup of Analysis extensions
- Installation and setup of Reporting extensions
- Dynamics AX SQL Server Reporting Services setup
- Assigning Role Centers

Installation and setup of Role Centers

The earlier mentioned list contains a number of components that when setup, all work in unison to provide Business Intelligence Role Center functionality. However, you can still have limited Role Center functionality if Reporting extensions or Analysis extensions are not set up. Depending on your setup, the Business Intelligence setup of Role Centers may require some specific modifications in configuration and setup such as Kerberos authentication as covered in *Chapter 5, Setting Up Kerberos Authentication*.

Before we begin installing and setting up Role Centers, you will need to have at least local administrator privileges on the machines that you are installing the Role Center components on. You may also be required to change network and domain controller settings; in that case you will need to have network administrator privileges. You will also need the Dynamics AX DVD. Be aware that Role Centers require report deployment, installation of the Dynamics AX analysis database, and a functional Enterprise Portal. The following server components are required to install and set up Role Centers:

- Web server
  - **Internet Information Server (IIS)** 7
  - Windows SharePoint Services 3.0 or Office SharePoint Server 2007
- Reporting server
  - SQL Server Reporting Services 2008 or 2008 R2
- Analysis server
  - SQL Server Analysis Services 2008 or 2008 R2

In some infrastructure scenarios, it is plausible to have the reporting server and web server combined into one server. Similarly, the analysis server and database server can also be combined into one server.

Your network infrastructure setup will determine where each component of the Role Centers will be installed. For example, the Enterprise Portal will be installed on the web server since that is where SharePoint and thus IIS is installed.

To help determine where each component will be installed, refer to the topology diagrams found in *Chapter 1*, *System Planning and Hardware Sizing*. You may notice in *Chapter 3*, *Setup and Configuration of the Enterprise Portal*, when installing the Enterprise Portal, you inadvertently installed the Role Centers as well, since the install option for both the Enterprise Portal and Role Centers are combined. However, even though the web page content files for Role Centers were installed, the Reporting and Analysis extensions for Business Intelligence in the Role Centers were not installed. The following sections will cover the installation of the Analysis and Reporting extensions as well as the steps to configure each component to work properly in order to have fully functional Role Centers for Dynamics AX.

Installation and setup of Analysis extensions

Analysis extensions are part of the Dynamics AX Business Intelligence framework. They are a set of predefined cubes (also known as default cubes) for SQL Server Analysis Services. Partnered with Reporting extensions and Role Centers, Analysis extensions complete the Business Intelligence capabilities of Dynamics AX. To install the Analysis extensions, you will need to be on the server in which you have SQL Server Analysis extensions installed. The Dynamics AX installation wizard will automatically install the Dynamics AX analysis database in the specified analysis server environment as depicted in the following steps:

Unfortunately, due to limitations with the Dynamics AX installation wizard, it can only install Analysis extensions on SQL Server Analysis Services 2005. Fortunately, there are two ways to circumvent this. You can either install Analysis extensions on SQL Server Analysis Services 2005 and then upgrade to SQL Server Analysis Server 2008 or copy the Analysis extensions database to SQL Server Analysis Server 2008. To install Analysis extensions on SQL Server Analysis Services 2008, refer to *How to install Analysis extensions on SQL Server Analysis Services 2008* in the *Appendix*.

1. Run the **Microsoft Dynamics AX Setup** wizard to add new components. In the **Add or modify components** screen of the wizard, mark **Analysis extensions**, as shown in the following screenshot and then click on **Next**

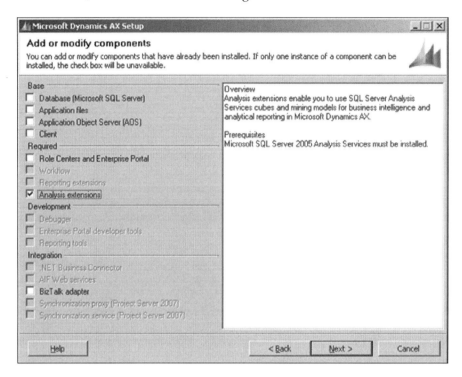

2. In the following screen of the wizard, select **Microsoft SQL Server** as the database server then click on the **Next** button:

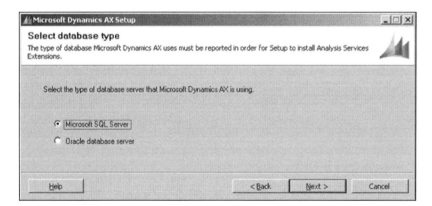

3. In the next section of the wizard, **Analysis extensions: Select an Analysis Services instance**, you will be asked to select the Analysis Server instance in which you want the Dynamics AX analysis database to be installed in. The wizard will install to the default analysis server instance. After you have the appropriate analysis server instance selected, click on **Next**.

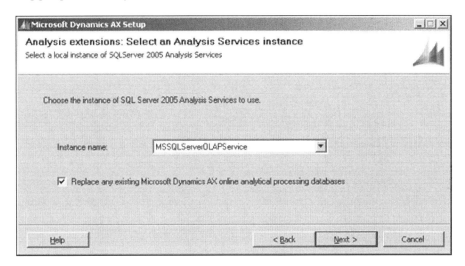

 Even if SQL Server Analysis Services 2008 or 2008 R2 are installed, the installation wizard for Analysis extensions will still say SQL Server 2005 Analysis Services. The installation process will however install to your SQL Server Analysis Services 2008 database.

4. In the following screen you will be prompted to complete the installation of the **Analysis extensions**. Click on the **Install** button to finalize the installation, as shown in the following screenshot:

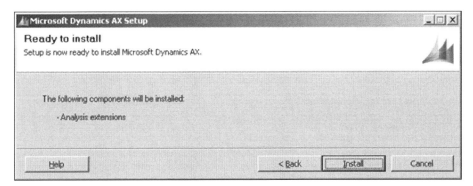

5. Once the installation of the Analysis extensions has completed, you will be prompted with the final screen of the wizard where you can confirm if the installation was successful or not, as shown in the following screenshot. When you are satisfied with the component's installation, click on the **Finish** button to complete and close the wizard.

Installation and setup of Reporting extensions

Reporting extensions is a utility that deploys a collection of Microsoft **SQL Server Reporting Services (SSRS)** reports. To install the Reporting extensions, you will need to be on the server in which you want to serve the SQL Server Reports. Make sure you can navigate to the SSRS report manager URL as well as the SSRS report server web service URL. After the Dynamics AX installation wizard installs the Dynamics AX Reporting extensions, you will manually have to run the Reporting extensions utility to deploy the reports. To install the Reporting extensions, perform the following steps:

The Dynamics AX installation wizard cannot install Reporting extensions on SQL Server Reporting Services 2008 without a hotfix. For more information on obtaining and installing this hotfix, refer to Knowledge Base article 957312 or go to: `https://mbs.microsoft.com/knowledgebase/KBDisplay.aspx?scid=kb;en-us;957312`.

1. Run the **Microsoft Dynamics AX Setup** wizard to add new components. In the **Add or modify components** screen of the wizard, mark **Reporting extensions**, as shown in the following screenshot and then click on the **Next** button:

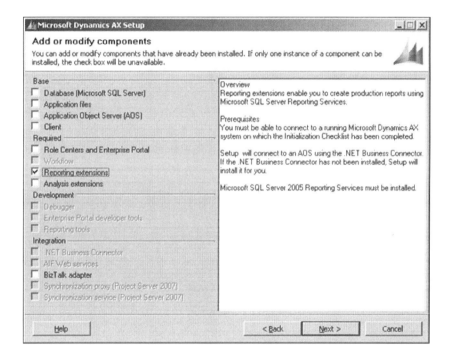

2. In the next section of the wizard, **.NET Business Connector proxy account information**, you will be prompted to enter the password for the Business Connector Proxy account, as shown in the following screenshot. This is necessary because once the Reporting extensions are installed, the Reporting extensions utility will need to access the specific AOS to which the reports will be associated to. After you have provided the appropriate password, click on the **Next** button to proceed to the next step.

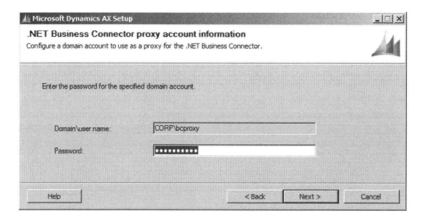

3. In the following section of the wizard, **Reporting extensions: Select a Reporting Services instance**, you will be prompted to select the appropriate SSRS instance, as shown in the following screenshot. Make sure you also mark the **Configure IIS and Report Server** checkbox so the installation wizard can automatically modify the SSRS configuration files and other settings in IIS that belong to the Report Server and Reports Manager website to appropriately integrate with Dynamics AX. Once the appropriate SSRS instance is selected, click on the **Next** button to proceed.

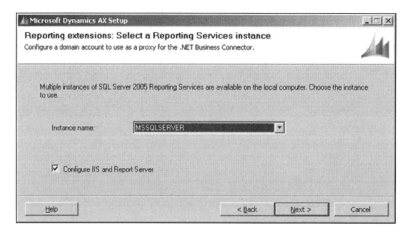

Even if you are installing the Reporting extensions on SQL Server 2008 or 2008 R2 Reporting Services, the install wizard will still display SQL Server 2005 Reporting Services. This is because the GUI of the installation wizard has not been updated. From now on, simply ignore it.

4. The next section of the wizard is basically a confirmation to install the Reporting extensions based on the settings provided in the previous sections. Make sure the **Restart IIS after installation is completed** checkbox is marked, as shown in the following screenshot. When you are confident with your settings, click the **Install** button to start the installation process.

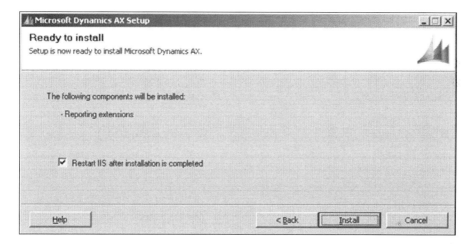

5. Once the installation process completes, you can determine if the SSRS and IIS were appropriately configured or not, as shown in the following screenshot. If the box next to the Reporting extensions label is not green, then you must open the log file to determine what went wrong. If the installation was successful, you can automatically run the Reports Deployment utility that was just installed to begin deploying the Dynamics AX SSRS reports. Otherwise, unmark the **Automatically launch Reports Deployment utility**, if you desire to do this at a later stage.

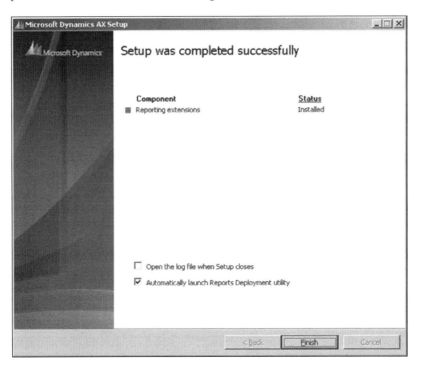

The previous steps outlined the process of installing **Reporting extensions**. This is indeed a straightforward process for installing in a single environment. However, while the database and Analysis extensions can be installed for multiple Dynamics AX 2009 environments, unfortunately, **Reporting extensions** cannot. Reporting extensions can only point to a single Dynamics AX environment on the server it is hosted on. Whatever the **Business Connector Configuration Target** is pointed to in the **Microsoft Dynamics AX 2009 Configuration Utility** in Windows' **Administrative Tools**, is the environment that **Reporting Extensions** will function with.

Deploying reports using the Report Deployment utility

After you have installed the Reporting extensions as we did in the previous section, you will need to run the Reports Deployment utility. If the utility did not automatically run after the installation, you can manually run it by going to **Start | All Programs | Microsoft Dynamics AX 2009 | Microsoft Dynamics AX 2009 Reports Deployment**. The **Reporting Deployment** utility will deploy reports for the Dynamics AX AOS that is specified in the **Business Connector Configuration Target**, in the **Microsoft Dynamics 2009 Configuration Utility**. Once you have the Reports Deployment utility running, perform the following steps to successfully deploy the Dynamics AX SSRS reports:

 In order for the Reports Deployment utility to run properly, ensure that Dynamics AX 2009 SP1, Visual Studio 2008 shell, and Windows Server 2008 SDK are installed.

1. Upon loading the Reports Deployment utility, it will automatically generate a list of report libraries from Dynamics AX that you can selectively deploy, as shown in the following screenshot. Typically, you will want to mark **<Select All>** to deploy all the available reports to your SSRS server. Once you have selected the appropriate report libraries, click on the **Next** button to begin extracting the libraries.

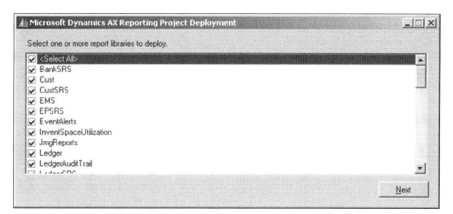

2. Once the libraries have been extracted, the utility will automatically begin building the report libraries and preparing them for deployment. The number of reports you selected will determine how long this process takes. If you have selected all report libraries, this process can take about half an hour to complete. Once these initial processes are completed, you will be prompted to modify the SSRS connection string for the reports, as shown in the following screenshot. Depending on your server setup, you may need to modify the **Data Source** property setting to connect to the appropriate Dynamics AX 2009 database. Once you are satisfied with the connection string(s), click on the **Next** button to proceed to deploy the reports.

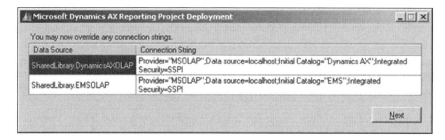

2. The following process is the actual report deployment process. This process can take more than one hour to run depending on how many reports you are deploying. Once the deploying completes, you will be prompted with a message log and a location of the deployment log file for review, in case there were any errors or warnings, as shown in the following screenshot. To complete and exit the utility, click on the **Finish** button.

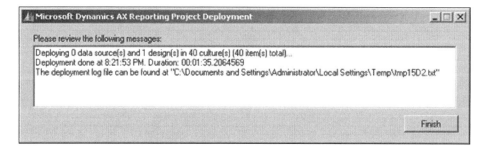

3. Once the deployment of Reporting extensions is successful, you should confirm that the reports have indeed deployed to the reporting services website. Simply navigate to your SQL Server Reporting Services (SSRS) Report Manager site with Internet Explorer, as shown in the following screenshot. Verify that the **Dynamics** folder is created and that the reports are deployed to it. You will see a similar screen depending on the number of reports that were deployed.

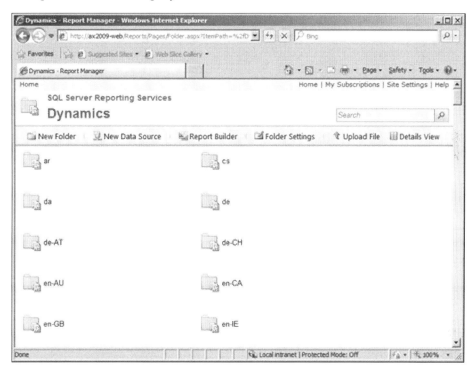

Dynamics AX SQL Server Reporting Services setup

Even though the installation wizard and the report deployment utility perform many automated tasks, there is still some manual setup that needs to be performed within Dynamics AX. We will need to notify Dynamics AX where the reporting server is and set various configuration settings. The following steps explain the process:

1. Run the Dynamics AX client. Once Dynamics AX loads, go to the **Administration | Setup | Business Analysis | Reporting Services** section. Click on the **Reporting Servers** link. The **Reporting Servers** form will load. Notice that the SSRS server information is already provided. This was automatically created during the installation of the Reporting extensions. If there is no information provided yet, there is a valid reporting server to use, simply create a new record and provide the information.

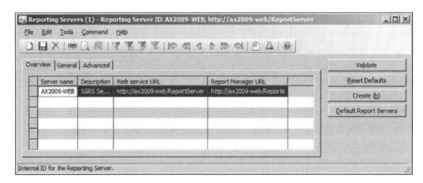

2. If specifying a new SSRS server, go to the **General** tab and begin entering the appropriate information for your current SSRS setup.

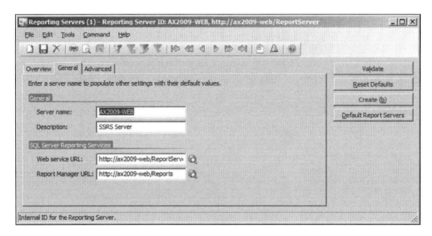

3. After you have filled out the appropriate fields in the **General** tab, click on the **Advanced** tab and enter the appropriate information.

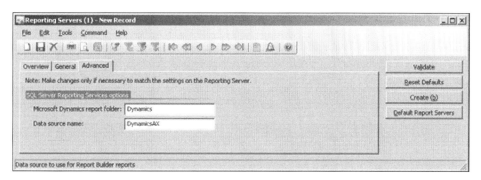

4. In SQL Server 2008 or 2008 R2 Reporting Services, the installation wizard for Reporting extensions may have not created the Dynamics AX data source even though it is specified. To create it, ensure that **DynamicsAX** is specified in the **Data source name** textbox and click on the **Create** button to automatically create the data source in the report server. An **Infolog** window will pop up determining whether the process was successful or not.

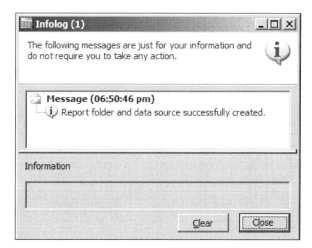

5. Once you have specified all the appropriate information, click on the **Validate** button to verify that Dynamics AX can access the reporting server and that all the reporting settings are properly set. If so, you will receive an **Infolog** message, as shown in the following screenshot:

Assigning Role Centers

Now that Analysis extensions and Reporting extensions are installed and configured, we can proceed to assign users to actual Role Centers. Within Dynamics AX, Role Centers are also referred to as **User profiles**. In fact, the form to assign Role Centers is in the **User profiles** form. To assign and understand the various options for assigning users to Role Centers, follow the steps outlined here:

1. To assign a Role Center to users, load the **User profile** form located in **Administration | Setup | User profiles**.

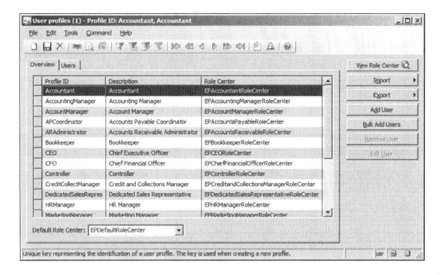

2. Let's assign several users to the **Accountant** profile. To do this, select the **Accountant** profile and click on the **Bulk Add Users** button.

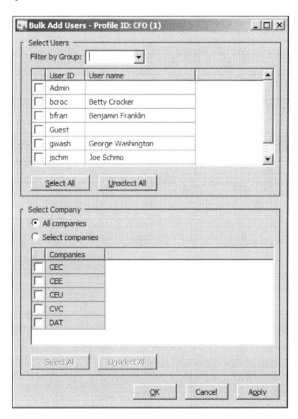

3. Select which users to assign to the **Accountant** profile. If the users are already organized in a Dynamics AX group (for example, an Accountant group), select the group in the **Filter by Group** drop-down to easily filter by user group. There is also an option to specify which company the profile will be active on. This is present because one user can have different profiles in separate companies. For example, a user can have an **Accountant** profile in company **CEU** while having an **AccountingManager** profile in company **CEE**. When the appropriate users are marked, click on the **OK** button to add the marked users to the **Accountant** profile.

4. Additionally, users can be assigned to profiles in the **Active Directory Import Wizard**, as shown in the following screenshot. This process is similar to the previously mentioned steps.

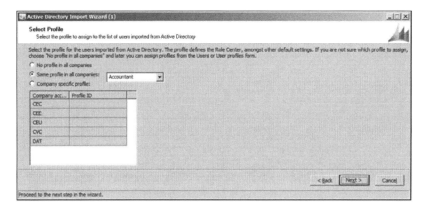

Since the selected users were mapped to a profile, they will now be associated to a **Role Center**. Individual users can be added one at a time by clicking on the **Add user** button, as shown in step 1. User profiles can also be saved to be exported and imported between Dynamics AX environments to simplify the process of creating duplicate user profile settings.

Summary

This chapter focused on the process of setting up the Enterprise Portal with Role Centers, SQL Reporting Services, SSRS, with Dynamics AX. Reporting extensions are a vital component for the Business Analysis features that Dynamics AX 2009 provides. Most reports query Dynamics AX directly while some query SQL Server Analysis Services cubes. Installing Reporting extension along with Analysis extensions are necessary in your arsenal for setting up Role Centers.

In order for users to be able to access and use the reports, permissions must be set up. In *Chapter 9, Security and User Administration* we will cover how to appropriate setup permissions on reports.

In the next chapter, we will cover the process of setting up Kerberos authentication. The setup and configuration of Kerberos authentication is required for Role Centers to function properly when each Dynamics AX server component is implemented across multiple servers. Otherwise, if Kerberos authentication is not appropriately set up, the Role Center web parts will fail to load properly.

5
Setting Up Kerberos Authentication

Typically, servers and services in a Windows Server environment are set up using **NT LAN Manager (NTLM)** authentication. When in a multiple distributed server and services environment, NTLM increases its level of vulnerability as it is easier for a hacker to gain access from one service by spoofing their identity or performing other malicious authentication attacks. At one time, NTLM was appropriate and easy to use; however, times have changed. Servers and services come aplenty and security is critical.

NTLM lacks in providing extra security measures that are needed. The word Kerberos is actually derived from the Greek name Cerberus. Cerberus was a mythological three-headed hound that guarded the gates of Hades. In other words, it was an extremely protective creature that thwarted any invaders from attempting to breach the gates of Hades. The Kerberos authentication protocol was developed with enhanced security measures in mind when authenticating users as they "pass through the gates" to access multiple services. Therefore, when one thinks of Kerberos authentication, one can also think of enhanced security authentication.

For Dynamics AX 2009, Kerberos authentication is not only nice to have for its security protocol, but is necessary for Role Centers to function properly in a non-developer environment. Without Kerberos authentication, Role Center web parts that contain reports from Microsoft SQL Reporting Services or Microsoft SQL Analysis Services will simply fail to load. The reason Role Centers will work in a developer environment is because all of the base and extended server components reside on the same server and there is really no need to authenticate on other servers. However, for other Dynamics AX 2009 environments, such as a production environment, the base and extended server components will be dispersed across multiple servers; hence, Kerberos authentication has to be properly set up.

In this chapter, we will specifically cover:

- Configuring Service Principal Names
- Configuring the Domain Controller for Kerberos authentication
- Configuring SharePoint for Kerberos authentication
- Configuring SQL Reporting Services for Kerberos authentication
- Configuring SQL Analysis Services for Kerberos authentication
- Setting up Office Data Connection (ODC) files
- Setting up Component Services
- Configuring Internet Information Services for Kerberos authentication

Setting up Kerberos authentication for Role Centers

Now that you have an understanding of what Kerberos authentication is, the next process is to set up your Dynamics AX 2009 environment to utilize Kerberos authentication. Depending on your infrastructure setup, some of the following items on the list may not be applicable. However, the following setup is considered optimal:

- Web server:
  - Office SharePoint Server 2007 or Windows SharePoint Services 3.0
  - SQL Server Reporting Services 2008 or 2008 R2

- Database server:
  - SQL Server 2008 or 2008 R2
  - SQL Server Analysis Services 2008 or 2008 R2

In the previous list, we have two servers. Depending on server load, you may also decide to have the SQL Server Analysis Services on a dedicated server or the SQL Server Reporting Services on a dedicated server. In this example, we have one server designated as the web server and the other as the database server. The web server contains anything related to serving web pages while the database server contains anything related to storing and retrieving data, as well as performing any calculations on that data. If you notice, the AOS server is not mentioned because it is not required to be set up for Kerberos authentication. However, each one of the components mentioned will have to be set up individually to utilize Kerberos authentication.

Configuring Service Principal Names

The **Service Principal Name (SPN)** can be considered as a link between the service and the Active Directory user account. By specifying the server name, domain name, and user account running a service (for example, application pool account or service account), `setspn.exe` is a utility that an administrator can use to list, register, delete, or update Service Principal Names. The SPN must be specified for both the Enterprise Portal application pool account (which should be the Business Connector Proxy account), SQL Server, and the SQL Server Analysis Services (SSAS) service accounts. There is no restriction on which server the SPN command can run on, as long as the server is within the same domain as the services whose accounts require to be set up as Service Principal Names. The following steps outline this process:

1. Open the Windows Command Prompt (**Start | Run | cmd**).

2. Register the SPN for the Enterprise Portal application pool account. To set it, enter the following:

   ```
   setspn.exe -A HTTP/<Enterprise Portal server name> <Application
   pool account name>
   ```

3. Where `<Enterprise Portal Server Name>` is the server name, but not the **Fully Qualified Domain Name (FQDN)** of the Enterprise Portal server. `<Application pool account name>` is the Active Directory user account running the application pool. This account is typically the Business Connector Proxy account.

```
C:\Users\Administrator>setspn -A HTTP/AX2009-DEV01 CORP\bcproxy
Registering ServicePrincipalNames for CN=Dynamics AX Business Connector Proxy Us
er,CN=Users,DC=corp,DC=ingnomics,DC=com
        HTTP/AX2009-DEV01
Updated object

C:\Users\Administrator>
```

4. Perform the same process as described in the previous step; however, this time, use the FQDN.

Now that the SPN is registered for the Enterprise Portal SharePoint site, the SPN must also be registered for the SQL Server Analysis Services (SSAS). To register the SPN for the SSAS server, enter the following commands in the Windows Command Prompt.

 If service accounts are the Network Service or Local Service accounts, use the `<Computer>$` format for the account names, for example, if the SSAS service account is a Network Service account, `AX2009-SSAS01$` would be the service account name to use when setting the SPN.

1. To set the SPN on a SSAS service account, use the following commands:

   ```
   setspn.exe -A MSOLAPSvc.4/<SSAS server name> <SSAS service account
   name>
   ```

 If using SQL Server 2005, replace **MSOLAPSvc.4** with **MSOLAPSvc.3**.

2. Where `<SSAS Server Name>` is the server name, yet not the FQDN of the SSAS server. `<SSAS account name>` is the Active Directory user account running the SSAS service.

3. Perform the same process as described in the previous step; however, this time, use the FQDN.

4. To set the SPN for the SQL Server Service account, perform the following command:

```
setspn.exe -A MSSQLSvc/<SQL server name>:1433 <SQL service account name>
```

5. Perform the previous step again, except use the FQDN of the SQL Server.

To verify that Kerberos authentication was set up properly, run the `setspn -L <account name>` command. For example, to verify that the HTTP service principal name was configured correctly, you would run the `setspn -L CORP\bcproxy`, where `CORP\bcproxy` is the business connector account. If the results point to the correct server, then you can be assured that the SPN was configured correctly for the HTTP service. Similarly, if you want to verify that the SQL Server Analysis Services was configured correctly, you need to run the `setspn -L AX2009-DEV01$` command. If the results point to the correct servers, then you can be assured that the SQL Server Analysis Services SPN was configured correctly. Remember, both the local hostname as well as the FQDN must be listed.

A useful tool that can assist you in verifying whether the SPNs have been successfully registered is **KerbTray**. This tool is included in the Windows Server 2003 Resource Kit Tools. KerbTray runs in the task bar tray and displays the Kerberos service tickets. Confirm that both the Enterprise Portal and the SSAS service tickets are listed. Similarly, if you are using Windows Server 2008, you can use the utility, `klist.exe` to view and delete service tickets.

Configuring the Domain Controller for Kerberos authentication

Various settings will need to be applied in the Domain Controller to fully support Kerberos authentication and for the Role Center web parts to display properly. Although many settings are already set during a Windows Server installation, there are some additional settings that must be appropriately set. This section covers each process necessary in the Domain Controller to accomplish this.

Raising the domain functional level

Before enabling Kerberos authentication on the individual server components, your network Domain Controller must be running at least in the Windows Server 2008 or Windows Server 2008 R2 domain functional level in order to be able to facilitate Kerberos authentication. The following steps describe this process.

Windows Server 2003 domain functional level is also supported.

1. Access the Domain Controller server and go to **Active Directory Users and Computers** by going to **Start | Administrative Tools | Active Directory Users and Computers**.

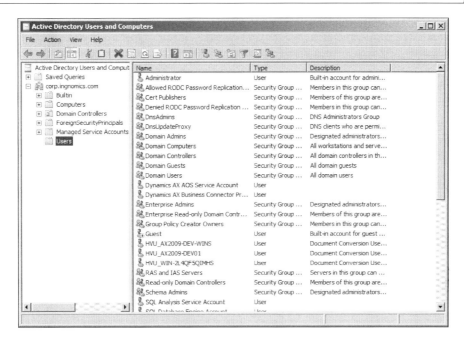

2. To raise the domain functional level, right-click on the domain and then select **Raise domain functional level...** from the drop-down menu. If using Windows Server 2003, raise the domain function level to **Windows Server 2003**.

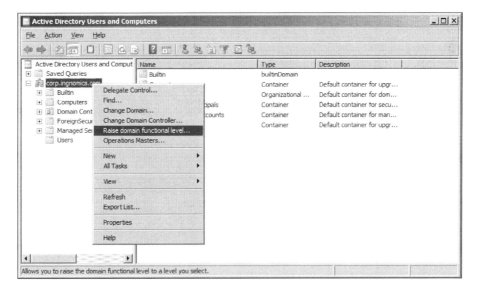

3. Select the domain functional level **Windows Server 2008** or **Windows Server 2008 R2**. When complete, click on the **Raise** button to raise the level and save the changes.

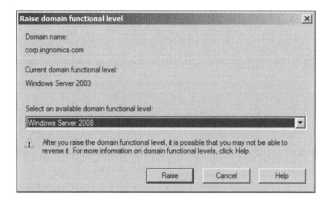

In order to complete the following steps in this section, the domain functional level must be raised appropriately.

As noted by the **Raise domain functional level** window, once you raise the level, you may not be able to reverse it. Therefore, verify that raising the domain functional level will not negatively impact other servers and applications before performing such tasks. Raising the domain functional level to **Windows Server 2003** may be a better approach because other server systems on your network may not support more recent versions. Verify that all systems on a network will work with either **Windows Server 2008** or **Windows Server 2008 R2** domain functional level. Dynamics AX 2009 and its components support all three of them.

Verifying account delegation

Now that the domain functional level has been properly set, we can proceed to modify the delegation options wherever needed. User accounts that will access Role Center pages, SSRS, or SSAS reports must have the capability to be delegated. Additionally, service accounts that have been set up as Service Principal Names (SPNs) must be trusted to perform delegation so that they can assume the identity of user accounts when user accounts are accessing other servers. For example, when a user logs in to a Role Center page, the Enterprise Portal application pool account will impersonate the user account accessing the page to authenticate the Report web parts.

To verify that a user account can be delegated, perform the following steps:

1. Access your Domain Controller server and go to **Active Directory Users and Computers (Start | Administrative Tools | Active Directory Users and Computers)**.

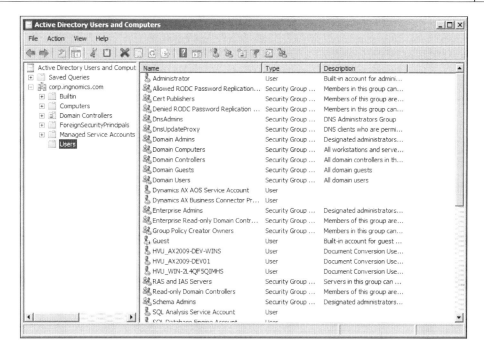

2. Select a user account that will access a Role Center page and go to **Properties**.

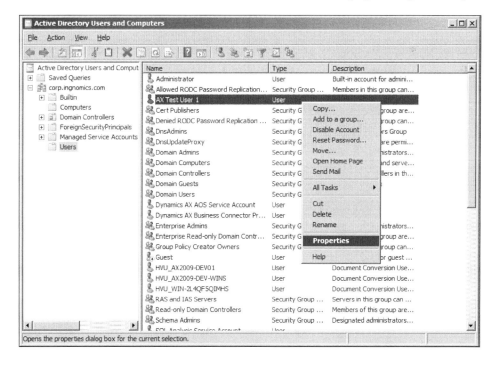

3. In the user's account properties, go to the **Account** tab and in the **Account options** group, verify that the checkbox **Account is sensitive and cannot be delegated** is unchecked.

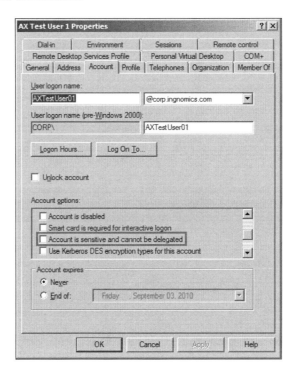

Additionally, the IIS Application Pool account for the Enterprise Portal must be updated to delegate user accounts. The following steps outline this process:

4. Access your Domain Controller server and go to **Active Directory Users and Computers** (**Start | Administrative Tools | Active Directory Users and Computers**).

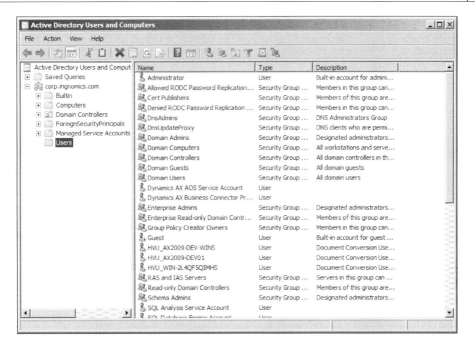

5. Select Enterprise Portal IIS application pool account. This should be the business connector proxy account. When selected, right-click on that user account and go to **Properties**.

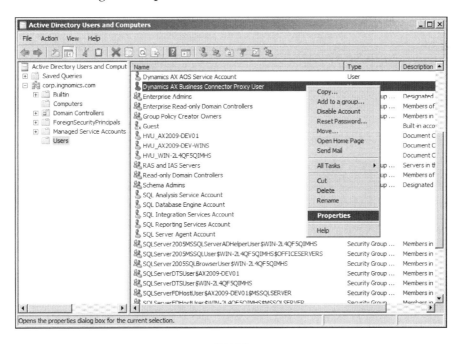

6. In the account properties, go to the **Delegation** tab to view the delegation settings for the user account. If the **Delegation** tab is not present, then verify that you set the SPN on this account correctly. Mark the option **Trust this user for delegation to any server (Kerberos only)**.

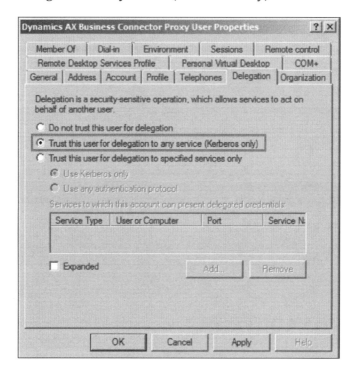

Additionally, perform the same process for the Report Server and Report Manager user accounts that are used in the application pool for those sites.

Configuring SharePoint for Kerberos authentication

This section assumes that the Role Centers and Enterprise Portal have already been installed on a SharePoint server as covered in *Chapter 3, Setup and Configuration of the Enterprise Portal* and *Chapter 4, Setup and Configuration of the Role Centers*. To set up Kerberos authentication on SharePoint, perform the following steps:

1. Connect to your web server and run the SharePoint **Central Administration**. In Windows, click on **Start | Administrative Tools | SharePoint <version> Central Administration**. This will open up Internet Explorer and connect you to the **Central Administration**.

2. Once the **Central Administration** page loads, click on the **Application Management** tab to go to the **Application Management** section.

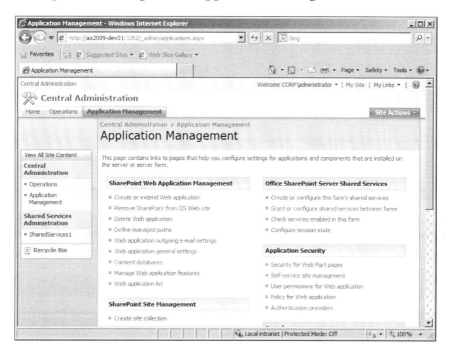

3. Since you have already set up your Enterprise Portal website, we will need to change its default authentication method. To do this, click on the **Authentication providers** link under the **Application Security** group.

4. In the **Authentication Providers** page, before continuing, make sure that the correct web application is selected. If so, click on the current zone. In this example, the zone is **Default**.

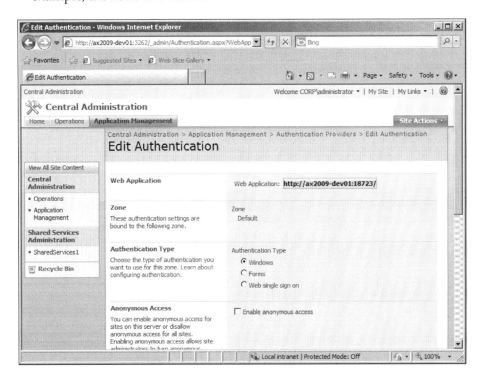

5. In the **Edit Authentication** page, make sure the **Integrated Windows authentication** mode is marked and select **Negotiate (Kerberos)** to use Kerberos authentication. Then click the **Save** button to apply the new settings.

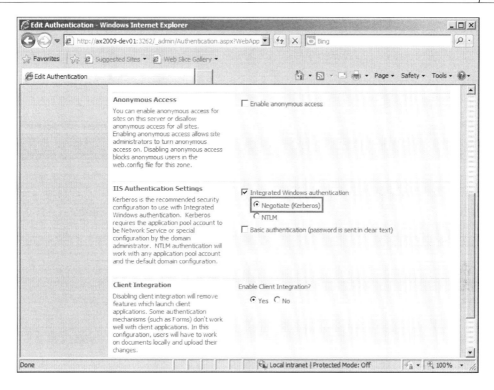

6. Repeat steps 2-5 for the **Shared Service Provider (SSP)** of the Enterprise Portal application.

7. Open the Windows Command Prompt (**Start | Run | cmd**) and type in **iisreset** to restart IIS.

Configuring SQL Reporting Services for Kerberos authentication

In order to set up the Reporting Services for Kerberos authentication, you will need to complete the following steps:

1. Open the `RSReportServer.config` file for editing in a text editor. The file is typically located in `<SQL Server Reporting Services Install Directory>\Reporting Services\ReportServer`.

2. Locate the `<AuthenticationTypes>` section.

3. Delete the NTLM configuration settings to disable NTLM authentication and instead add the following to enable Kerberos:

   ° `<RSWindowsKerberos />`

   ° `<RSWindowsNegotiate />`

 Ensure that you make a backup of the files before they are edited.

Configuring SQL Analysis Services for Kerberos authentication

If SSAS is running on a server that does not have SQL server installed, then the connection must be capable of communicating using Kerberos authentication. By default, the connection string for the SQL Server Analysis Services database lacks the capability to connect using a Kerberos authentication method. This requires us to manually modify the connection string. To modify the connection string, perform the following steps:

1. Log in to the Analysis Services server in the **SQL Server Management Studio**.

2. On the SSAS server, navigate down to the data source and right-click on the **Dynamics AX** data source and click on **Properties**.

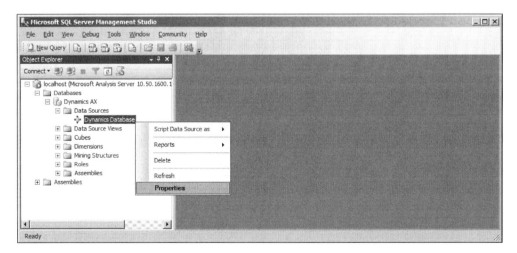

3. At the very end of the connection string, place ;sspi=Kerberos.

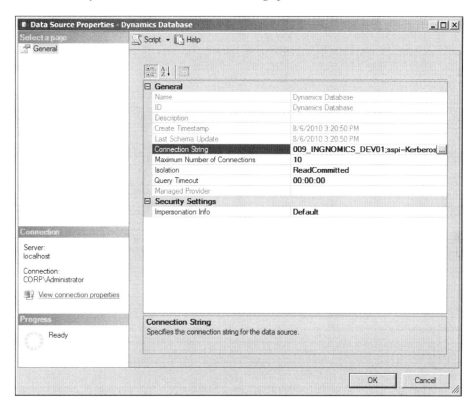

4. Click on **OK** to save the changes.

Setting SQL Report Services connection string

The final step for setting up Kerberos authentication for Report Services is to modify the connection string. The following steps outline this process:

1. Access the **Report Manager** website and open the Dynamics AX reports directory (for example, **Dynamics** folder).

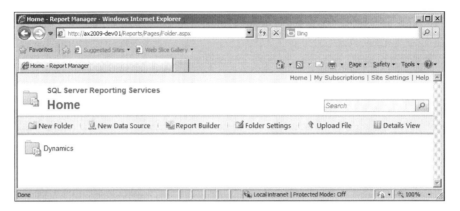

2. Click on the **SharedLibrary.DynamicsAXOLAP** data source connection to open and edit the connection string.

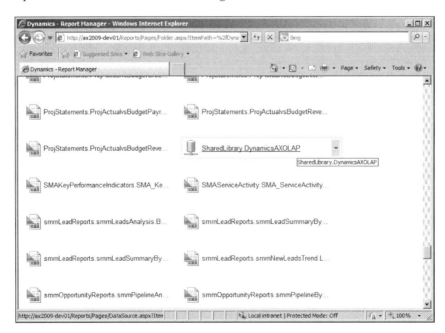

3. Append `;SSPI=Kerberos` to the end of the connection string and then click on the **Apply** button to save the changes.

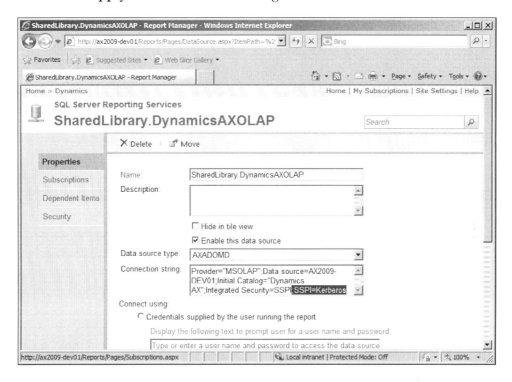

Setting up Office Data Connection (ODC) files

Office Data Connection (ODC) files are resource files with connection information such as the data connection type, data source address, and so on. It is the method used by SharePoint sites to connect to data sources such as an OLAP server. ODC files are utilized by the Enterprise Portal site so that the embedded OLAP reports can connect to the OLAP server to retrieve data. Without the ODC files, the Dynamics AX 2009 OLAP reports will fail to load. Microsoft Dynamics AX 2009 has a utility within the Administration module that will automatically generate the ODC files and deploy them to the Enterprise Portal SharePoint site. However, custom modifications must be done to the main ODC file in order for the connection to allow Kerberos authentication. The following steps cover the process of deploying the ODC files and also modifying the default ODC file to work with Kerberos authentication:

1. Load the Microsoft Dynamics AX 2009 client.

2. Open the **OLAP Administration** form in **Administration | Setup | Business analysis | OLAP | OLAP Administration**.

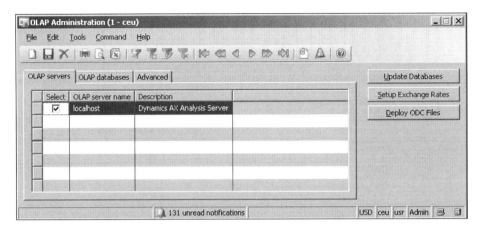

3. In the **OLAP Administration** form, click on the button **Deploy ODC Files** to deploy the ODC files. If this does not work, make sure you have installed Analysis Extensions for Dynamics AX 2009, Role Centers, and Enterprise Portal, and then try again.

4. Now that the ODC files are deployed, the next step is to edit the default ODC file. To do this, go to the Enterprise Portal SharePoint website.

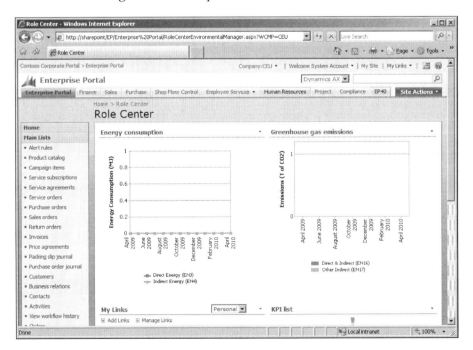

5. In the Enterprise Portal SharePoint site, click on **Site Actions | Site Settings**.

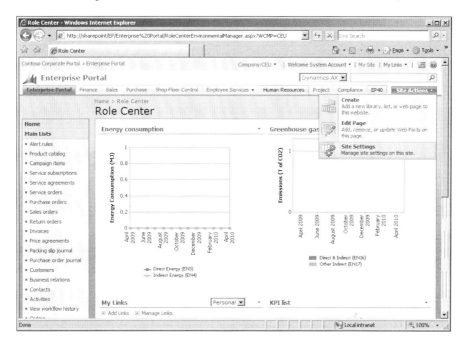

6. In the **Site Settings** page, click on **Master pages** located in the **Galleries** group.

7. Once in the **Master Page Gallery** page, click on the **View All Site Content** link on the left of the menu.

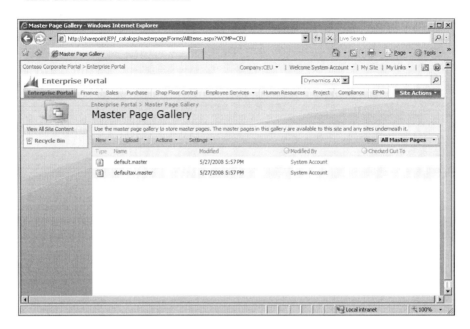

8. In the **All Site Content** page, click on the **Data Connections** link, located in the **Document Libraries** group.

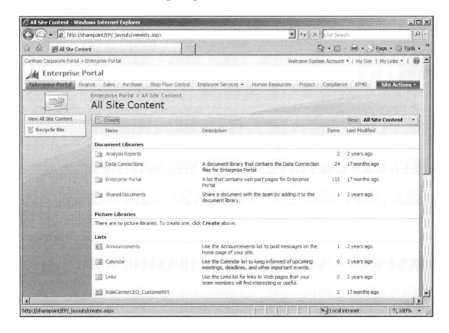

9. In the **Data Connections** page, right-click on the **Dynamics AX** ODC file and save the file to your hard drive. `Dynamics AX.odc` is the default ODC file.

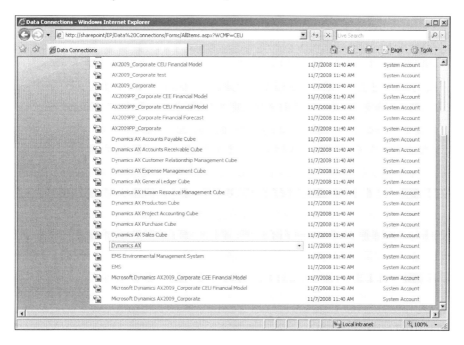

10. After the `Dynamics AX.odc` file is downloaded, open it in **Notepad**. Add `;SSPI=Kerberos` at the end of the connection string located in the `<odc:ConnectionString>` tag. Then save the file and close the **Notepad**.

11. Now that the `Dynamics AX.odc` file has been modified for Kerberos authentication, the next step is to upload it back into the Enterprise Portal SharePoint site. To do this, go back to the **Data Connections** page, as shown in step 9. In the toolbar menu, click on **Upload**.

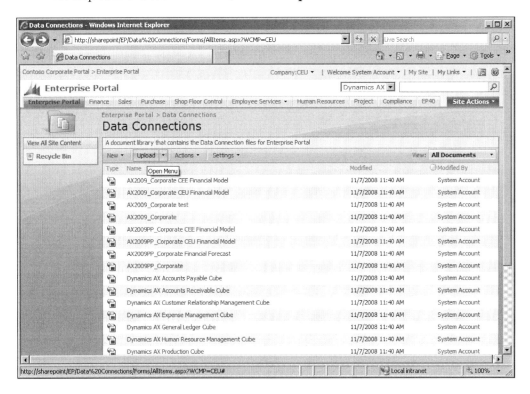

12. In the **Upload Document: Data Connections** page, browse the newly modified `Dynamics AX.odc` file on your hard drive. Once selected, make sure that the **Overwrite existing files** option is marked and then click on the **OK** button.

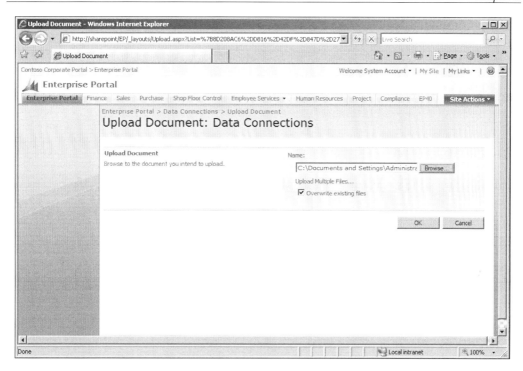

13. Finally, restart IIS by running **iisreset** in the Windows Command Prompt.

Setting up Component Services

For the IIS server to function properly with Kerberos authentication, the component service accounts permissions must be updated. To do so, perform the following steps:

1. Load the **Component Services** applications by going to **Start | Administrative Tools | Component Services**.

2. Collapse the **Component Services** node and all the child nodes until you reach the **DCOM Config** node.

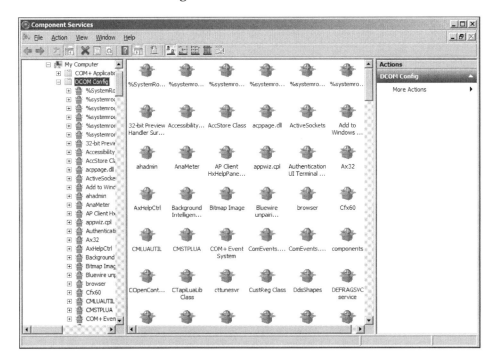

3. Under the **DCOM Config** node, select and right-click on the **IIS WAMREG admin Service** and go to **Properties**.

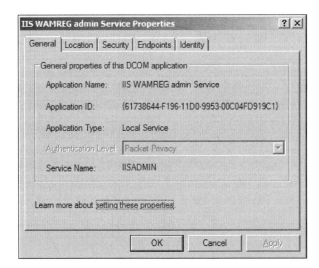

4. In the **IIS WAMREG admin Service** properties, click on the **Security** tab. Ensure that **Customize** is marked. When complete, click on the **Edit** button.

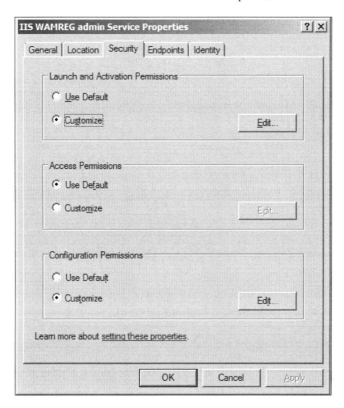

 In Windows Server 2008 R2, the **DCOM Config** properties window may be read-only, even if you are the administrator. Refer to the *Modifying Component Services Properties in Windows Server 2008 R2* section in *Appendix B*.

5. In the **Launch and Activation Permissions** group, make sure **Customize** is selected and click on the **Edit** button. Click on the **Add** button, which is located in the user account that is running the IIS application pool accounts for the Reports Manager, Report Server, and Enterprise Portal SharePoint site. This user account is typically the Business Connector Proxy account. At the very minimum, these accounts must have **Allow** access on the **Local Activation** permission. Once completed, click on **OK** to save.

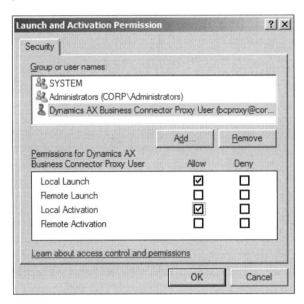

6. To ensure that the changes take effect, restart IIS by running **iisreset** in the Windows Command Prompt.

Configuring Internet Information Services for Kerberos authentication

Internet Information Services (IIS) 7 requires specific modifications to accommodate Kerberos authentication due to the feature of kernel mode authentication. For more information regarding kernel mode authentication, refer to: http://blogs.msdn.com/b/sudeepg/archive/2009/02/08/iis-7-kernel-mode-authentication.aspx. The following steps outline the process required to configure kernel mode authentication to work with Kerberos authentication. This process will need to be completed for the Enterprise Portal site, Reports Manager site, and the Report Server site.

1. With a text editor, open the configuration file: `C:\Windows\System32\inetsrv\config\applicationHost.config` on the web server.

> Authentication can also be modified from the IIS Manager interface or the command line. For more information, refer to `http://technet.microsoft.com/en-us/library/cc754628(WS.10).aspx`.

2. Locate the appropriate site to modify in the **<location>** block. For example, the Enterprise Portal site is located in **<location path="AX2009_INGNOMICS_DEV01 – SharePoint – 18723">**.

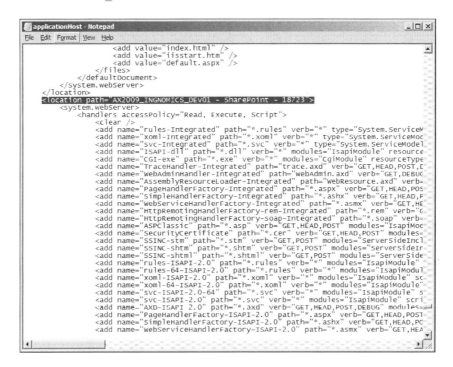

3. In the `<security>` block under `<authentication>`, change `<windowsAuthentication enabled="true">` to `<windowsAuthentication enabled="true" useKernelMode="true" useAppPoolCredentials="true">`. Once complete, save the modifications.

4. Open the Windows Command Prompt and run **iisreset** to ensure that the modifications will take effect.

Summary

Setting up Kerberos authentication is not only a secure feature, it is also necessary. Without Kerberos authentication being set up, SSAS reports and SSRS reports will fail to load in the Enterprise Portal. Therefore, Kerberos is essential in order to take advantage of the powerful Business Intelligence capabilities that Dynamics AX 2009 has to offer.

Kerberos authentication setup is by far the most involved process of setting up the Role Centers for Dynamics AX 2009. However, by breaking the process into sections and performing each section individually and confirming that each section was performed properly, it will ensure that Role Centers will operate successfully. Keep in mind that since each server and network may be set up differently, this process may need to be tweaked further.

The licensing scheme of your Dynamics AX 2009 environment will also determine the presentation of the reports displayed. For example, after successfully setting up Kerberos authentication if a report fails to load, consider the possibility that either your licensing schema does not include tables that are required to calculate data displayed in the web parts and KPIs or that your system lacks the required data. Another reason why reports may not load may be because the appropriate data required to make the specific calculations is missing in the underlying tables. Since each implementation has specific licenses, it will be necessary to manually modify the OLAP cubes using the SQL Server Business Intelligence Studio to fully synchronize the default OLAP cubes that are shipped with Dynamics AX 2009. Typically, this process is done by either a Developer or Database Administrator (DBA).

In this chapter, we have covered the essential process of setting up and configuring Kerberos authentication for Role Centers. In the next chapter, we will cover the process of setting up and configuring the workflow.

6
Setup and Configuration of the Workflow

So far we have covered the new business intelligence features in Dynamics AX 2009 such as the Role Centers. In this chapter, we will embark on the implementation of yet another powerful new feature in the Dynamics AX 2009 component arsenal, Workflow.

The workflow system in Dynamics AX 2009 has been completely redesigned. In short, it is a web application that implements the **Windows Workflow Foundation (WF)** framework. Windows Workflow Foundation has been part of the Microsoft .NET Framework instance since version 3.0. If you have had experience setting up and defining custom workflow configurations in Microsoft SharePoint, then you will be familiar with the same terminology and interface.

A batch process must also be available to process Workflow events in Dynamics AX. The purpose of the batch process is to communicate the Workflow tasks generated in Dynamics AX to the Workflow web service. Additionally, the batch process also generates appropriate messages.

In this chapter, we will specifically cover:

- The prerequisites required for Workflow
- How to install Workflow
- How to appropriately set up and configure Workflow
- Testing Workflow

Workflow prerequisites

Before we begin installing and setting up Workflow, you will need to have administrator privileges on the machines in which you are installing Workflow on. The following prerequisites are required:

- **Internet Information Services (IIS)** 7
- .NET Framework 2.0
- Business Connector

The Workflow component for Dynamics AX utilizes the Business Connector to communicate directly to Dynamics AX from its web service. Although it depends on the number of users and computing resources available, it is best practice to implement the Workflow web service application on its own server.

Workflow accounts setup

The Workflow system in Dynamics AX utilizes two accounts to function properly. If these accounts are not specified, workflow will still function; however, it is best practice to have dedicated accounts. One account is the service account. This account is responsible for the communication between Dynamics AX and the Workflow web service. The other account is the execution account. This account is responsible for executing Workflow tasks and processes. Similar to the Business Connector proxy account, these two accounts must be created with the following criteria:

- The password must never expire
- It must not be interactive
- It must not be associated to any Dynamics AX users

Once the Workflow accounts have been created, the next process is to ensure that the Dynamics AX Workflow system will use the accounts. To do this, perform the following steps:

1. Log in to Dynamics AX 2009.

2. Go to **Administration | Setup | Security | System service accounts**.

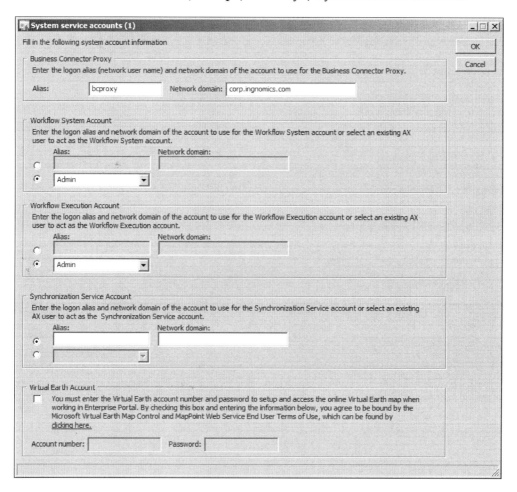

3. In the **System service accounts** form, specify the **Workflow System Account** and the **Workflow Execution Account**. To specify the accounts that were created in the Active Directory, mark the **Alias** field radio boxes. When complete, click on the **OK** button.

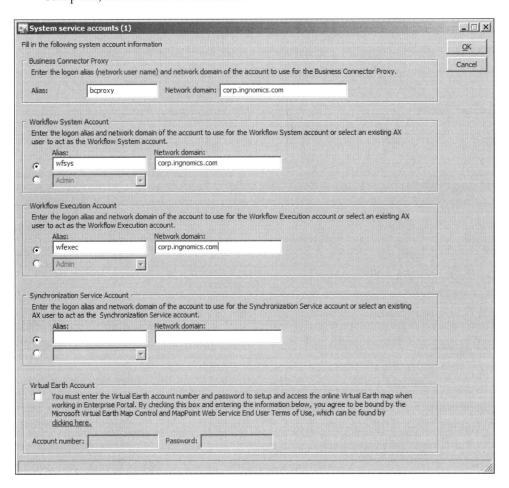

Now that the Workflow accounts have been specified, the Dynamics AX Workflow system can utilize these accounts when communicating with the Workflow web service. It is also possible to create a user within Dynamics AX but not Active Directory, and use the Dynamics AX user accounts as the Workflow Service and Execution accounts. These accounts may appear as different users in Dynamics AX; however, these accounts will be impersonated by the AOS service account to the Workflow web service. This can make troubleshooting and connection auditing more difficult and therefore, it is not recommended.

Installing Workflow

Since Workflow consists of various parts that function together to create the Dynamics AX 2009 Workflow system, we will break down each part's setup and complete each setup individually.

Creating a website for Workflow

Before we can install the Workflow extended server component, we must have a website available to install upon. It is possible to use the default website that is on port 80. However, it is not recommended; therefore, a new website must be created. For information regarding how to create a website in IIS 7, refer to `http://technet.microsoft.com/en-us/library/cc772350(WS.10).aspx`.

Installing the Workflow component

By now you should be accustomed to the process of installing the extended components for Dynamics AX. Installing Workflow is no different. The following steps will guide you through the process:

1. Run the **Microsoft Dynamics AX Setup** wizard to add new components. In the **Add or modify components** screen of the wizard, mark the **Workflow** checkbox, as shown in the following screenshot and then click on the **Next** button:

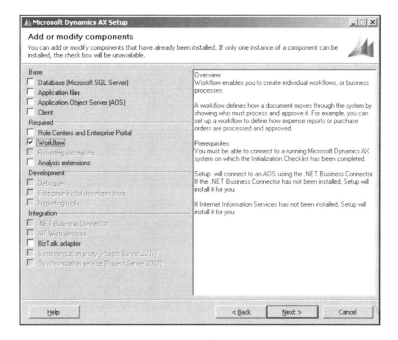

2. In the following screen of the wizard, specify the password for the .NET Business Connector proxy account, and then click on the **Next** button:

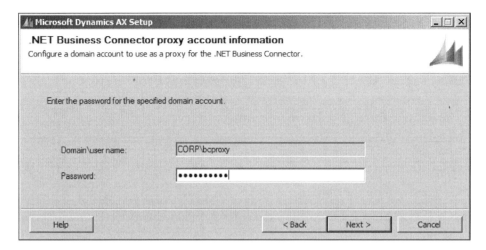

 The **Domain\user name** field will automatically be populated if the Business Connector proxy user is specified in the **Administration | Setup | Security | System service accounts** form in the **Business Connector Proxy** group.

3. In the next section of the wizard, you will be prompted to tweak the Workflow service. In other words, you can select which website you want to install the Workflow service into. By default, the wizard will select the default website in IIS. However, it is recommended to install Workflow on its own dedicated site and port, you have the flexibility to do so. When you are satisfied with the settings on this page, click on the **Next** button.

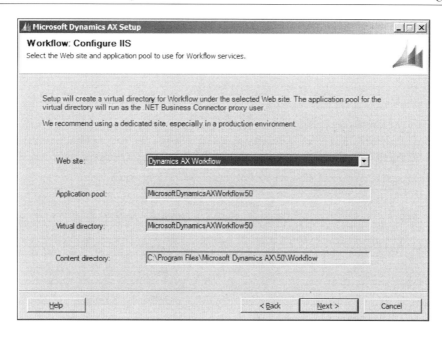

4. In the following screen you will be prompted to specify the AOS account for the Workflow service to grant permissions to. If there is more than one AOS and each AOS service account is different, provide the accounts for each AOS so that they can access the Workflow service.

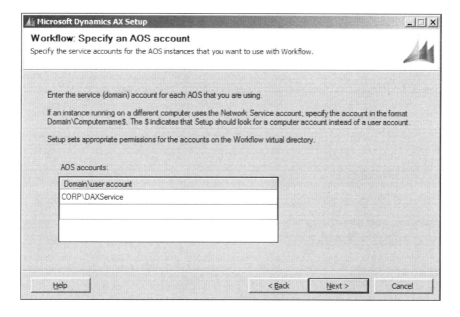

5. In the following step, you are prompted to complete the installation of the Workflow by clicking on the **Finish** button. You will want to restart IIS after the Workflow has been successfully installed. Therefore, leave the option checked at the bottom, as shown in the following screenshot:

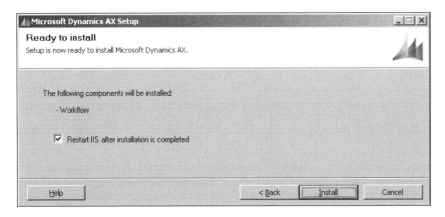

6. Once installed, you will be prompted with the final screen. The final screen will display the result of the installation of the Dynamics AX 2009 Workflow system. If the installation is successful, you will see a green box next to the installed component. Otherwise, if the box is orange or red, you should open the log file after you close the wizard by marking the checkbox at the bottom.

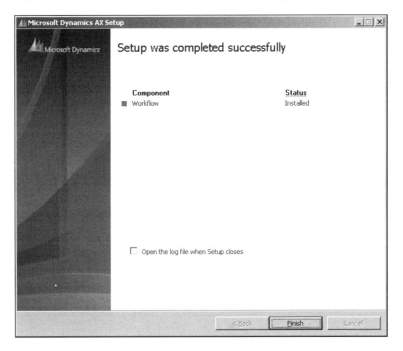

Enabling Workflow in Windows Server 2008 R2

In Windows Server 2008 R2, additional setup is required to enable the Workflow web service. The Workflow web service application pool must be enabled to run 32-bit applications. Otherwise, the Workflow service will fail. To set up the application pool to run 32-bit applications, perform the following steps:

1. Go to the IIS console and access the web server that you installed the Workflow web service on.

2. Under **<Your web server>** | **Application Pools**, select the **Dynamics AX Workflow** application pool.

3. Under **Actions**, go to **Advanced Settings...**. In the **Advanced Settings** window, set the **Enable 32-Bit Applications** property to **True**. When complete, click on the **OK** button to save the changes.

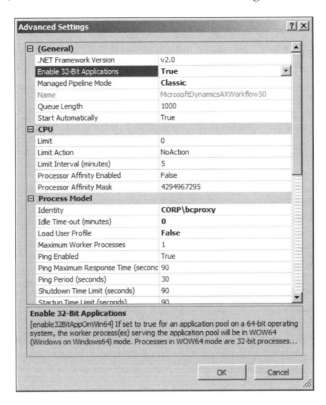

After performing these steps, the Workflow web service can then be used by Dynamics AX to process Workflows. Next, we will set up Dynamics AX to use the Workflow web service.

Setting up Workflow

Now that the Workflow service for Dynamics AX has been successfully installed, we can begin to configure it for use. Dynamics AX will not utilize the Workflow service after it has been installed. Therefore, in order to properly configure the Workflow system, we must do so within Dynamics AX 2009.

Workflow configuration prerequisites

Before we begin configuring the Workflow system, we need to ensure that the following is set:

- A dedicated Workflow batch group has been created
- An AOS is set up as a batch server

Creating a dedicated batch group is not required but recommended since, there is no batch group dedicated for Workflow. Since Workflow uses batch jobs to generate notifications and run Workflow processes, a batch server is required.

Creating a dedicated Workflow batch group

The following steps cover the process of verifying whether an AOS is a batch server and how to create a Workflow batch group:

1. To create a dedicated Workflow batch group, go to **Administration | Setup | Batch groups**.

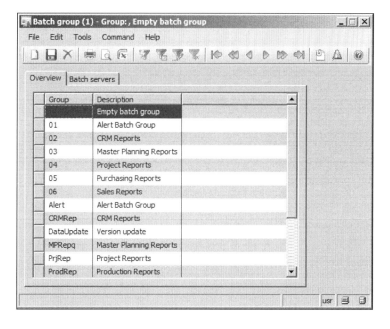

2. Create two new records in the **Batch group** form—one group that will execute Workflow commands and another that will process Workflow due date notifications.

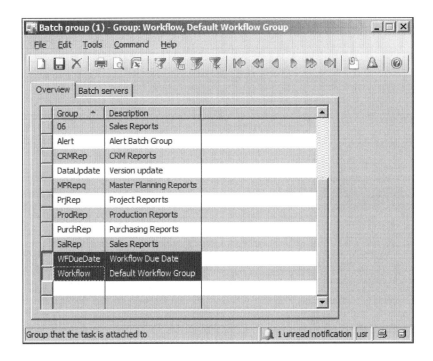

Setting up the AOS as a batch server

Since Dynamics AX workflow uses a batch job to send workflow tasks to the web service in order to be processed in Dynamics AX, we need to ensure that there is at least one AOS that is designated a batch server. Without the batch job, the Workflow web service would sit idle, waiting for a workflow request even though a user may have initiated a workflow task in Dynamics AX. In this section, we will cover the process of setting up an AOS as a batch server and ensuring that a Workflow's batch group will be associated to a designated batch server.

1. To view and modify the current batch server set up on an AOS or group of AOSs, go to **Administration | Setup | Server Configuration**.

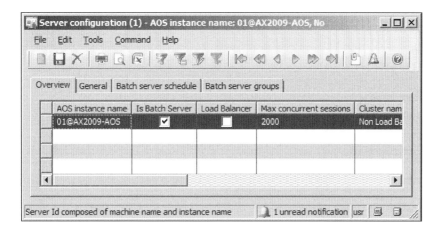

 An AOS can be set up as a batch server and service users. However, depending on the performance and resource requirements for an implementation, it is recommended to have an AOS as a dedicated batch server.

2. Select the appropriate AOS that should run as the batch server and then click on the **General** tab and ensure that the **Is Batch Server** checkbox is marked.

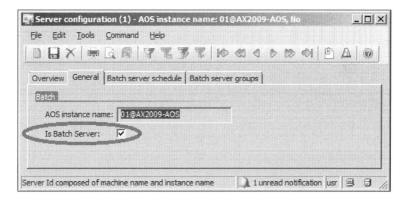

3. Go to the **Batch server groups** tab, and add the Workflow batch groups that we created.

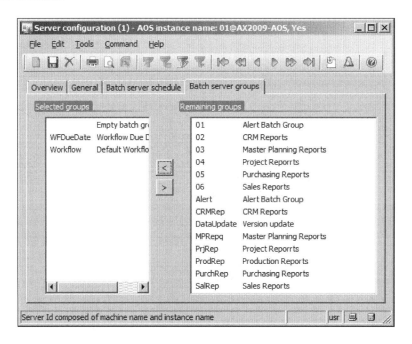

4. To specify the number of batch threads/processes that can run simultaneously and the time the batch processes can run, go to the **Batch server schedule** tab and provide the desired values. The following batch schedule is the default schedule and runs eight threads at any time of the day:

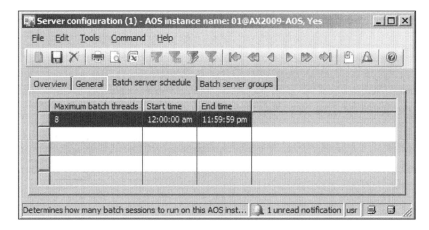

Configuring Workflow

Now that we have an AOS that can run Workflows in a batch server, we must configure the batch processes. This section will guide you through the process of:

- Configuring Dynamics AX to use the Workflow service
- Specifying Workflow parameters for notifications and general use

Running the Workflow infrastructure configuration wizard

The Workflow infrastructure configuration wizard allows you to quickly specify the Workflow web service address, Workflow batch groups, and specify when the Workflow batch jobs should run. It also validates the Workflow web service and ensures that it is accessible by the AOS. In this section, we will cover the process of running the wizard.

1. Go to the **Administration** module and in the **Setup** section, open the **Workflow infrastructure configuration wizard**. Once in the **Workflow infrastructure configuration wizard** form, click on the **Next** button, as shown in the following screenshot:

2. In the next section of the wizard, you may specify the URL of the Workflow web service, which you created as described in *Creating a website for Workflow* section of this chapter. By default, this field will already be populated if you installed the Workflow service correctly. However, if you want to modify this field, you certainly have the option to do so. Be sure to click on the **Validate** button to confirm that the URL is accessible by Dynamics AX, as shown in the following screenshot:

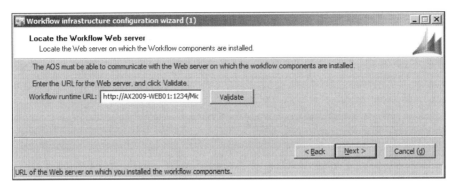

3. In the following section of the wizard, you will be able to see which batch group is designated to execute Workflow batch jobs. Verify that the appropriate batch group is assigned and then click on the **Next** button.

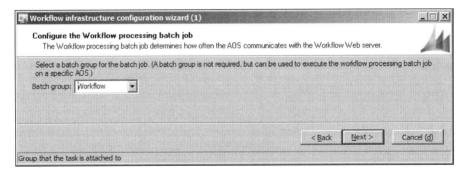

4. In this section of the wizard, you can specify how many times you want the batch server to repeat the Workflow batch process. The lowest value you can enter is **1**. The wizard will allow you to enter in **0**; however, the batch system only accepts **1** as the lowest value. Once you have specified the appropriate value, click on the **Next** button.

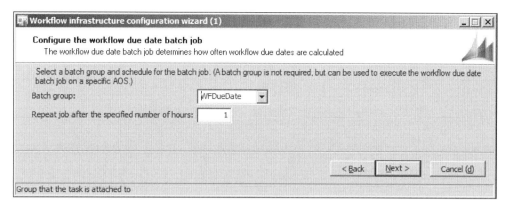

5. The next and final screen of the wizard displays a summary of all the settings that were specified. Click on the **Finish** button to apply these new settings and to make Dynamics AX start using the Workflow service.

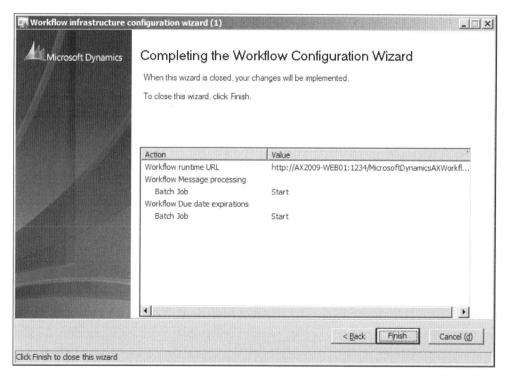

Specifying Workflow settings

The Workflow infrastructure configuration wizard assists in setting up common Workflow settings that are shared between companies. However, company specific settings for Workflow must also be specified such as **Number sequences**. Additional settings can be customized but are not required, such as specifying custom e-mail templates or another Workflow web service URL. In this section, we will cover the process of specifying company-specific workflow settings.

1. Go to **Basic | Setup | Settings for workflow**. In the **General** tab, provide a custom template for **Approval and task notifications**. By default, no template is specified. In this case, a generic e-mail template will be used.

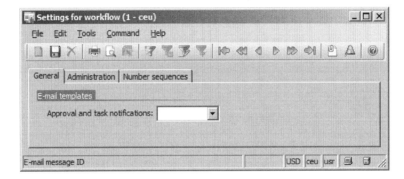

2. In the **Administration** tab, verify that the correct Workflow web service is listed and verify that the system can access the service by clicking on the **Validate** button.

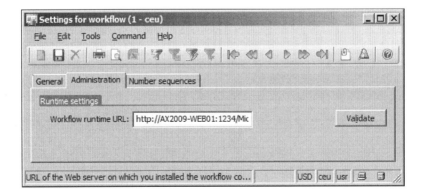

3. In the **Number sequences** tab, ensure that **Number sequences** are mapped to the appropriate **Reference**.

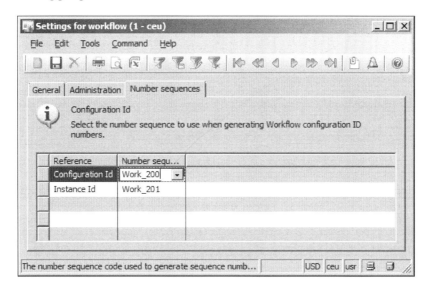

If number sequences are not mapped, it may be because the number sequence wizard never ran. To run the number sequence wizard, go to **Basic | Setup | Number sequences** to load the **Number sequences** form. In the **Number sequences** form, run the wizard by clicking on the **Wizard** button. Dynamics AX will automatically check which number sequences need to be set up and associate number sequences to their reference.

Testing Workflow

At this point, you have performed all the steps required to process workflows. Running an actual Workflow is the best way to test the Workflow system. Depending on your license scheme, Dynamics AX will be equipped with default Workflow templates. In this example, we will cover the process of testing the Workflow system using the Purchase requisition workflow template.

1. In Dynamics AX, go to **Account Payable | Setup | Workflow configurations** to load the Workflow configuration form specific for Accounts Payable business processes.

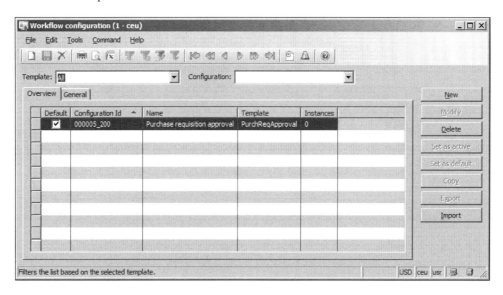

2. In the **Workflow configuration** form, select the **PurchReqApproval** template from the **Template** drop-down.

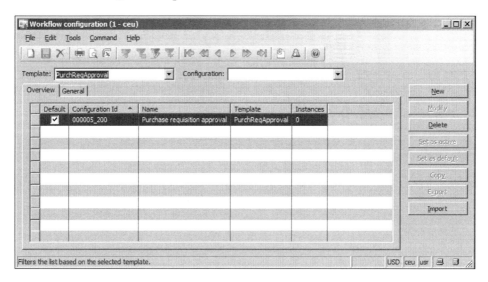

3. To create a new Workflow configuration for Purchase requisitions, click on the **New** button. The **Create configuration: Select a template** form will load. Select **Purchase requisition approval** and click on the **Create configuration** button to start creating the new configuration.

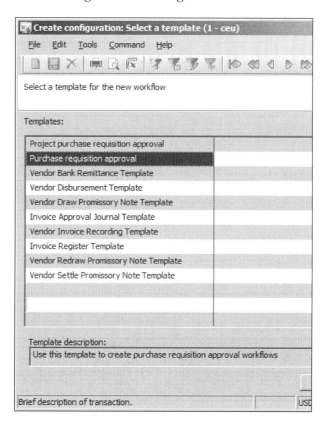

4. After you have clicked on the **Create configuration** button, a new form **Workflow: Purchase requisition approval** will load.

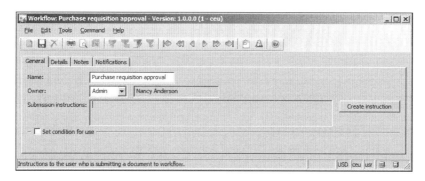

5. Provide the relevant field information in the current view. Various fields are required to be filled out in order to save a configuration. In this view, we must provide text in the **Submission instructions** field. You can set a specific condition that will allow this workflow to initiate. If the condition isn't satisfied, the workflow will not proceed. For example, perhaps you would want the workflow to be used for Purchase requisitions that have a specific value. Instead of waiting for the workflow to run in order to verify that it works on specific conditions, you can simply test the conditions as you create them by clicking on the **Test condition** button. This will allow you to test your conditions on existing Purchase requisitions.

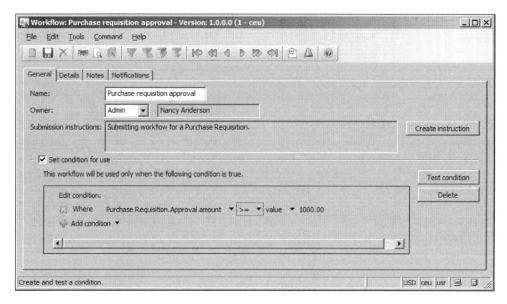

6. In the next step, we must specify the required parameters for the complete and approval stage of the Purchase requisition workflow template. Each workflow may have different stages and each stage has fields that are required to be populated. To specify the parameters for the complete and approval stages in the Purchase requisition workflow, click on the **Details** tab.

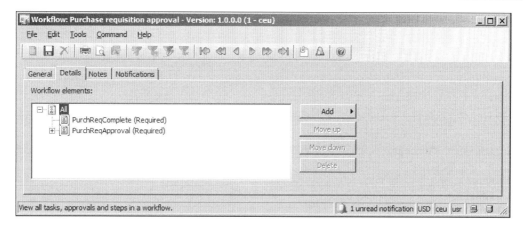

7.   Select the **PurchReqComplete** task to specify the parameters for the complete stage as you did when you were in the **General** tab. When you have specified the required fields, collapse the **PurchReqApproval** task and select **Step 1**.

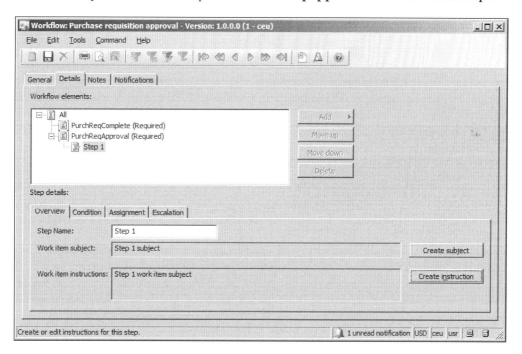

8. You must also assign a user, group, or role that can approve the **PurchReqComplete** task. To specify a user, click on the **Assignment** tab.

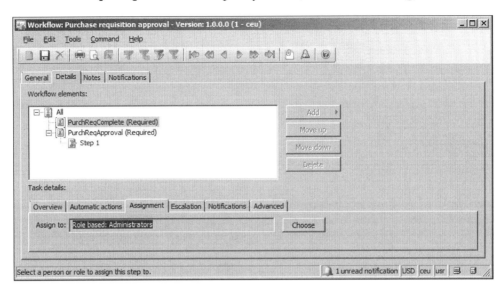

9. To specify a user, click on the **Choose** button. This will load the **Assignment** form where you can select a specific user, group, role, or hierarchy. You can also specify a time limit for how long a task must be approved by until it expires. Once you have specified the appropriate parameters, click on the **OK** button.

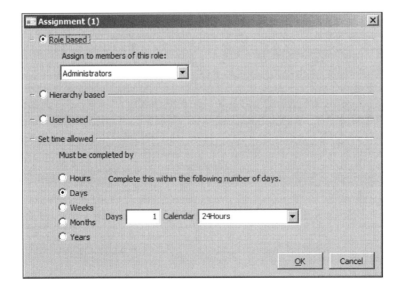

10. In the **Step 1** step of the **PurchaseReqApproval** task, you must specify the same parameters in both the **General** and **Assignment** tabs as you did in the previous step.

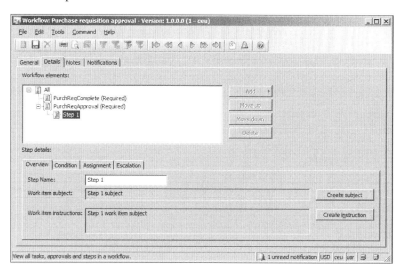

11. When complete, save the workflow configuration by closing the form. You should be back in the **Workflow configuration** form in the **General** tab. You will also notice a record has been created with a version number and checkbox field, which—when marked—activates the current Workflow configuration version. To mark the checkbox, click on the **Set as active** button. Every time you modify a Workflow configuration version, a new version is automatically created. In order to activate a new version, ensure that you deactivate the previous version before activating the version you want to work with, by clicking on the **Set as inactive** button. Once you have activated the **PurchReqApproval** workflow, it will now be used to process Purchase requisition workflows.

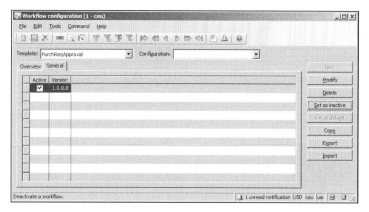

12. Now that we have created the workflow configuration for Purchase requisitions, the next step is to perform a Purchase requisition workflow. To start this process, open the **Purchase requisitions** form by going to **Accounts Payable | Common Forms | Purchase Requisition Details**.

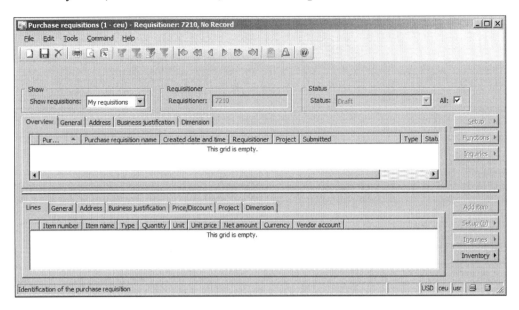

13. Create a new Purchase requisition by creating a new record in the form. This will load the **Create purchase requisition** form. In the form, specify the mandatory fields. When complete, click on the **OK** button to create the Purchase requisition.

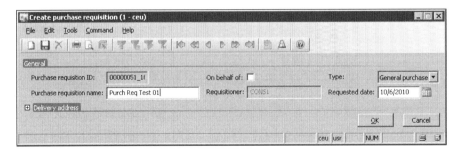

14. Now that the Purchase requisition has been created, you must add at least one item to the Purchase requisition. To add an item, click on the **Add item** button or create a new line in the **Lines** section and select an item to add.

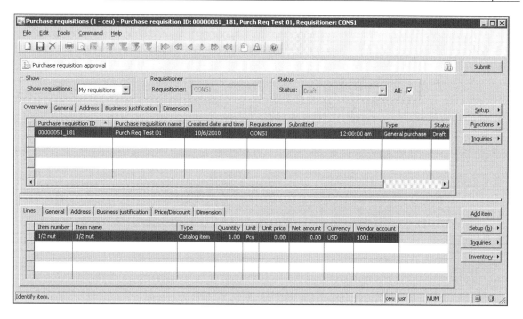

15. Once you have added an item and saved the record, the workflow info area will appear at the top of the form that states the workflow template name and a button to submit the current step. Click on the **Submit** button to submit the Purchase requisition. This will also load a form that provides a textbox to enter a comment for you submission. After specifying a comment, click on the **Submit** button to finally submit the workflow.

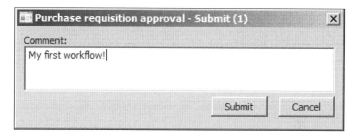

16. Once you submit the workflow, the Purchase requisition workflow info area will be updated with the employee name and the time of the last submission on the selected Purchase requisition.

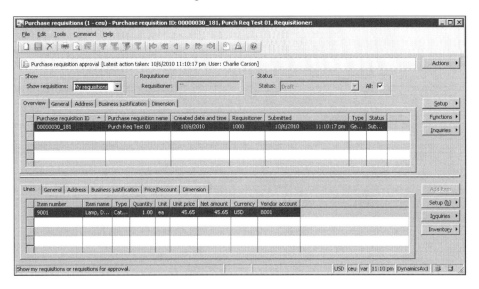

17. Once you submit the workflow, it will be sent to the workflow batch job that was created earlier in this chapter. You can press *F5* to refresh the Purchase requisition form to view the latest workflow status. The batch job will communicate with the workflow web service, which will process the workflow logic. Once it is processed, the results will be sent back to Dynamics AX that will update the workflow. To see the current progress of the workflow, click on **Actions | View history**.

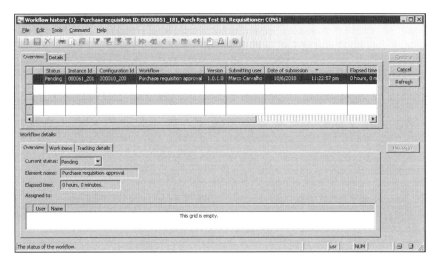

18. In the **Workflow history** form, you will be able to view the workflow details of the current Purchase requsition. To view the most recent status of the workflow, click on the **Refresh** button.

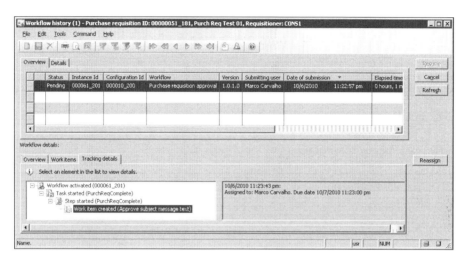

19. In the **Purchase requisitions** form, refresh the form by pressing *F5*. Once updated, the **Actions** button should now list additional options such as **Complete**, **Reject**, **Request Change**, and **Delegate**. Select the appropraite task to continue the workflow until it is complete, where it will automatically create a Purchase Order based on the Purchase requisition.

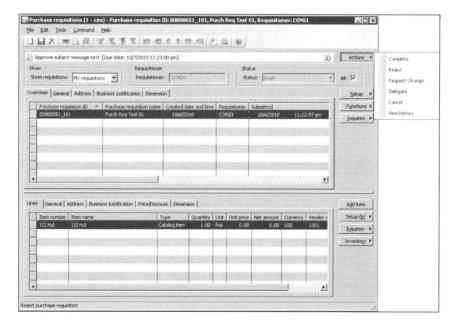

In this section, we initiated an actual Purchase requisition workflow to test if the Workflow system is functioning properly. If you were able to successfully submit a workflow without any errors, then the Workflow system is working properly. Errors can result from permissions not being set up properly on the Workflow web service or the Business Connector pointing to the wrong AOS or employee setup. The **View history** form and **Windows Event Log** will assist in determining the source of any errors.

Summary

Although Dynamics AX 2009 has many workflow processes which can be customized and extended, the actual workflow engine is a separate component. A workflow batch process is needed in Dynamics AX to execute the workflow process, which communicates with the Workflow service to determine the logical steps a workflow should take.

The Workflow is a very powerful and useful feature in general. In Dynamics AX, you can assign workflows to any facet of the system. However, by default, many common processes for which workflow would seem logical to have, already do so outside the box.

In the next chapter, we will cover yet another powerful component of the Dynamics AX 2009 arsenal of components, the Application Integration Framework (AIF). The AIF is a powerful yet simple framework, which is used to integrate third-party systems or other data sources into the Dynamics AX system.

7
Setup and Configuration of Application Integration Framework

Exchanging data between two systems, either between two separate businesses (B2B) or applications (A2A) is becoming increasingly common. Such a scenario is quite common when a business needs to exchange information with its trading partners using **Electronic Data Interchange (EDI)**. To adapt to this need, Dynamics AX 2009 is packaged with the **Application Integration Framework (AIF)** component to provide a flexible framework for data exchange. When certain business processes in Dynamics AX require the exchange of information with one or more external systems, AIF becomes a useful tool for integration.

The AIF provides a flexible framework for Dynamics AX to exchange XML data (commonly referred to as "documents") or messages without the requirement of developing a proprietary system. Custom adapters can be created if necessary; however, AIF comes with the capabilities to exchange documents using web services, MSMQ, BizTalk, or flat files. In Dynamics AX, these methods are referred to as **Transport Adapters**.

If AIF is intended to be used for document exchanges using web services or BizTalk, then the AIF extension must be installed. Otherwise, additional transport adapters that are included in the standard installation of Dynamics AX 2009 do not require the installation of the AIF web service extension.

In this chapter, we will specifically cover the following:

- Configuring AIF in Dynamics AX
- Setting up AIF to use the filesystem adapter
- Managing and troubleshooting AIF document exchanges
- Setting up AIF to use web services

Configuring AIF in Dynamics AX

Before the AIF can be used, it must be set up and configured. For example, endpoints must be specified to determine which company in Dynamics AX, AIF will exchange data with. This section will cover the rudimentary configuration of the AIF, regardless of the transport adapter used. The following checklist outlines the required steps before you can begin to implement an adapter for document exchange:

1. Specify global settings.
2. Provide local endpoints.

Specifying global settings

Various general settings are available to tweak the AIF. Some of these settings can be overridden in the individual implementation either in the adapter or services themselves. For example, the default encoding format can be specified but can also be overridden, if necessary. The purpose of these settings is to streamline typical settings when creating services. Additionally, these settings can also be manipulated to tweak performance, such as the cache lifetime or resource locking. To modify these settings, go to **Basic** | **Setup** | **Application Integration Framework** | **Global settings**.

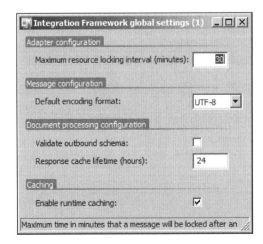

Specifying local endpoints

Local endpoints determine where a document or message will ultimately be received or sent from, in Dynamics AX. There can be multiple local endpoints for a single transport method of document exchange. Since Dynamics AX provides a multi-company setup, it is possible to have multiple local endpoints point to multiple companies at the same time. There is at least one company for any local endpoint. In this section, we will cover the process of setting a simple local endpoint.

1. To begin the process of specifying an endpoint, go to **Basic | Setup | Application Integration Framework | Local endpoints**.

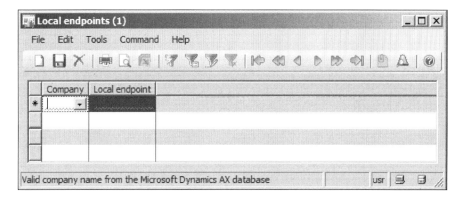

2. In the **Local endpoints** form, create a new line and select the company account that will be the local endpoint for document exchange and provide a name for the endpoint.

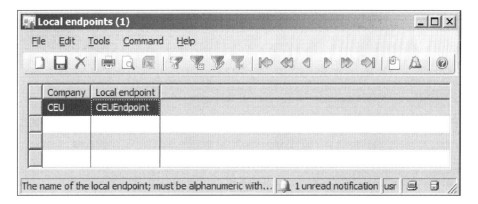

Setting up AIF to use a filesystem adapter

At times, data is exchanged between two systems using a filesystem. In other words, files are placed in a directory and read from a directory. For Dynamics AX to process documents in a filesystem, the AIF must be set up to use a filesystem adapter. To set up a filesystem adapter, perform the following steps:

1. First, we must create a filesystem adapter. To specify the transport adapter, go to **Basic | Setup | Application Integration Framework | Transport adapters**. In this example, we will be using the filesystem adapter. Create a new record and select the **AifFileSystemAdapter** class.

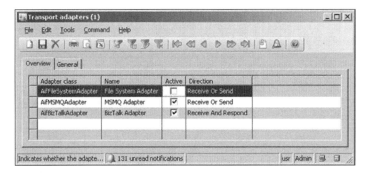

 When you create a new record in the **Transport adapters** form, the system scans for any classes in the AOT that implements the interface class **AifIntegrationAdapter**. In this example, we will be using the filesystem adapter.

2. Now that you have created the transport adapter, the next step is to activate the transport adapter. To do this, mark the **Active** field for the **AifFileSystemAdapter** record.

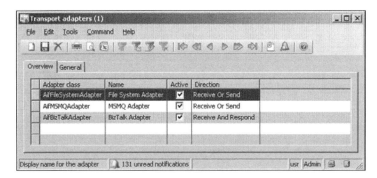

Specifying channels

Since we have activated the transport adapter that implements the
`AifFileSystemAdapter`, a channel must also be created. A **channel** defines the
transport method for processing documents. Depending on the type of adapter in
use, an address or location is specified for document exchanges. To create a channel,
perform the following steps:

1. Before we can set up the channel, we must create the appropriate inbound
   and outbound folders since we are using the filesystem adapter. Open
   Windows Explorer and create a new folder called **AIF** (for example: `C:\AIF`).

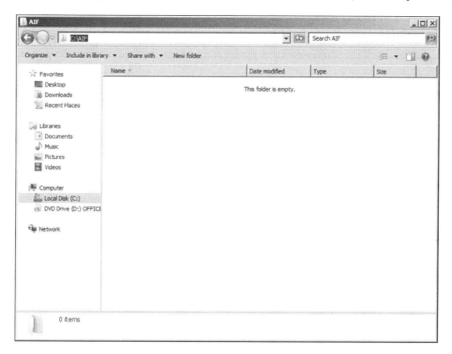

2. Within the newly created **AIF** folder, create two folders: one called **Inbound**, which will contain documents received for Dynamics AX to process, and another called **Outbound** for Dynamics AX to place documents that will be sent.

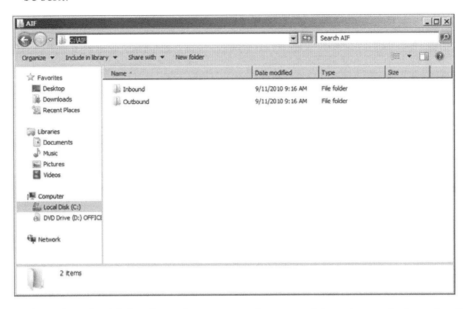

3. Now that the folders have been created, we need to set permissions for the **AIF** folder to allow the AOS service account to be able to modify the folder contents. To do this, right-click on the **AIF** folder and click on **Properties**.

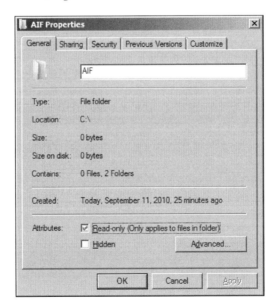

4. In the **AIF Properties** window, go to the **Security** tab.

5. Click on the **Edit...** button to modify the permissions on the folder.

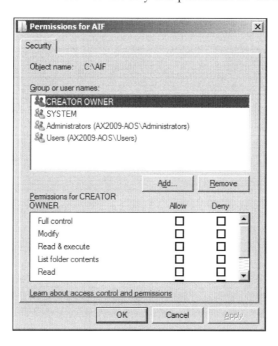

6. Click on **Add...** to add the AOS service account. When complete, click on the **OK** button.

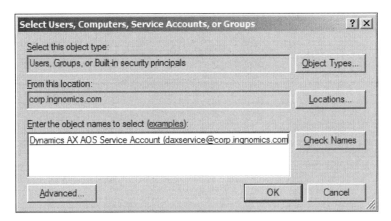

7. Now that the AOS service account has been added, we need to allow **Full Control** permissions. When completed click on **OK** to save the changes.

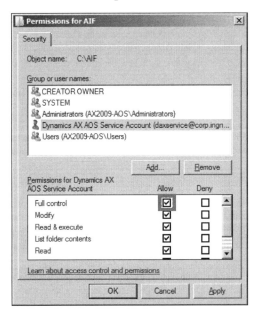

8. Now that the folders are created and the permissions are set, we can specify the folders as appropriate channels for the filesystem adapter. Go to **Basic | Setup | Application Integration Framework | Channels**. Create a new record and then click on the **General** tab and fill in the appropriate fields. In this step, we will create an **Inbound Channel**, which is the channel that will handle incoming documents.

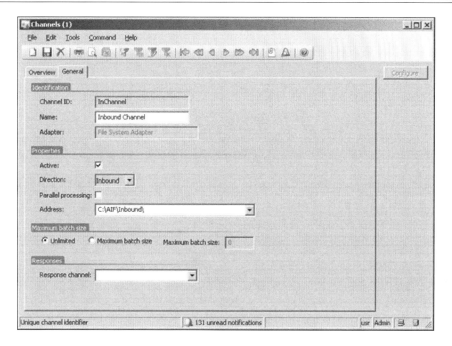

9. In order to process data and send data to be processed by other systems, we must now create an **Outbound Channel**. The process is the same as when configuring an **Inbound Channel**, as shown in the following screenshot:

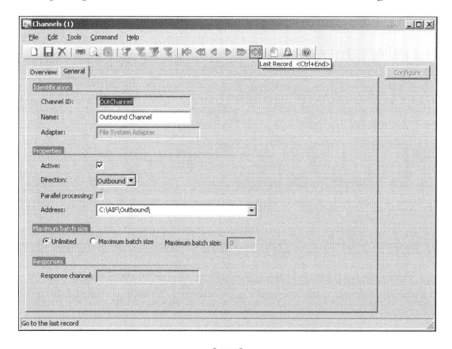

10. In order to associate the **Outbound Channel** to the **Inbound Channel**, we must explicitly specify that relation. To do this, select the **Inbound Channel** previously created in the **Channel** form and specify the **Response channel** to the newly created **Outbound** field, as shown in the following screenshot. Therefore, the system can respond independently to the **Inbound Channel** after incoming requests.

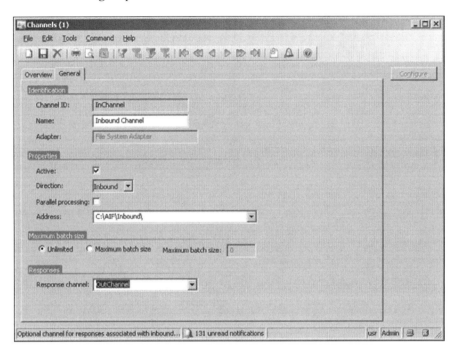

 In a multi-AOS environment such as a clustered or load-balanced setup, any AOS can process documents if they are available to do so. To enable this feature, mark the **Parallel processing** checkbox. This method allows documents to be processed more quickly.

11. After one or more channels have been set up, you must define actions that can be utilized by the AIF service. To do this, go to **Basic | Setup | Application Integration Framework | Action**. You have the flexibility to enable up to six actions per service (create, read, find, findKeys, update, and delete). To enable an action, simply mark the action's **Enabled** field.

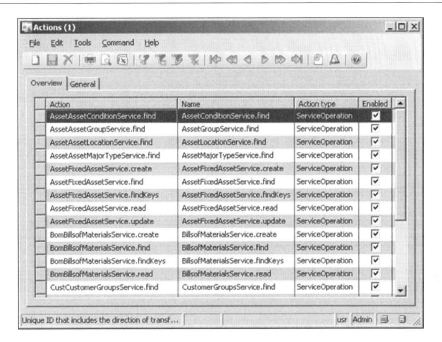

Specifying external endpoints

External endpoints in Dynamics AX are simply referred to as **Endpoints**. When an endpoint is set up, you can control various options, such as which services and actions are available to external systems. There can be multiple endpoints for a single transport method of document exchange. In this section, we will cover the process of setting a simple endpoint.

1. In Dynamics AX, go to **Basic | Setup | Application Integration Framework | Endpoints** to load the **Endpoints** form.

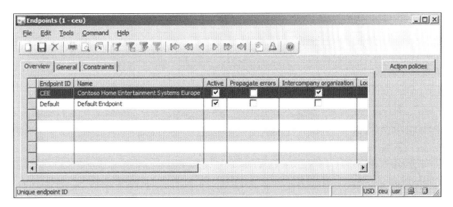

2. In the **Endpoints** form, create a new record. Specify the local endpoint that we previously created and save the record.

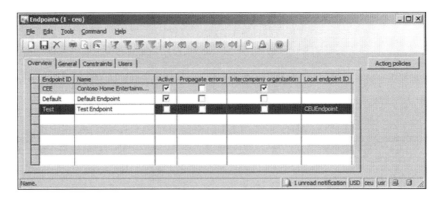

3. Before we can proceed, we must disable or enable constraints. Constraints are used to control which data is available to specific warehouses, vendors, customers, and so on. In this example, we will disable constraints.

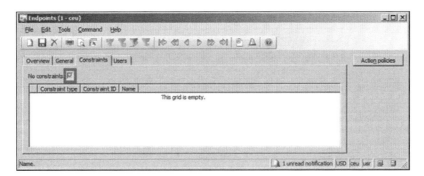

4. Now we can enable actions that will be available for use to an external system. To create an action, click on the **Action policies** button.

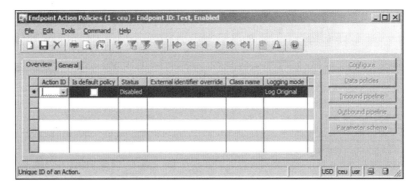

Endpoint actions will be available only if they are enabled on the specified service in **Basic | Setup | Application Integration Framework | Services**.

5. In this example, we will simply allow a read action on a specific service. To do this, click on the lookup button on the **Action ID** field and select a read action on an available service (for example: **CustCustomerService.read**).

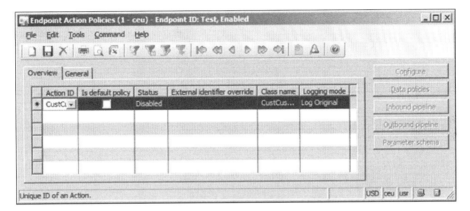

6. By default, the action is disabled. To enable the action, so that it is available to an external system, change the **Status** field value to **Enabled**.

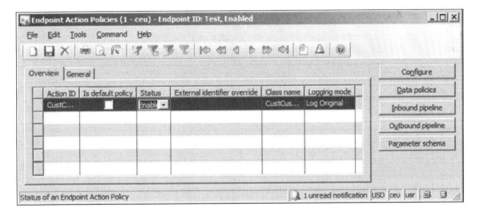

7. With the endpoint's action now enabled, we can specify further restrictions or policies, such as which fields are permitted. To do this, click on the **Data policies** button. This will open the **Parameter Data Policies** form.

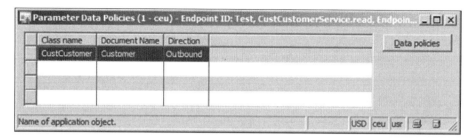

8. Click on the **Data policies** button to open the **Endpoint action data policies** form.

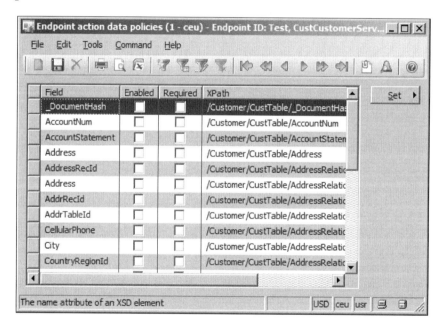

9. To make a field available on the service for an endpoint, it must be enabled. To enable a field for access, mark the **Enabled** field (to quickly enable all fields click on **Set | Enable all**). To make a field as a required field when inserting a new record or querying a service, mark the **Required** field. Some fields may already be marked **Required** if they are mandatory fields because on the table level, the fields have been specified as mandatory fields.

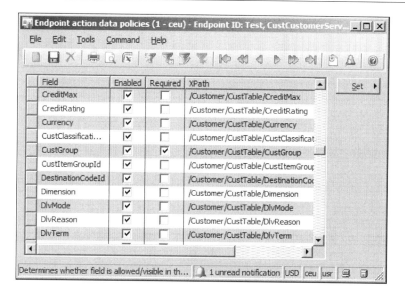

10. In the **General** tab, specify an **Outbound channel ID** and mark the **Active** field to enable the endpoint.

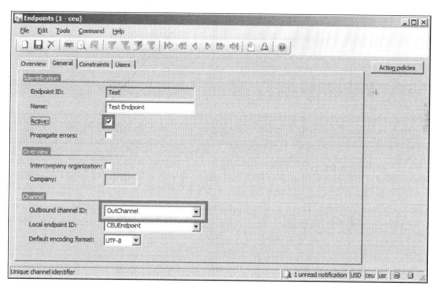

Now that we have specified all the steps necessary for creating a file adapter for document exchange, documents can now be created and placed in the **Inbound** folder. Dynamics AX will then read the documents in the **Inbound** folder in the order they are created, process them, and output results in the **Outbound** folder for access. If this process does not work as expected, the following section will show you how to troubleshoot such issues.

Managing and troubleshooting AIF document exchanges

In this section, we will cover the process of common management and troubleshooting tasks on the AIF.

Managing AIF document exchanges

In Dynamics AX, we can check document logs, view document messages, or manually import messages. We can also peak at which documents are in the pipeline for Dynamics AX to process. This can all be accomplished using the AIF **Queue manager** form. To access the **Queue manager** form in Dynamics AX, go to **Basic | Periodic | Application Integration Framework | Queue manager**.

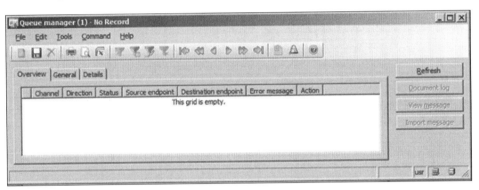

To view a history of document exchanges in Dynamics AX, go to **Basic | Periodic | Application Integration Framework | Document history**. The **Document history** form contains detailed information on documents and how they are to be processed.

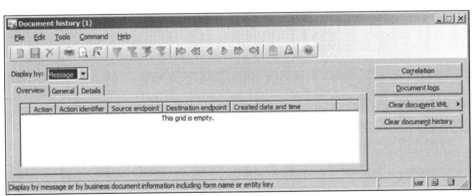

Methods for troubleshooting

When attempting to diagnose issues with the AIF, there are a couple of methods at your disposal that will assist in isolating issues. The following is a list of possible methods:

- Consult the AIF Exception Log
- Consult the Windows Event Log
- Consult endpoint's logs

The AIF exception log can be accessed in Dynamics AX by going to **Basic | Periodic | Application Integration Framework | Exceptions**.

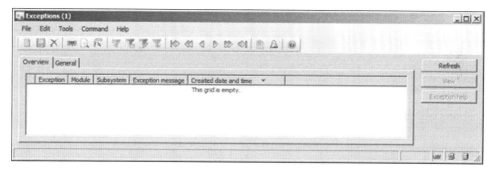

 For additional AIF troubleshooting tips refer to: `http://technet.microsoft.com/en-us/library/aa548693.aspx`.

Setting up AIF to use web services

In some cases, setting up a filesystem transport adapter, as we did in the previous section, can satisfy simple document exchange needs. However, most document exchange methods utilize web services to transfer documents. Most web services utilize the **Simple Object Access Protocol (SOAP)** to transfer XML messages. For more information on web services and what they are, refer to: `http://en.wikipedia.org/wiki/Web_service`.

The following section provides the process of how to set up AIF to exchange documents using web services. Much of the process is the same as using and setting up the filesystem adapter since we must also specify both local and external endpoints and channels. We can even reuse the settings we already created for the filesystem adapter without having to reconfigure for web services. However, additional steps are required for specifically using web services as a means of document exchange.

Creating an AIF website

Before we install the AIF web service extension, a website in IIS must be created to successfully run the installer. This allows you to also determine which port the AIF web service will listen on. The process of creating a website for the AIF is no different than creating a generic website in IIS. For more information on creating websites in IIS, refer to: `http://technet.microsoft.com/en-us/library/cc772350(WS.10).aspx`.

Installing the AIF web service extension

By now you should be accustomed to the process of installing the extended components for Dynamics AX. The following steps will guide you through the process of installing the AIF integration component:

1. Run the **Microsoft Dynamics AX Setup** wizard to add new components. In the **Add or modify components** screen of the wizard, mark the **AIF Web services** checkbox, as shown in the following screenshot and then click on the **Next** button.

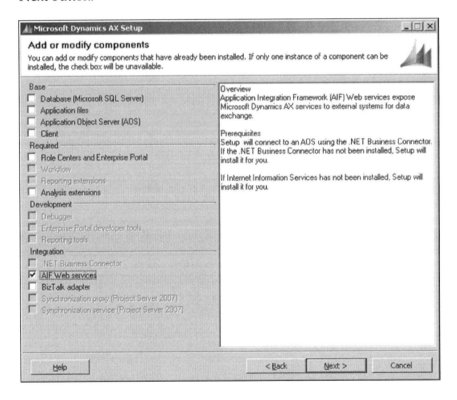

2. In the following screen of the wizard, specify the password for the .NET Business Connector, and then click on the **Next** button when complete.

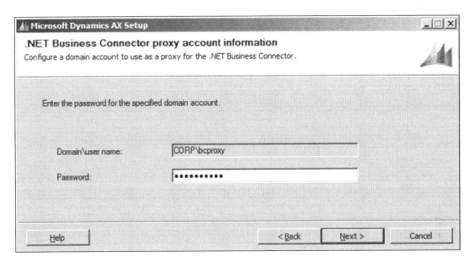

3. In the next section, you can select which website you want to install the AIF web service component into. Select the website that you recently created the AIF web service for. Additionally, you have the option to specify the application pool and virtual directory name if desired, but its not required. When the parameters have been set with the appropriate settings, click on the **Next** button.

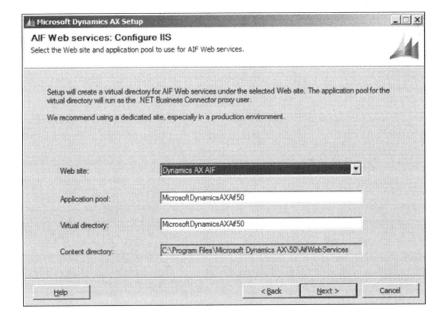

During this step, the installer prepares to update Dynamics AX with the settings provided. However, this may not fully complete in Windows Server 2008 or 2008 R2. The succeeding sections will provide the necessary steps to successfully set up the AIF web service.

4. In the following screen, you ensure that the AOS service account is provided in order for the wizard to properly assign permissions to allow the AOS to access the AIF web service.

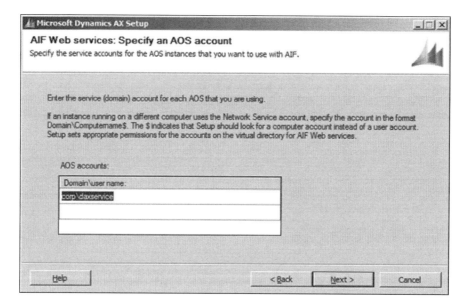

5. In the following step, you are prompted to complete the installation of the AIF by clicking on the **Finish** button.

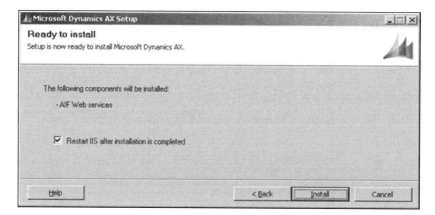

6. Once installed, you will be prompted with the final screen. The final screen will display the result of the installation of the Dynamics AX 2009 AIF system. If the installation was successful, you will see a green box next to the installed component. Otherwise, if the box is orange or red, you will want to open the log file after you close the wizard by marking the checkbox at the bottom. It is recommended that IIS be restarted after AIF has been successfully installed.

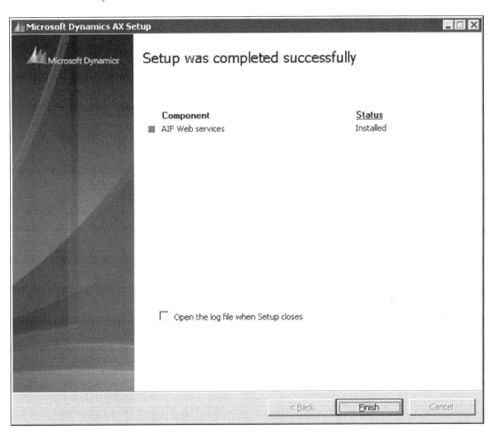

If any warnings or errors appeared during the installation of the AIF, review the log file that was generated to find and isolate the issue. In Windows Server 2008 and 2008 R2, it is possible that permissions were not appropriately set on folders that were generated in Dynamics AX. Additionally, the website for the AIF may have not been updated in Dynamics AX. In the following section, we will cover the process to manually set these up.

Creating and configuring an AIF website

Up to this point, the installer will have created and installed the appropriate libraries. However, in Windows Server 2008 and 2008 R2, the permissions and website setup in Dynamix AX may not have completed. The following process is what is required, so that the AIF website is properly set up for use:

- Apply appropriate permissions
- Specify an AIF website
- Generate an AIF web service
- Specifying the authentication method for an AIF web service
- Accessing the AIF web service

Applying appropriate permissions

During the installation of the AIF web service extension in the *Installing the AIF web service extension* section, a **Content directory** was specified in step 3. That directory was created to store the AIF web service files. The installation wizard went ahead and automatically created a network share of the folder. However, due to limitations of the installers in a Windows Server 2008 or 2008 R2 environment, the permissions will not work. The AOS will need access to this directory in order to create, modify, or delete AIF services. To allow this functionality, we need to permit the AOS service account to be able to do this. The following steps outline this process:

1. In Windows Explorer, navigate to the **Content directory** that was specified in step 3 of the *Installing the AIF Web Service Extension* section (for example: C:\ Program Files\Microsoft Dynamics AX\50).

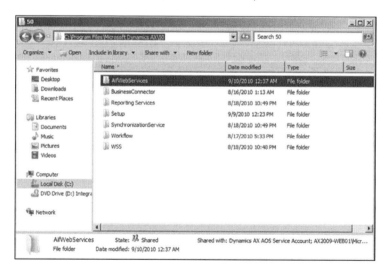

2. Right-click on the **AifWebServices** folder and go to **Properties**.

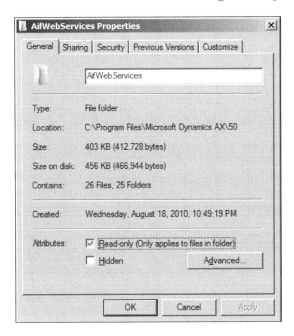

2. Go to the **Security** tab and click on the **Edit** button to edit the permissions on this directory.

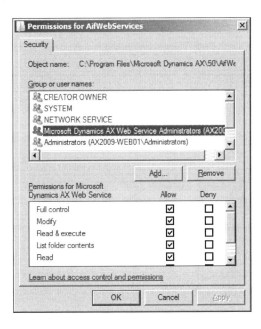

The installer originally created a group **Microsoft Dynamics AX Web Service Administrators** on the server and assigned the AOS service account as a member of that group. Regardless, you will still have to manually add the AOS service account and apply the appropriate permissions.

3. In the **Permission for AifWebServices** window, click on the **Add...** button and then add the AOS service account and click on the **OK** button.

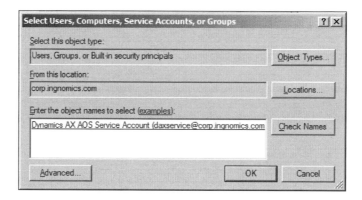

4. Now we must specify the permission level for the AOS services account. In the **Permissions for AifWebServices** window, ensure that the newly added AOS service account is selected and allow **Full Control**. When complete, click on the **OK** button to save the modifications.

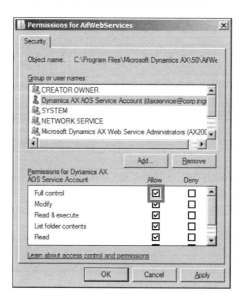

Specifying an AIF website

Now that we have applied the appropriate permissions to the AIF web service directory, the AOS will now be able to access and modify the directory and contents. This is necessary if you want to use AIF for web services. When services are created in AX, the AIF will be able to generate standard WCF web services and place them in the **Content directory**. In this section, we will cover the process of specifying this directory.

1. In Dynamics AX, go to **Basic | Setup | Application Integration Framework | Web sites**.

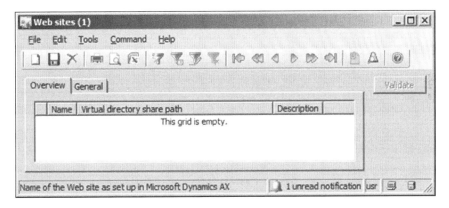

2. In the **Web sites** form, create a new record and specify the network share location of the AIF **Content directory** (it may be easier to go into the **General** tab and browse the folder manually).

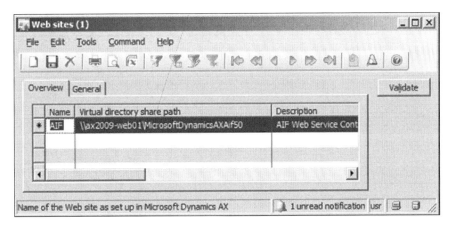

The **Web sites** form automatically validates the directory upon creating the record. If the validation fails and the record cannot be created, verify that the permissions are correct and that the directory exists and is shared.

3. Now that the record with the AIF **Content directory** location has been provided, click on the **Validate** button to ensure that the AOS will be able to access and modify it appropriately. An **Infolog** window will display whether the validation was successful or not.

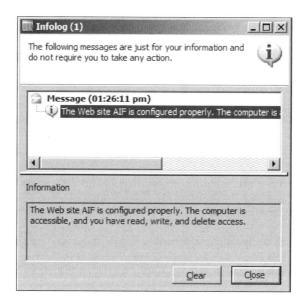

Generating an AIF web service

Now that we have configured the AIF web service in Dynamics AX, we can generate services right from Dynamics AX that will be available for use. Services can be created by developers but Dynamics AX 2009 comes pre-packaged with several services, depending on your licensing scheme. In this section, we will go over the process of generating services.

1. In Dynamics AX, services are specified in the **AOT** under the **Services** node.

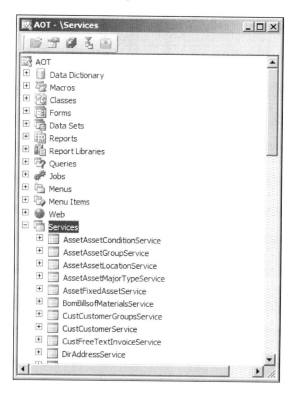

2. To enable the use of the services in the AOT, go to **Basic | Setup | Application Integration Framework | Services**.

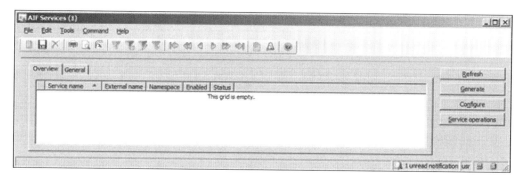

3. In the **AIF Services** form, click on the **Refresh** button. This may take a while because the form will query Dynamics AX for the available services.

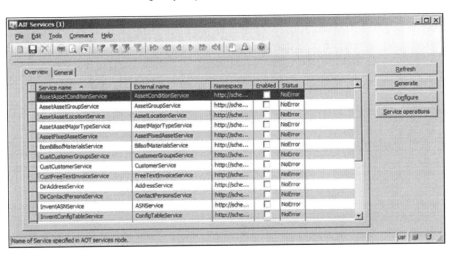

4. To choose which services will be available as a web service, select the appropriate service and mark the **Enable** field.

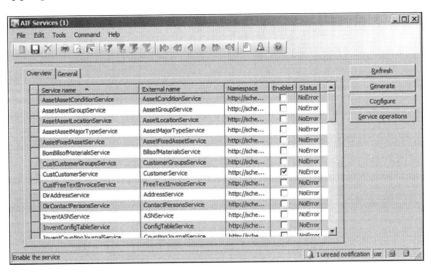

5. Now that the desired services have been selected to be enabled, the next step is to automatically generate the web services. To generate these services, click on the **Generate** button.

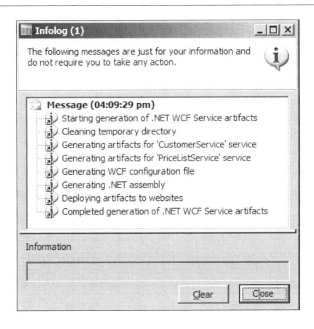

Specifying the authentication method for an AIF web service

Since an AIF web service is a WCF service, all the same rules apply when it comes to specifying authentication methods and many other settings. Such settings allow greater flexibility when customizing web services to enhance security, performance, and compatibility. When you generate a web service for the AIF, the default method for authentication is **basicHttpBinding**. However, in most scenarios, the binding method for authentication should be **wsHttpBinding**. For more information on **wsHttpBinding**, refer to `http://msdn.microsoft.com/en-us/library/ms751418.aspx`. To change the authentication binding method, we must edit the configuration file of a web service that was created when the service was generated.

The following steps describe the process of editing the AIF web service configuration file:

1. In Dynamics AX, go to **Basic | Setup | Application Integration Framework | Services** to load the **Services** form.

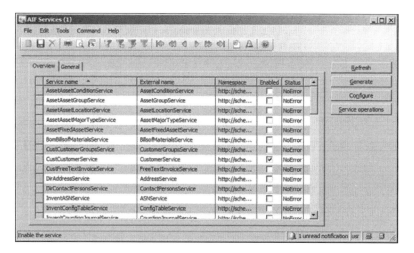

2. Select the service to change the authentication binding method and click on the **Configure** button. This will load the **Microsoft Service Configuration Editor**.

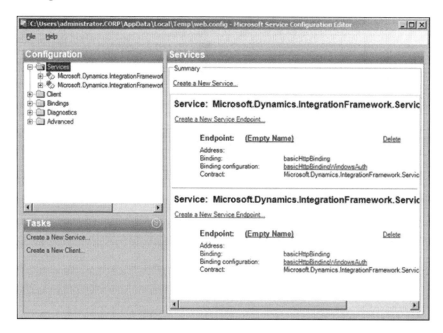

The **Microsoft Service Configuration Editor** comes with the Microsoft .NET 3.5 Framework SDK or Windows Server 2008 SDK. This must be installed in order to properly edit the web service configuration. Although you can use a text editor to make modifications to the configuration file, it is not best practice, nor is it recommended. The configuration editor ensures that configuration settings are properly formatted.

3. In the **Microsoft Service Configuration Editor**, collapse the **Bindings** node to view the current binding. Notice that the default binding method is **basicHttpBinding**.

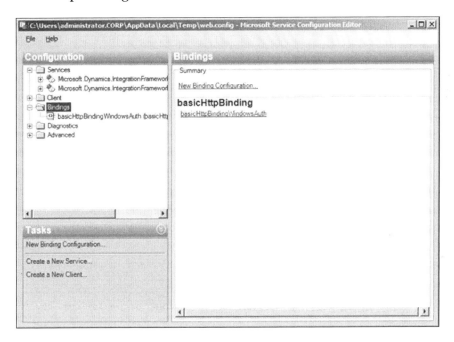

4. We will need to create a **wsHttpBinding** method for authentication. To create a new binding, right-click on the **Bindings** folder and click on **New Binding Configuration....** In the **Create a New Binding** window that pops up, select **wsHttpBinding** and click on the **OK** button.

5. A new binding method of type **wsHttpBinding**, will be created under the **Bindings** folder. In this example, we will rename it to **wsHttpBindingAif**.

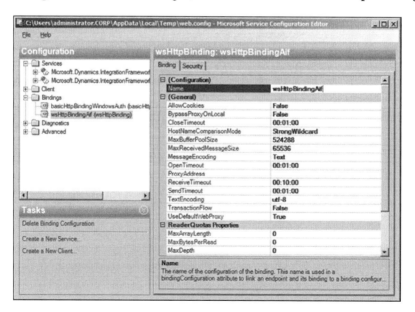

6. Now that we have created an appropriate binding method for an AIF service, we must associate the binding to the service that was generated, so that it may be used as a binding method. In the **Services** folder, collapse the appropriate service (for example: `Microsoft.Dynamics.IntegrationFramework.Service.CustomerService`) and collapse the **Endpoints** folder. Select the listed endpoint, and change the **Binding** property to **wsHttpBinding**. Then in the **Binding Configuration** property, select the **wsHttpBindingAif** that we created.

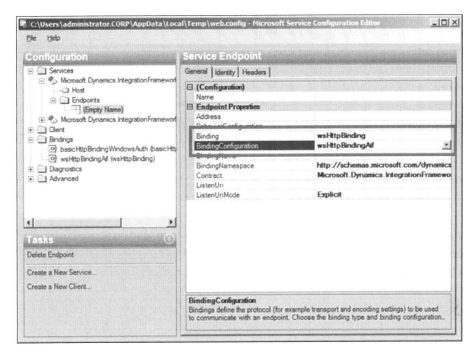

7. Now that the correct binding is set, close the **Microsoft Service Configuration Editor** and save the modifications that were made. To ensure that the settings take immediate effect, open the Windows Command Prompt and run `iisreset` on the web server.

Setting the appropriate authentication binding method will ensure that developers, external servers, and end users will be able to access the service appropriately. Additional methods can be implemented to ensure a stronger security implementation such as SSL.

For information regarding the set up of SSL on a web service, refer to:
`http://msdn.microsoft.com/en-us/library/ms734679.aspx`
or `http://blogs.msdn.com/b/imayak/archive/2008/09/12/wcf-2-way-ssl-security-using-certificates.aspx`.

For setting up and configuring AIF to use a BizTalk transport adapter, refer to the white paper *Microsoft Dynamics AX 2009 AIF BizTalk Adapter Configuration White Paper Part I* that can be found on Partner Source or Customer Source *(login required)*.

Accessing the AIF web service

Now that the AIF web services were generated and the appropriate authentication methods have been specified, the next step is to verify that they can be accessed. In this section, we will cover the process of testing the web services that were created.

1. On the server in which the AIF web service extension was installed on, go to **Administrative Tools | Internet Information Services (IIS) Manager**.

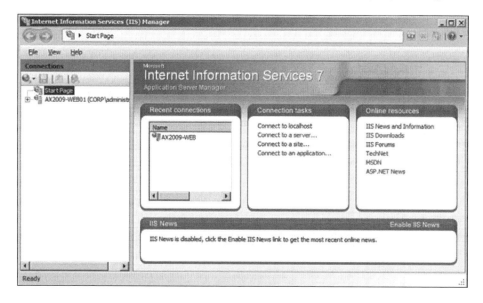

2. In the IIS manager, collapse the web server instance node and navigate all the way to the AIF web service that was created when you installed the AIF web service extension.

3. In order to simplify the process of validating that the AIF web services are accessible, make the **MicrosoftDynamicsAXAif50** virtual directory browseable. To do this, select the **MicrosoftDynamicsAXAif50** directory and under **IIS**, open **Directory Browsing**.

4. Once the **Directory Browsing** view opens, click on **Enable** on the right pane to enable **Directory Browsing**.

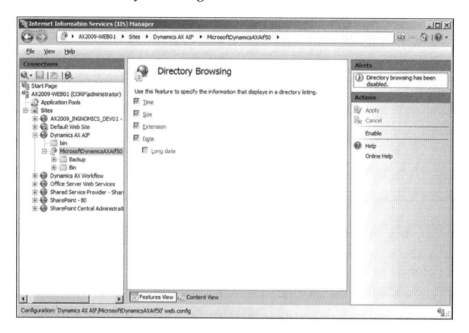

5. Now that browsing has been enabled, right-click on the **MicrosoftDynamicsAXAif50** node on the left, a go to **Manage Application | Browse** to open the site.

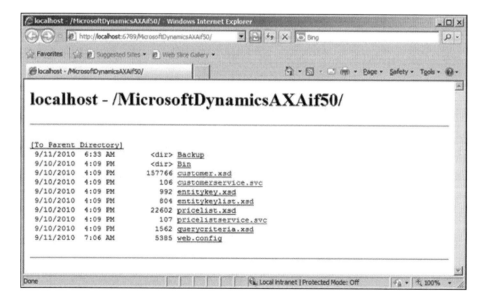

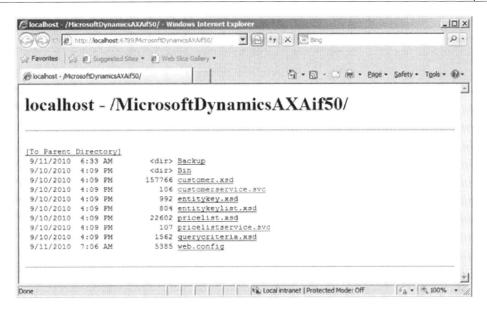

6. In the directory list page view, click on any *.svc to view the service and the available methods.

If the site is unavailable, ensure that the Web Server and Application Server (with Web Server support) role is installed on the server.

Now that the AIF web services have been validated to be accessible, developers can access the web services to exchange documents with Dynamics AX. In the next chapter, we will cover the process of changing authentication methods of a web service.

Summary

This chapter guided you through the process of configuring a filesystem adapter for the AIF, so that Dynamics AX can exchange documents using a filesystem. We also covered the process of installing and configuring the Dynamics AX AIF to exchange documents using web services. Furthermore, we covered the various requirements and settings that show the great flexible potential of AIF. Whenever there is a requirement to integrate third party systems or applications with Dynamics AX, AIF provides a powerful, industry standard, and highly flexible solution.

In the next chapter, we will start to focus on how to migrate data from existing or legacy systems into Dynamics AX. This process is important for any organization that is implementing Dynamics AX for the first time or would like to import data into Dynamics AX.

8
Data Migration

As with any ERP implementation, whenever Dynamics AX is implemented, it will more than likely run into a situation in which you need to import historical or third-party data into Dynamics AX. However, at times this process is not as straightforward as it seems. For example, you may need to convert, eliminate, or clean up data as it is imported into Dynamics AX. There are various methods to migrate data into Dynamics AX.

In the previous chapter, we covered the setup and configuration of the AIF system. Theoretically, a correct setup of the AIF adapter can migrate data into Dynamics AX; however, this is not the most efficient method when importing large sets of data, especially during the initial stages of an implementation. In this case, the best and most common approach would be to import data using a Microsoft Excel spreadsheet. If using Microsoft Excel, at the very least version 2003 must be installed. For extremely large sets of data (over 65,000 rows), it is recommended to implement a custom importing system.

There are many reasons due to which you may need to move large sets of data within, into, and out of Dynamics AX. For example, you may need to export data from one company in a Dynamics AX instance and import it into another company in the same instance. Or, you may need to import the customer, vendor, inventory, or ledger data from an old system into Dynamics AX. Another scenario may be for the simple means of backup data. In this chapter, we will cover the most common processes and methods for migrating data into Dynamics AX, specifically:

- The data migration process
- Generating an Excel spreadsheet
- Importing data from an Excel spreadsheet
- Advanced data migration features

The data migration process

Dynamics AX has built-in tools that allow the user to import and export data in and out of Dynamics AX with little or no programming experience required. Dynamics AX can utilize various file types for importing or exporting data. The following table specifies the various types of files:

Excel spreadsheet	For documents that end in Microsoft Office Excel format (`*.xls` or `*.xlsx`).
Custom (comma delimited)	Delimited files. Typically, these files are comma delimited (for example: `*.csv`) however, you have the option to specify a custom delimiter.
Standard (data file)	Actual data serialized and dumped into a data file (`*.dat`). An accompanying definition file (`*.def`) is also created that contains table information such as names, IDs, record counts, and so on. The definition is not required to be available but is recommended when importing.

The following describes the typical sequence for exporting data from Dynamics AX:

1. Generate a spreadsheet.
2. Create or select a definition group.
3. Export data.

The following is the typical sequence required for importing data into Dynamics AX:

1. Create or select a definition group.
2. Import data.

Both the export and import processes are similar. A definition group that is used to export data can also be used to import data. For example, you can use a definition group to import and export inventory data in Dynamics AX. This will ensure that the structure of the data is the same, both when importing and exporting.

Generating an Excel spreadsheet

A spreadsheet is typically used when importing or exporting data. Spreadsheets can either be delimited spreadsheets, such as comma delimited spreadsheets (`*.csv` files) or Excel spreadsheets (`*.xsl` or `*.xsls`). Dynamics AX contains a wizard that will automatically generate an Excel spreadsheet and definition group. In this section, we will cover the process of using this wizard. The following steps show an example of generating a spreadsheet that can be used to import or export inventory data:

1. To initiate the **Excel Template Wizard**, go to **Administration | Periodic | Data export/import | Excel spreadsheets | Template Wizard**. Click on the **Next** button to start the process of creating the Excel spreadsheet template.

2. In the following step, you are prompted to specify the name of an existing Microsoft Excel workbook to add a new spreadsheet to. However, if you do not have a pre-existing workbook, as in many cases, simply specify a new filename and the wizard will create a new Excel workbook for you. Once you have either selected or created an Excel workbook, click on the **Next** button.

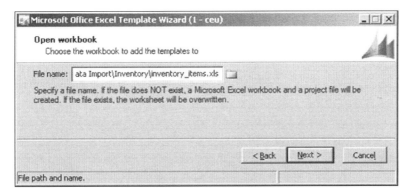

3. In the following **Select tables** screen, you will need to specify which tables in Dynamics AX you want the template to be created for. You are allowed to select more than one table. By default, only the main module tables in Dynamics AX are visible. To view every available table in Dynamics AX, custom tables, or tables that are from third-party modules, select the **Show all tables** option. For each table you select, a new spreadsheet within the workbook will be created. After selecting the appropriate table(s), click on the **Next** button to proceed. In this example, since we will be importing inventory items, we need to select the **InventTable**, as shown in the following screenshot:

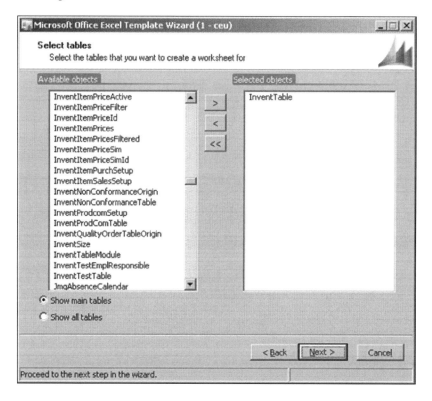

4. The following section of the wizard generates the field list that will be used for the columns in the Excel spreadsheet. If the process was successful, click on the **Next** button. Otherwise, if there was an error, you may have to check the table itself in the **Application Object Tree (AOT)**. Make sure the table compiles without errors and synchronizes properly.

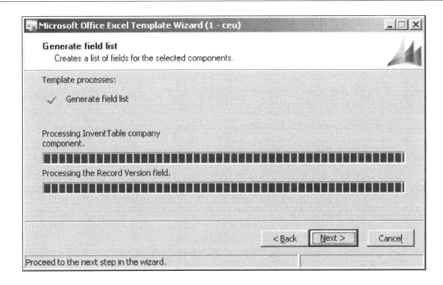

5. In the next section of the Excel template wizard, you can select the fields, which you want to include in your Excel spreadsheet. As in many cases, you may not need to import data for each field and therefore you can select only the specific fields, which you want to import data from. Once you have selected the appropriate fields for the spreadsheet, click on the **Next** button.

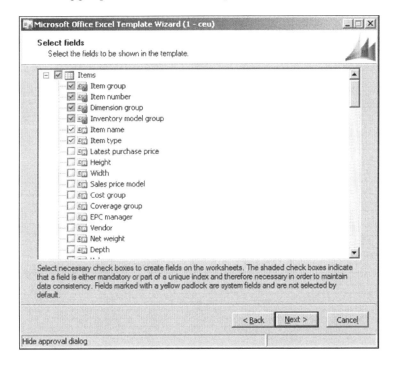

Depending on the table setup, you will notice some fields have a red lock icon next to the field name, this means that the field is required to have data in Dynamics AX and therefore, you cannot add or remove it from the field list.

6. The following section of the wizard prompts you with the option to create a definition group. A definition group is required to properly import or export data. Also, if you want to be able to modify and reuse the import, creating the definition group will save the settings that you recently specified for the Excel template. From now on, it is recommended to have the **Create import definition group?** option marked. Once this has been done, click on the **Next** button to continue.

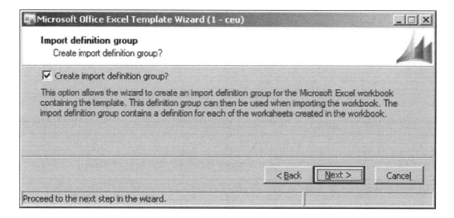

7. The next screen in the wizard contains various options to further automate the import or export process. If you wish to have data of the tables you specified automatically exported, mark the **Export data** checkbox.

8. Oftentimes, tables in Dynamics AX depend on relating tables for data. Also known as relations, these tables can also be included in the Excel workbook as separate spreadsheets. If you wish to include these tables, mark the **Create supporting tables worksheet** checkbox. To simply create another Excel workbook, mark the **Create a Microsoft Office Excel project file** checkbox.

9. To create the template and export data, mark the **Export data** field and the **Create a Microsoft Office Excel project file** field. Otherwise, to just create a template and populate the data, mark the **Export data** checkbox only. When you have marked or unmarked the desired options, click on **Next** to complete the wizard.

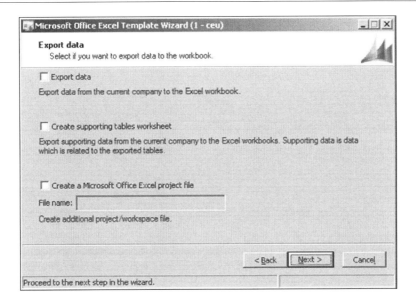

10. This is the last step in the Excel template creation wizard. Simply click on the **Finish** button. Dynamics AX will generate the Excel spreadsheet based on the options that were specified in the wizard. Upon completion, if you want Excel to open up the spreadsheet, mark the **View workbook after creation?** checkbox.

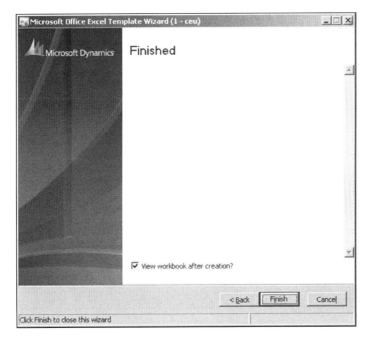

11. The following is an example output of the Inventory Table in Dynamics AX based on the options specified in the earlier mentioned example. Highlighted columns determine what fields are required, as specified while creating the wizard earlier.

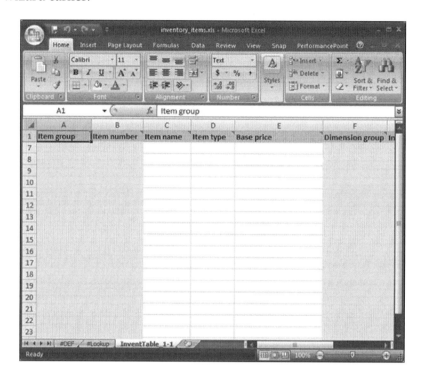

Now that you have successfully generated a spreadsheet, you can populate the spreadsheet with relevant data in Dynamics AX. A spreadsheet is an easy-to-use method for storing data that can be imported into Dynamics AX. For example, a non-technical person can key or paste data into the spreadsheet to import data into Dynamics AX.

Importing data from an Excel spreadsheet

In the previous section, we covered the process of creating a sample import and export template for the Inventory Table in Dynamics AX. Since the option for creating a definition group was marked, it is possible to modify or import and export data on demand. The following steps will cover the process of importing data from an Excel spreadsheet. It will be a continuation from the previous example, which created an inventory table spreadsheet.

1. To begin the process of importing data from the spreadsheet, we must confirm that the Excel spreadsheet contains data, as shown in the following screenshot:

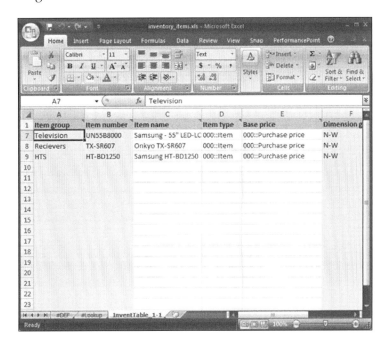

2. Once we have confirmed that the import data is correct, we can now begin to proceed with the import process. To start the import process, we need to use the appropriate definition group for our import file. From the previous section, a definition group was automatically created in the wizard. To find the definition group and run the import, we must go to the definition group form. To go to the definition group form, go to **Administration | Data export/import | Definition groups**.

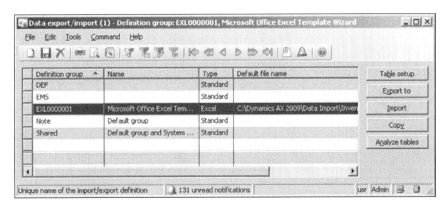

3. From the **Definition groups** form, select the appropriate definition group for the file you wish to import from. In this example, the definition group for inventory items is **EXL0000001**. Once the appropriate definition group is selected, click on the **Import** button to begin the data import. This will initiate the **Microsoft Office Excel import** form.

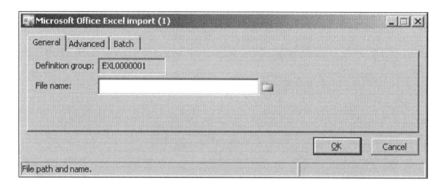

4. Although you have the option to specify a filename, it is not necessary because by default, the definition group already has an associate import file. If you wish to override the import options such as only importing new records, clearing table contents before import, and various other options, click on the **Advanced** tab. This example will use the default settings stored in the definition group and therefore the import rule will be set to **Use Definition group settings**, which will append the existing table data in Dynamics AX with data from the Excel spreadsheet. If you want to include system and related table information as discussed in the previous section, mark the **Include system and shared tables** checkbox. Once satisfied with the settings, click on the **OK** button to start the import.

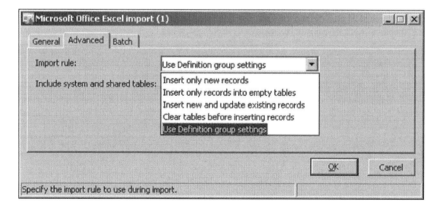

5. Once the import is completed, the **Infolog** will appear with a summary of the import. If the import was successful, you will receive a view, as shown in the following screenshot:

Otherwise, you will see a view similar to the following screenshot:

Since a definition group has already been created and set up for an Excel file type, importing data is very straightforward. All that is required is that you populate the import file with relevant data and ensure that the required fields are provided. The wizard that was used to generate the Excel spreadsheet and definition group took a lot of burden from having to set up the features manually. However, at times, it is necessary to be able to customize a definition group even further such as converting data as it is imported, generating log files, and so on. In the next section, we will cover more advanced methods of importing and exporting.

Advanced data migration features

The previous two sections discussed the basic process of creating an Excel spreadsheet for import and export as well as importing data into Dynamics AX. However, often, this process does not satisfy the import or export requirements. Nonetheless, Dynamics AX provides even more control over the customization of data import and export.

The advanced features for data migration can be found in the **Definition group** form.

- Load the **Definition group** form by going to **Administration** | **Data export/ import** | **Definition groups**.

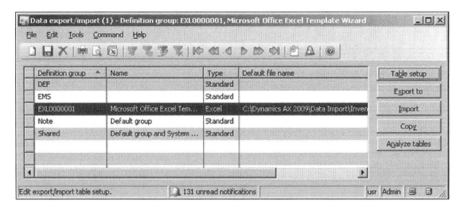

- Selecting the appropriate definition group and clicking on the **Table setup** button will show you more advanced options.

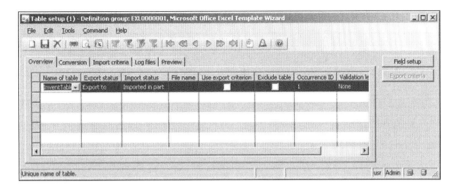

The following table describes each field option in the **Overview** tab:

Name of table	Specify a table in Dynamics AX.
Export status	A flag that specifies the status of the last export. In order to export normally, this field must be set to **Export to**.
	Export to: Export normally.
	Exported in part: Previous attempt only exported partially.
	Exported in total: Previous export attempt exported fully.
Import status	This field is similar to the previous field. To import normally, this field must be set to **Import**.
	Delete and import: Clear table contents in Dynamics AX before importing.
	Import: Import normally.
	Imported in part: Last import attempt did not fully import.
	Imported in total: Last import attempt imported fully.
File name	Specify a filename for the export or import file.
Use export criterion	Specify a specific range (criteria) of records based on user defined filters from the table for export. When checked, the **Export Criteria** button will appear in the tab in which you can specify a Dynamics AX query.
Exclude table	Exclude a table in the definition group from import or export.
Occurrence ID	Which spreadsheet the table appears in, in the workbook.
Validation level	Perform validation procedures on the data that is imported. This ensures that the data meets the table's business logic requirements.

The **Conversion** tab contains the feature of performing custom data conversions on data that is imported into Dynamics AX. The method has been hardcoded and therefore, only the body of the method is needed. The data conversion code is X++ expressions and requires knowledge in X++ to complete. After filling in the text area with X++ code, click on the compile button on the upper-right corner to make sure that the code is valid. Otherwise, the import will fail. By default, the **Run conversion** checkbox is not marked. To enable the custom data conversion, the checkbox needs to be marked.

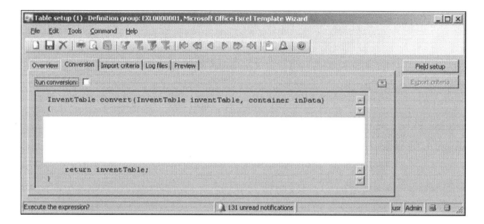

The **Import criteria** tab is similar to the **Conversion** tab. The difference in this tab is used to provide a custom layer of validation to the import sequence.

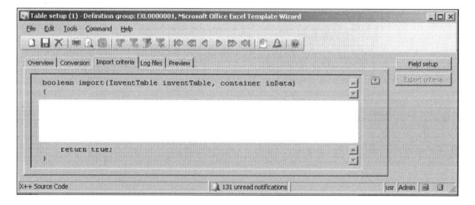

The **Log files** tab contains statistics of recent importing and exporting attempts. It also provides the option to specify a log file to be created for importing. This log file contains a list of records that were not imported.

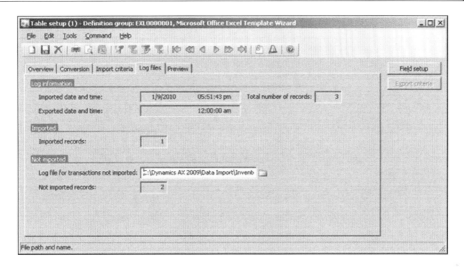

The **Preview** tab provides a simple table preview based on all the options specified. This will only show the first line of data in the spreadsheet used for import.

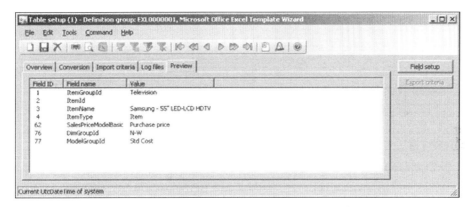

In the **Table setup** form, you will also notice that there is a **Field setup** button on the right side. The **Field setup** button opens up a form in which you can specify the following features:

- Which fields to import or export
- Whether the fields are active or not
- Specify the order in which the fields will be exported in the spreadsheet as well as the order in which to import
- Add a new field from the table by creating a new record in the grid

- Remove an existing field by deleting the record in the grid

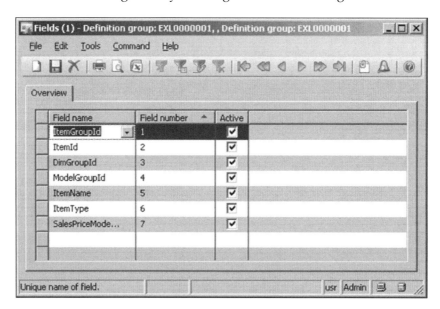

Using the available features in the definition group will allow you greater control and flexibility when importing and exporting data. Since you have the option of converting data as it's imported, it makes using a definition group an ideal method for importing data into Dynamics AX. However, with large sets of data, it is recommended that you break them into smaller, more manageable sets that the AOS can process efficiently. Otherwise, other import methods that can handle large sets of data should be considered.

Summary

In every implementation, there is always the need and requirement to import data from an old system to a newer system. Typically, this is only required with two separate systems and not systems that are simply newer versions of a pre-existing system. Often, many of these processes are the responsibility of a programmer or database administrator. However, Dynamics AX provides a solid set of tools to simplify this process. With such a simplified process, data importing procedures can be performed by anyone with IT knowledge and the length of time it takes to perform data conversions can be shortened significantly and therefore allow more focus on the implementation itself.

In the next chapter, we will cover the security and user administration in Dynamics AX where you will discover the automated features of importing users directly from the Active Directory and also how to set up their specific permissions in Dynamics AX. Security in Dynamics AX is not set up at the user level but rather at the group level and can be further expanded into what are referred to as "domains".

9
Security and User Administration

Whenever information is being shared and transferred, security is always a sensitive topic. As with any ERP system, security is a top priority. Dynamics AX contains many security features that ensure that specific personnel will only have access to information that they are supposed to have. The Dynamics AX system as a whole also adheres to Microsoft's security initiative. For more information on Microsoft's security initiative, please see the following website: `http://technet.microsoft.com/en-us/library/cc723542.aspx`.

Since Dynamics AX consists of base and extended server components, security must also be set up on each server component; otherwise, users may not be able to access or modify data. For example, the Enterprise Portal, Reporting Services, and Analysis Services all contain their separate security setup. Otherwise, unauthorized users can access data that should be confidential. Additionally, even though a user has access to specific data in Dynamics AX, they may not have access to data outside of Dynamics AX such as in the Enterprise Portal. Third-party and custom modifications will also need to be considered to ensure that they too adhere to the Dynamics AX security model.

The advanced Business Intelligence and Reporting features in Dynamics AX require security in not only Dynamics AX to be set up but also in their own specific server system as well. Advanced security settings and infrastructure must also be setup for external Enterprise Portal deployments. Below is a list of the components in Dynamics AX that have specific security requirements and will be covered in this chapter. It can also be used as a checklist to confirm that you have set up the security requirements for each component. However, some components may not be applicable to your implementation if they are not installed.

- Application Object Server (AOS)
- Application File Server
- Database Server
- Business Connector
- Enterprise Portal
- Workflow
- Application Integration Framework (AIF)
- Reporting Server
- Analysis Server
- Dynamics AX Client

In this chapter, we will cover the following topics:

- Security requirements
- Dynamics AX security model
- Setting up User Access in Dynamics AX
- Setting user permissions for the Enterprise Portal
- Specifying user permissions for Reports
- Setting user permissions for Analysis Cubes

Security requirements

Dynamics AX contains server base and extended components, which have unique security prerequisites and requirements. Before installing any of the server bases or extended components, it is necessary to understand the function that each component has to successfully determine the appropriate security settings. Dynamics AX utilizes other Microsoft server technologies such as Internet Information Services (IIS), SharePoint Server, and SQL Server, just to name a few. For more detailed information on setting up the security settings on each Microsoft technology used by Dynamics AX components, consult their individual security documentation. The following tables in this section contain the security requirements for each component.

Security requirements for the base server components

Dynamics AX exists as three base server components, the AOS, database, and application files. In order to properly run and access Dynamics AX, all three must be set up in harmony. For example, not only does the AOS require both the database and application files to run, it also requires appropriate permissions to access both resources. The following are the security requirements for the base server components:

Application Object Server (AOS)	During the installation, the Network Service account is sufficient for running the AOS. However, using a specific service account is best practice.
Application File Server	The AOS Service account should have access to the Dynamics AX application file folders and should only be accessible by the AOS service account and the Administrator.
Database Server	The AOS service account should be a valid user on the database with the 'db_datareader', 'db_datawriter' and 'db_ddladmin' role assigned as well as have execute permissions on the 'CREATESERVERSESSIONS' and 'CREATEUSERSESSIONS' stored procedures.

Security requirements for the extended server components

Although setting up security in Dynamics AX will restrict or provide user access to specific objects or data, additional security setup is required on the extended server components to either restrict or allow user access. Since other server technologies outside of Dynamics AX are used, it's best to consult the appropriate server documentation for general security setup.

The following are the security requirements for the extended server components:

Role Centers and Enterprise Portal	Since the Enterprise Portal runs on Windows SharePoint Services 3.0 or Office SharePoint server 2007 and thus Internet Information Services (IIS). Kerberos Authentication must be set up appropriately.
	Please refer to the vendor documentation for security best practices in SharePoint or go to: `http://technet.microsoft.com/en-us/library/cc262331.aspx`. Secured Socket Layers (SSL) is supported but not required.
	Since Role Centers utilize Microsoft SQL Reporting Services and Analysis Services, please refer to the appropriate vendor documentation for setting up security in Reporting Services and Analysis Services. For information on the Reporting Services security, go to: `http://msdn.microsoft.com/en-us/library/ms156014(SQL.90).aspx`. Similarly, for information on Analysis Services security, go to: `http://msdn.microsoft.com/en-us/library/ms175386(SQL.90).aspx`.
Workflow	Workflow security is dependent both on user security in Dynamics AX 2009 as well as integrated windows security in Internet Information Services (IIS). Secure Sockets Layers (SSL) is supported but not required. Since the Workflow service is a Foundation (WCF) service, additional security settings, specific for a WCF may be considered useful. For WCF security documentation, go to: `http://msdn.microsoft.com/en-us/library/ms735093.aspx`.

Security requirements for integration components

The integration components, such as the Business Connector and AIF, are specific components that are used to integrate Dynamics AX with outside systems. Since these components directly communicate with the AOS, security access to Dynamics AX data and objects is handled by the AOS. However, specific settings are required for the use of these components to work properly and securely. The following are the security requirements for the integration components:

Business Connector	Security for the Business Connector is governed by security settings specified on the Business Connector Proxy User. Since this is an Active Directory user, this user must not have interactive login rights and a password that does not expire.
Application Integration Framework (AIF)	If the AIF can be set up to exchange documents through a file system, web service, BizTalk, or by MSMQ. As a web service, then security for Internet Information Services (IIS) should also be considered. Since a web service is essentially a website in IIS, it means that an AIF web service can utilize Secured Sockets Layers (SSL). Otherwise, if the AIF is running on a third-party adapter, refer to the specific vendor documentation for that particular adapter. For example, if using the MSMQ adapter, refer to `http://msdn.microsoft.com/en-us/library/aa926452.aspx` for information on security set up.

Dynamics AX security model

Unlike other Microsoft server technologies, user security in Dynamics AX is not controlled in Active Directory. Instead, Dynamics AX implements its own security model to control access in the environment. This security model consists of licensing, security keys, and configuration keys. The following lists explain the constituent parts of the Dynamics AX security model:

- **Licensing:** Licenses are distributed by Microsoft for Dynamics AX or by vendors of third-party modules and features. Licensing can be modified in the **License information** form by going to **Administration | Setup | System | License information**, as shown in the following screenshot:

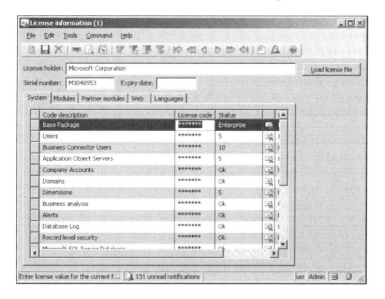

- **Configuration Keys:** The administrator can enable or disable certain features in Dynamics AX through configuration keys. Even though a security key can unlock a certain feature, it may still be hidden because a configuration key is not active. To enable or disable configuration settings in Dynamics AX, go to the **Configuration** form in **Administration | Setup | System | Configuration**, as shown in the following screenshot:

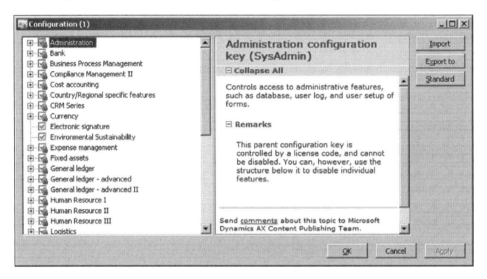

- **Security Keys**: The administrator can control access to specific elements in Dynamics AX such as Forms, Tables, Menus, Buttons, Fields, Web menus, Web content in Dynamics AX through security keys. The administrator can control whether the environment will have a specific feature enabled or not. Security keys can be enabled or disabled for a specific user group in the **User groups** form located in **Administration | Setup | User groups**. After selecting the appropriate user group in **User groups** form, you can modify its permissions by selecting it then clicking on the **Permissions** button, as shown in the following screenshot:

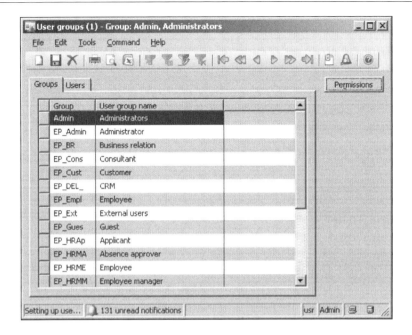

In this section, we covered the security model for the Dynamics AX environment that enables or disables specific features. In the following sections, we will cover the process of specifying security at the user and group level.

Setting up user access in Dynamics AX

There are a couple of processes required to successfully provide user access to Dynamics AX. In this section, we will cover the following:

- Importing users into Dynamics AX
- Specifying user permissions in Dynamics AX
- Using the Security Profiler Tool
- Assigning employees to users
- Creating and setting up Domains
- Setting up Record Level Security

Importing users into Dynamics AX

By default, after installing and setting up the Application Object Server, Application Files, and Database, only the administrator or user who installed Dynamics AX will have access to the AOS. In order for users to have access to Dynamics AX, they will have to be imported from the Active Directory. You can either import Active Directory users or groups. It is recommended that you have logical groups (for example, by department and security level) created in Active Directory. This will ease the process of importing and setting permissions on users in Dynamics AX, especially in large implementations where hundreds or thousands of users must be imported. The process of importing Active Directory users or groups into Dynamics AX is outlined as follows:

1. Go to **Administration | Common forms | Users**.

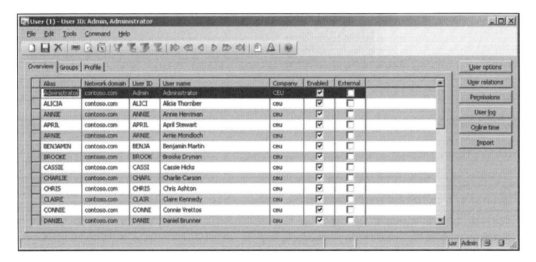

2. In the **User** form, click on the **Import** button. This will launch the **Active Directory Import Wizard**.

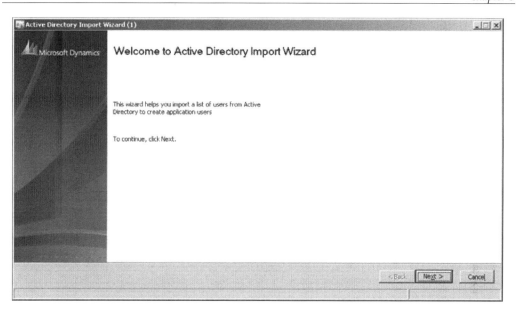

3. To start the wizard, click on the **Next** button. In the following wizard step, you can provide filter parameters to retrieve a specific subset of users in a certain domain. For a large implementation, it would be beneficial if users were already in logical user groups in the Active Directory. Each field can accept an '*' as a wildcard, as shown in the following screenshot. Once you are ready, click on the **Next** button.

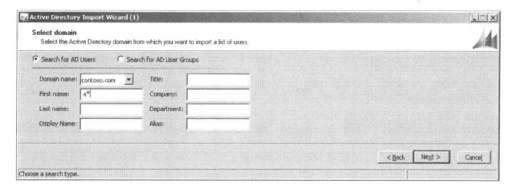

4. In the following screen of the wizard, you can select one or more users at once to import. When selected, click on the **Next** button.

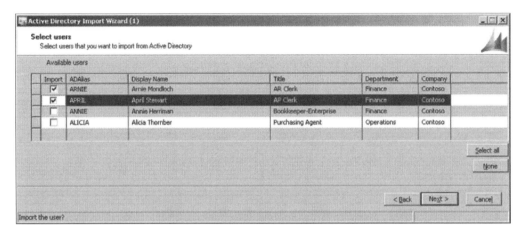

5. The next screen displays which users will be imported. When satisfied, click on the **Next** button.

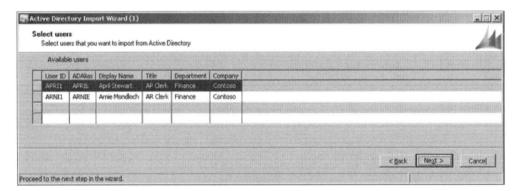

6. The following screen enables you to assign one or more user groups to the newly imported users. To create a new user group, follow the instructions in the next section; otherwise, select and add the available user groups and click on the **Next** button.

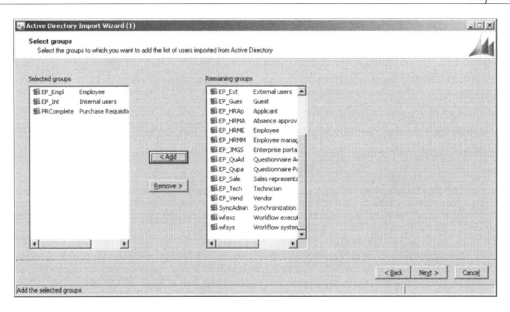

7. The following screen of the wizard is where you can also assign a profile for the newly imported users. The profile is the Role Center page that a user will see upon logging into Dynamics AX or the Enterprise Portal. This is also known as the home page.

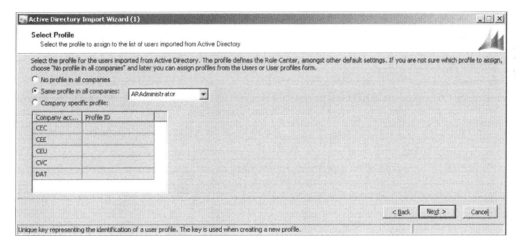

8. To complete the wizard and apply the settings for importing users, click on the **Finish** button.

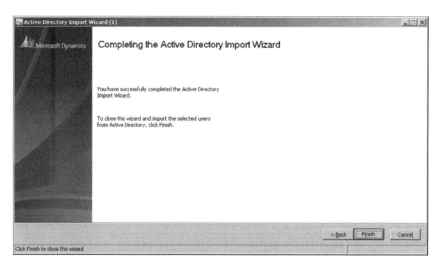

Specifying user permissions in Dynamics AX

To restrict or allow access to a specific element in Dynamics AX, the administrator must assign a specific user to a group and then enable or disable specific security keys for that group. The following steps outline the process of setting user permissions in Dynamics AX:

1. To begin modifying permissions, go to the **User groups** form located in **Administration | Setup | User groups**.

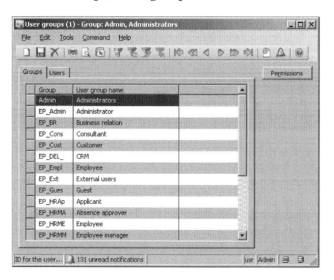

2. From here you can create or select a specific user group. In this step, create a new group by creating a new record in the grid. Name this user group, **AR Clerk** and then save this user group.

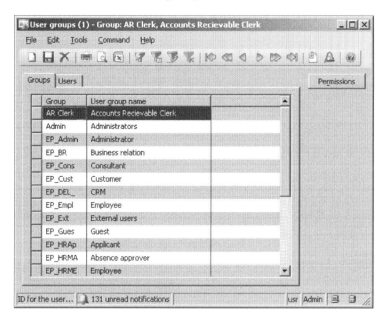

3. To assign users to this newly created group, click on the **Users** tab.

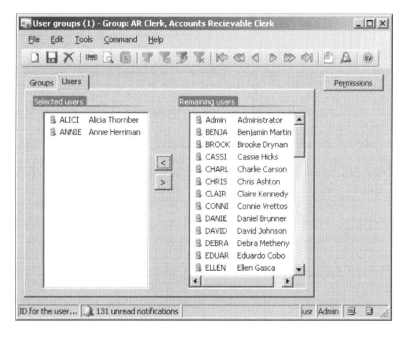

4. To specify the permissions for the group, click on the **Permissions** button.

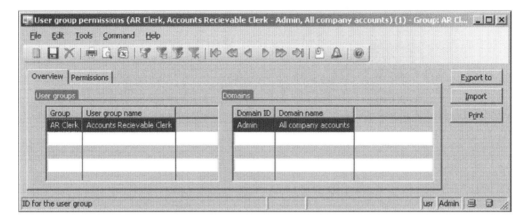

5. Click on the **Permissions** tab to start assigning permissions and select the **Accounts receivable** node.

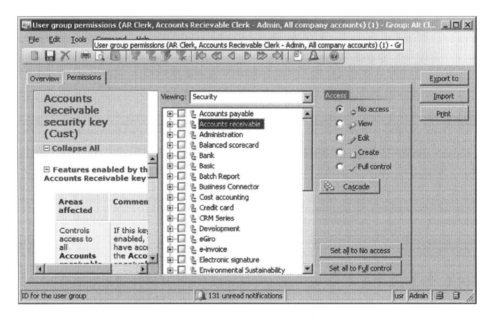

6. After selecting the **Accounts receivable** security key, click on the **Full control** option in the **Access** group and then click on the **Cascade** button to apply the permission to all the child nodes.

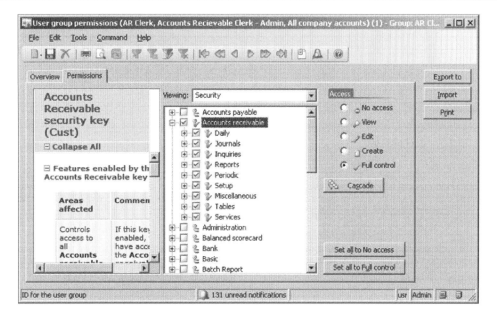

7. At this point, the permissions have to be applied to the current user group and assigned users. To save the current permission settings to a file so that you can quickly import the permissions settings in another environment without having to go through the same process again, simply click on the **Export to** button. Alternatively, to open a saved permission file, simply click on the **Import** button.

In other systems, permissions can be set on either a user or group. However, in Dynamics AX, you can only set permissions on groups. When it comes to general security, this is actually best practice. In the next section, we will cover the use of a tool, called the Security Profiler tool that will ease much of the detective work in figuring out which Security Keys are required when determining permissions on certain objects in Dynamics AX.

Using the Security Profiler tool

Setting up security in Dynamics AX can consume more time than one would like. Fortunately, there is a tool, the Security Profiler, that not only speeds up the process but simplifies it as well. The EMEA Dynamics AX Support Team created and released the Security Profiler tool and it can be downloaded from:
`http://blogs.msdn.com/b/emeadaxsupport/archive/2010/05/25/ax-2009-securityprofiler-tool.aspx`.

When the Security Profiler is running, it "scans" the security keys on various objects in Dynamics AX, such as forms, reports, buttons, and menu items and logs the information. This information can then be used to determine which security keys are required for specific objects. Currently, it cannot profile Enterprise Portal content; however, in the future, this may be supported. In this section, we will cover the process of setting up the Security Profiler as well as show an example of how to use it.

> The Security Profiler tool should not be installed on a Production environment.

1. After downloading Security Profiler, import (*Ctrl+Shift+I*) the XPO into Dynamics AX. When the import is complete, log out and then log back in to Dynamics AX. This ensures that the menu items will appear.

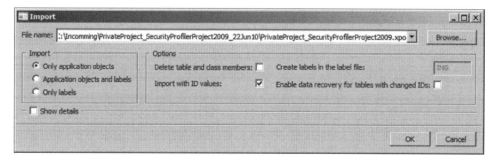

2. Once you log back in to Dynamics AX, go to **Administration | Common Forms | Security Profiler** to open the **Security Profiler** form. Click on the **Start Profiling** button to start the Security Profiler and keep it open.

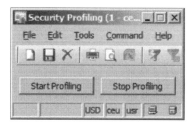

3. Now that the **Security Profiler** is active, open a form or report, such as the **Sales Order Details** form. Once it is open, go to the already running **Security Profiler** and click on the **Stop Profiling** button. This will load up the **Profiling Results** form, which displays the security key information from the **Sales Order Details** form. To print out the results, simply click on the **Print Report** button.

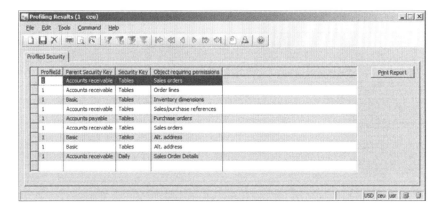

4. Based on the result, assign the appropriate security permissions on any group, as shown in the previous section.

The Security Profiler helps to determine not only which security keys a group will need for access but also which specific security permissions. For example, even if a form is part of a Security Key, assigning an entire security key may provide additional privileges that a group should not have. Therefore, knowing the specific object permissions in a Security Key that are required will increase security and prevent unnecessary access.

In the earlier mentioned example, if a group requires access to the **Sales Order Details** form, you would go to the **User group permissions** form (as described in the previous section) and collapse the **Accounts Receivable** node, then collapse the **Tables** node, and finally mark the **Sales orders** node. Each permission on the **Profiling Result** form grid must be set to successfully provide access to the Sales Order Detail form. To access the profiling results in the future, simply open the **Security Profile Results** form by going to **Administration | Common Forms | Security Profile Results**. This would avoid having to run the Security Profiler on objects that you already profiled and thus save time.

Assigning employees to users

At this point, users that have been imported and assigned to groups can access Dynamics AX and use the system, depending on their permission level. However, when creating Purchase Requisitions or working on other forms in Dynamics AX that require employee information, there is no way of telling which employee the current user is unless this information has been specified. Employees in Dynamics AX are not considered users and thus are not used to control permissions. Employee information is treated as data and is stored in tables. In the following section, we will cover the process of associating an employee to a user.

1. In Dynamics AX, go to **Administration | Setup | User relations** to open the User relations form.

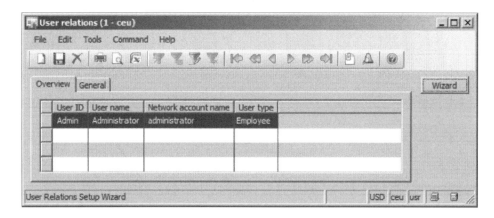

2. Click on the **Wizard** button to initiate the **User Relations Setup Wizard** and click on the **Next** button to begin the process.

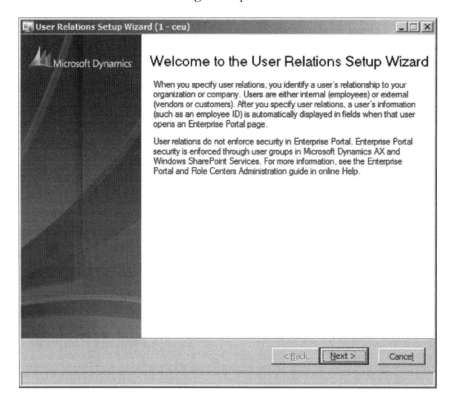

3. In the **User type** step, select the appropriate user type. In this example, since we are going to set up an employee, the **Employee** type is selected. When ready, click on the **Next** button.

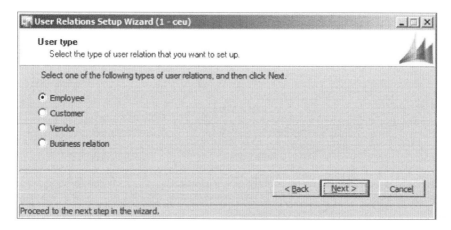

4. In the **Select an employee** section, choose which employee to associate to a user in Dynamics AX then click on the **Next** button to continue.

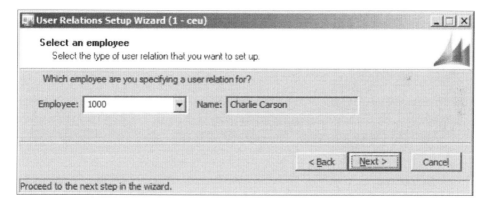

5. In the **Select a user** section, select a user that has been imported, that you want to associate to an employee in Dynamics AX then click on the **Next** button.

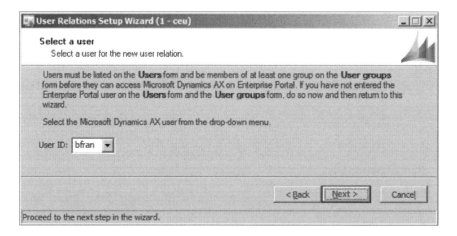

6. Review the parameters and click on the **Finish** button to apply the relation.

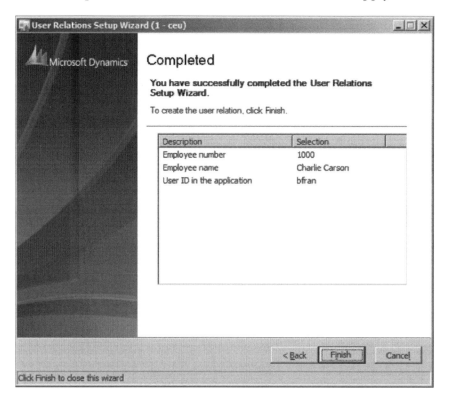

In the previous example, we associated the imported Active Directory user **bfran** to the employee **Charlie Carson** in Dynamics AX. Now, whenever the user **bfran** logs in to Dynamics AX, he will automatically be represented as the employee **Charlie Carson** and therefore, when creating Purchase Requisitions or for tracking Commissions or responsible users, his employee information will automatically be specified.

You may have also noticed that other user types can be imported. This is useful in other scenarios. For example, perhaps a vendor should have access to view their orders on an Enterprise Portal page. You can automatically accomplish this by creating an Active Directory user, importing that user and then setting up a user relation of type **Vendor**. Then, when the vendor logs in to the Enterprise Portal to view their orders, they will only see their orders. The process and concept is the same for user type **Customer** or **Business relation**.

Creating and setting up domains

To put it simply, **domains** specify which user groups have permissions in specific company accounts. By default, when you create a user group, that user group has access to whichever forms or reports that you specify regardless of the company account the user accesses. Domains provide an extra layer of security. In some cases, especially in smaller implementations, they may be acceptable. However, in larger implementations, this is not the case and may propose a security risk or it simply does not make sense.

For example, consider the scenario where there are two company accounts. One company account is a USA company account that handles United States financial information while another company account specific to Europe, handles European financial information. If you created two user groups such as "USA_Sales" and "EU_Sales", with the same permissions because the users will have to access the same forms in Dynamics AX, there is no way to differentiate which company account the groups have access to. This is where domains become useful. You can create a "USA" domain for the USA company account and assign the "USA_Sales" user group to that domain and a "Europe" domain for the European company account and assign the "EU_Sales" to that domain. This way, users in the "USA_Sales" group cannot access data specific to the "EU_Sales" group and vice versa.

The following steps describe the process of setting up domains. Before starting these steps, ensure that you have existing user groups.

1. In Dynamics AX, go to **Administration | Setup | Domains** to load the **Domains** form.

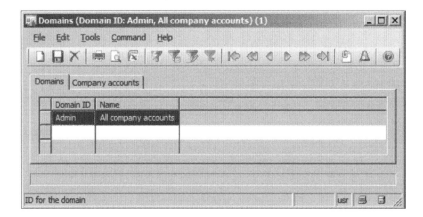

2. In the **Domains** form, create two new domains. For example, one with the **Domain ID USA** and one with **Europe**.

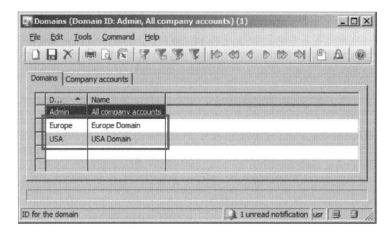

3. Select the **Europe** domain and then click on the **Company accounts** tab.

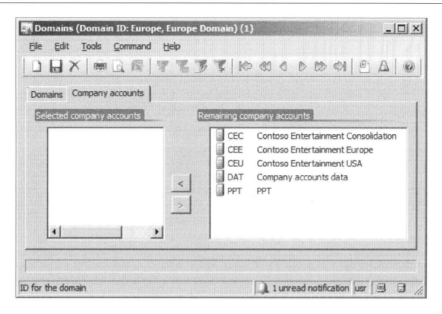

4. In the **Company accounts** tab, add the company account that should have access in the **Europe** domain.

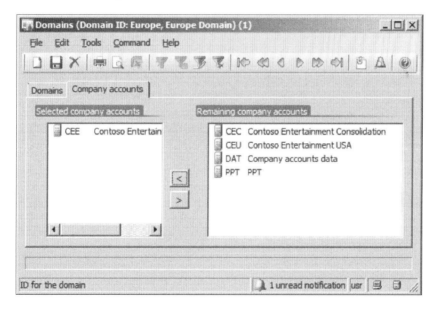

5. Perform the same steps for the USA domain but add a company account that should have access to the USA domain.

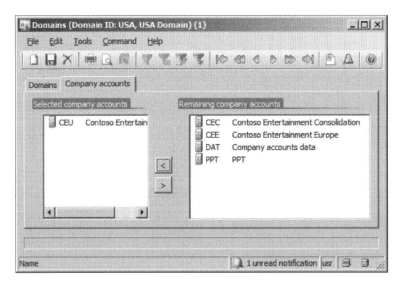

6. Now that you have set up the domains for specific accounts, the next step is to assign appropriate user groups to the domains. To do this, go to **Administration | Setup | User groups** to open the **User group** form.

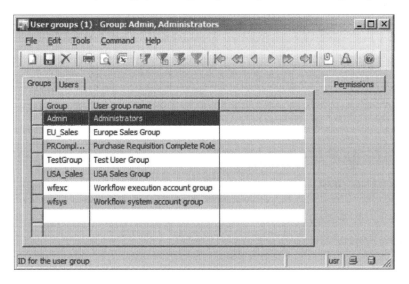

7. Select the **USA_Sales** group and then select a **USA Domain** in which to set specific permissions on.

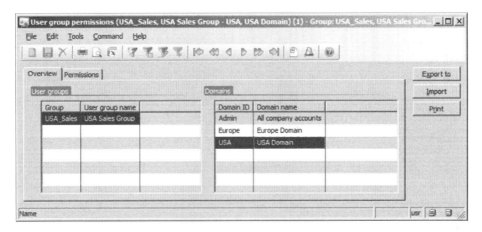

8. Then click on the **Permissions** tab to choose which permissions the group should have in the selected domain. In this example, the **USA_Sales** group has view permissions on the **Accounts payable** security key and full control on the **Accounts receivable** security key in the **USA Domain**.

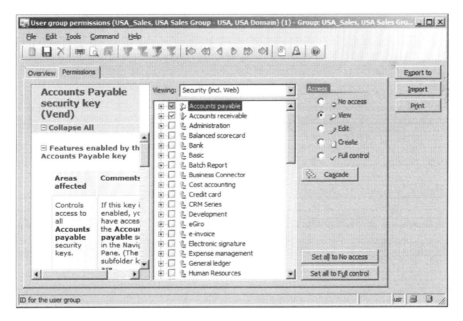

9. Click back on the **Overview** tab and then select the **Europe Domain**.

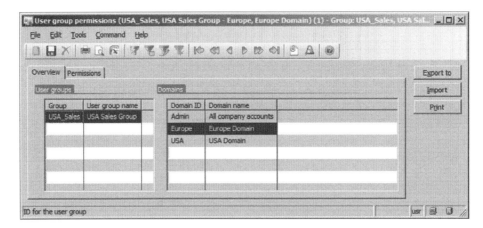

10. Click on the **Permissions** tab to set the appropriate permissions. In this example, the **USA_Sales** group cannot access anything in the **Europe** domain.

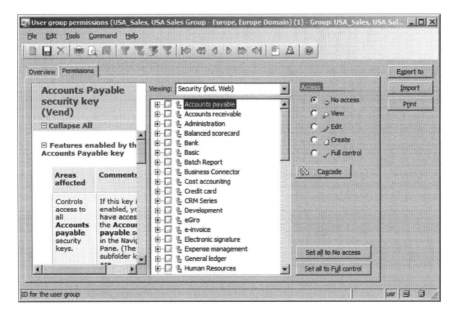

11. After completing these steps, any user that is in the **USA_Sales** group can access the Accounts Receivable section in the CEU company account. However, the same users will not be able to access it or anything else in the CEE company account.

Setting up Record Level Security

Up until now, we have covered the process of setting up security on specific objects in Dynamics AX such as forms, reports, menu items, and so on. However, what if you want to apply security on the data itself? For example, consider two separate sales divisions in a company. One sales group controls customers in the east coast while two groups with the appropriate users added to them were created (for example, Sales_East and Sales_West). Both should have access to the Sales Order Details and Customer form in the same company; however, both should only see their Customers or Sales Orders. This is where Record Level Security (RLS) comes in handy. Record Level Security allows you to apply security for groups against data thus restricting what data a user will see. In the following steps, we will cover the process of setting up Record Level Security with such an example:

1. In Dynamics AX, go to **Administration | Setup | Security | Record Level Security** to open the **Record level security** form.

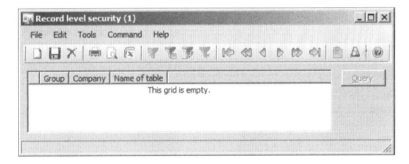

2. Create a new record in the form (*Ctrl+N*) to begin the process of setting up **Record level Security**. When the **Record level security** wizard opens, click on the **Next** button.

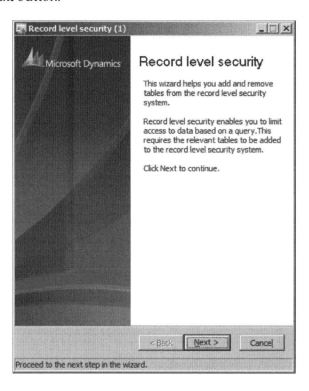

3. In the **User groups** section of the wizard, select the appropriate group to set up the Record Level Security on, then click on the **Next** button.

4. In the **Tables** step, a list of tables is organized into logical groups that
    resemble the modules in Dynamics AX. By default, only main, common,
    tables are shown but you can show all tables by marking the **Show all tables**
    radio button. Select the table or tables that you want to apply RLS on, for the
    group, then click on the **Next** button.

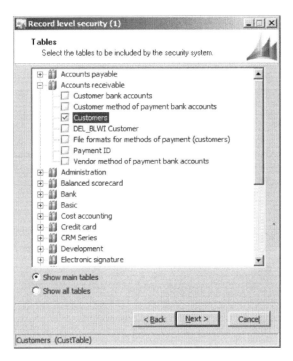

5. In the last step, click on the **Finish** button to apply the settings that have been applied in the earlier mentioned steps.

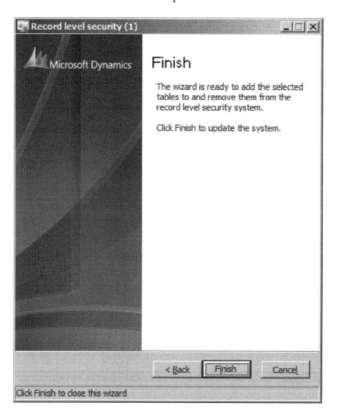

6. Once the wizard is complete, a new record is created in the **Record level security** form.

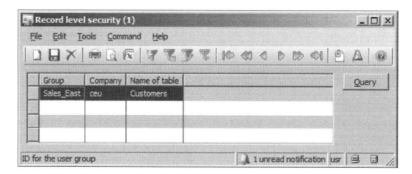

7. Although we specified the tables that RLS will be applied to for the group, we still need to specify a query that will filter that data. To do this, we need to create a custom for that table. To do this, ensure that the appropriate table is selected and click on the **Query** button. This will load a Dynamics AX query interface.

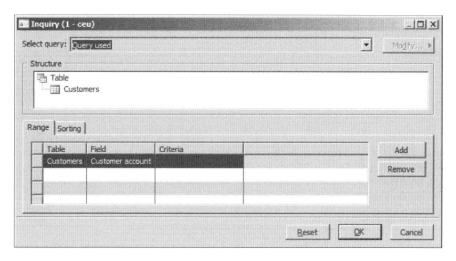

8. In the **Inquiry** query form, you can now add appropriate filters to the underlying data source of the **Customers** table. By default, the **Customer account** field is added in the **Range** tab. To filter by a specific set of customers, click on the **Criteria** field for the **Customer account** and select the appropriate Customer that the user group should be able to see. To add multiple customers or any other field, simply click on the **Add** button. When complete, click on the **OK** button to save the query.

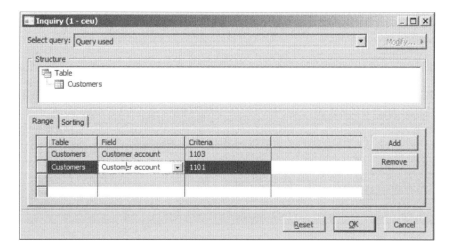

9. Once the user logs in to Dynamics AX and opens the Customer Details form, they will only see records for Customers 1103 and 1101.

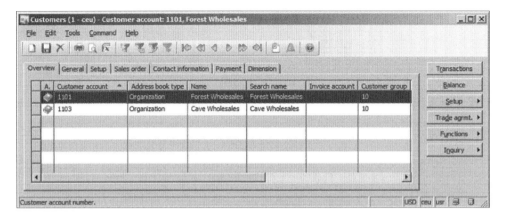

In this section, we covered the process of setting up security in Dynamics AX. The Dynamics AX security model is very flexible and adheres to common security best practices. Since the extended server components utilize other Microsoft technologies such as SharePoint, SQL Server Reporting Services, and SQL Server Analysis Services, additional security procedures are required to successfully provide and secure access to users. In the following sections, we will cover the process of setting up security across various extended server components such as the Enterprise Portal, Reports, and many more.

Setting user permissions for the Enterprise Portal

Even though you may have specified user permissions for the data from Dynamics AX in the Enterprise Portal in the **User group permissions** form, as described in the section *Specifying user permissions in Dynamics AX,* you still need to specify additional user permissions to allow access to Enterprise Portal and Role Center pages. User permissions for the Enterprise Portal are controlled both in Dynamics AX as well as on the SharePoint site. After you have specified the web content user permissions for a specific user group in the **User group permissions** form, permissions on the SharePoint site must also be assigned. The following steps outline this process:

 Dynamics AX has a wizard that automatically generates common user groups for the Enterprise Portal. To run this wizard go to **Administration | Setup | Internet | Enterprise Portal | Configuration wizard**.

1. Open the Enterprise Portal website. To do this, go to **Administration | Setup | System | Internet | Enterprise Portal | Web sites**. Select the Enterprise Portal website and click on the **View in Browser** button.

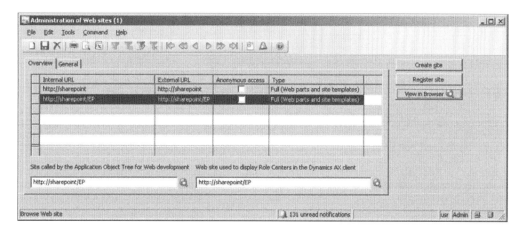

2. Once the Enterprise Portal website is opened, click on the **Site Actions** button and then click on the **Site Settings** button.

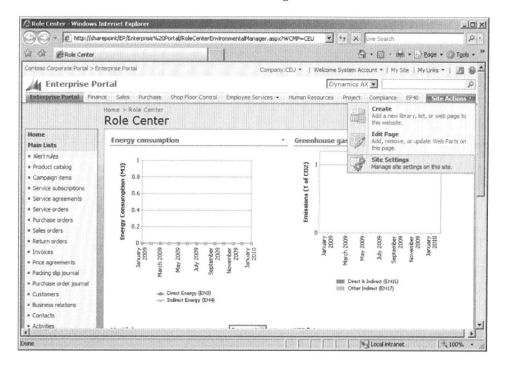

3. In the **Site Settings** page, click on the **People and groups** link.

4. In the **People and Groups** page, click on the **New** drop-down button on the toolbar and then click on the **Add Users** button to add a new user.

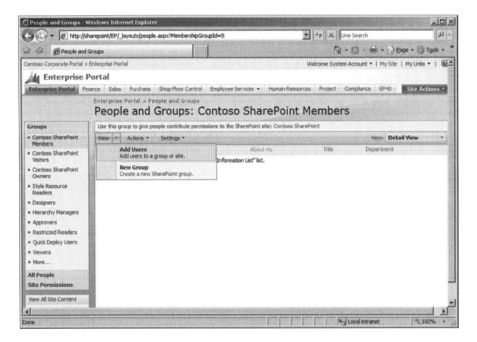

5. On the **Add Users** page, add the Active Directory user or group in which to provide access to the Enterprise Portal page then click on the **OK** button. In order for a Dynamics AX user to have access to the Enterprise Portal, they must have **Viewer** permissions.

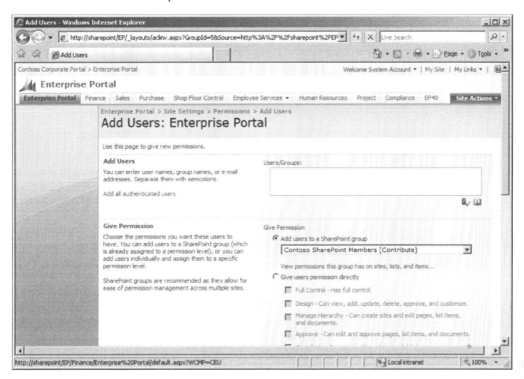

Specifying user permissions for reports

By default, reports will only be visible to the administrator. In order for users to view the reports after they have been deployed, you must specify the appropriate permissions. To specify the appropriate permissions, follow these steps:

1. Navigate to the SQL Server Reporting Services (SSRS) Report Manager site in Internet Explorer and then click on the **Dynamics** folder to open it.

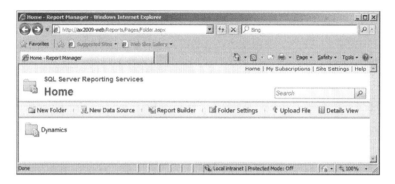

2. In the **Dynamics** folder view, click on the **Folder Settings** tab.

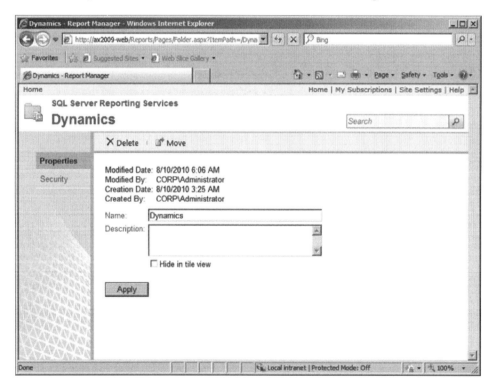

3. In the Folder Settings page, click on the Security link on the menu on the left side. You will notice that only Administrators have the default Content Manager group permission.

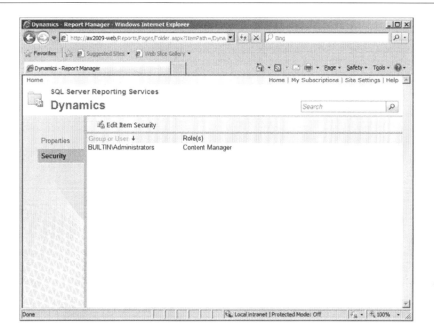

4. To manually start adding new permissions, click on the Edit Item Security button. Then, to create, add, or modify permissions for a user or group, click on the New Role Assignment button.

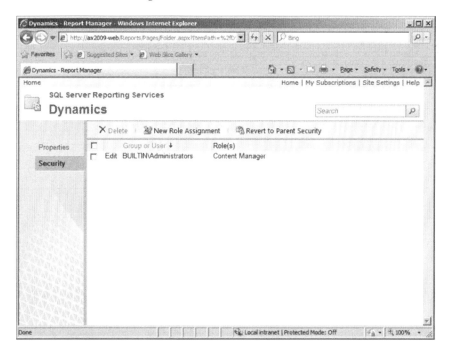

5. In the New Role Assignment page, add a user or group in the first textbox and check the appropriate Role, which will provide specific permissions as stated in the description field. In this example, we are adding the group "Everyone", browser access to the reports. This will allow every user in the domain to only view the reports. Once you are satisfied with your permissions settings, click on the OK button to apply the new role assignment.

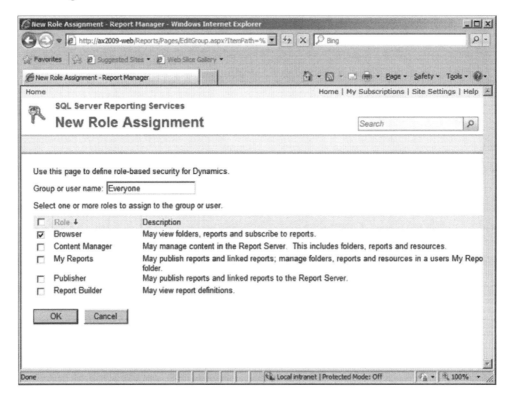

6. In the Security page, you should now see your newly created Group or User assigned to its role.

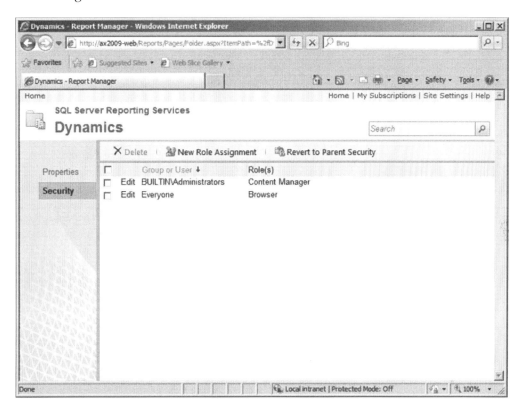

Setting user permissions for Analysis Cubes

Since some reports, Key Performance Indicators (KPIs) or Business Data Lookups (BDL) utilize OLAP cubes to calculate report data, user permissions must be set not only in the SQL Server Reporting Services Report Manager, but also in the SQL Server Analysis Services OLAP Database.

The following steps outline this process:

1. Open **SQL Server Management Studio**. Select **Analysis Services** for the **Server type** and then connect to the appropriate server that contains the Analysis services database.

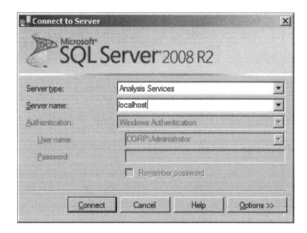

2. Once connected to the SSAS database, collapse the Dynamics AX SSAS database and then collapse the **Roles** folder to view the entire list of roles for the SSAS database.

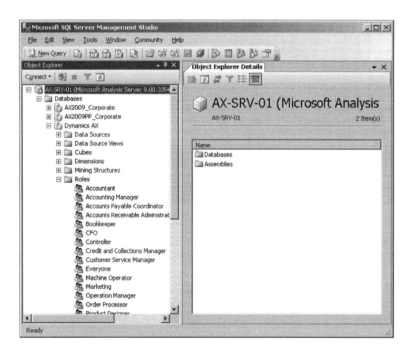

3. Right-click on each individual role and go to **Properties** to open the **Edit Role** window.

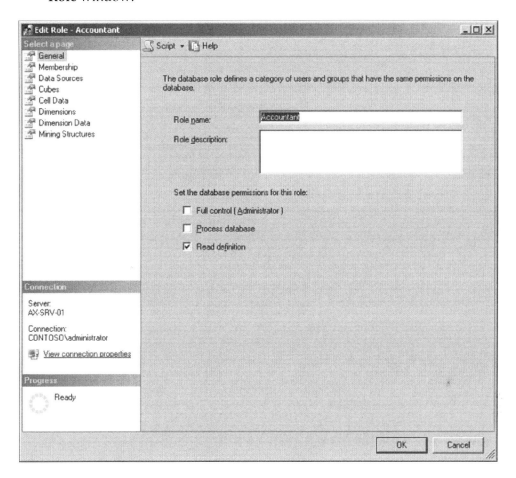

4. In the **Edit Role** window, click on the **Membership** page.

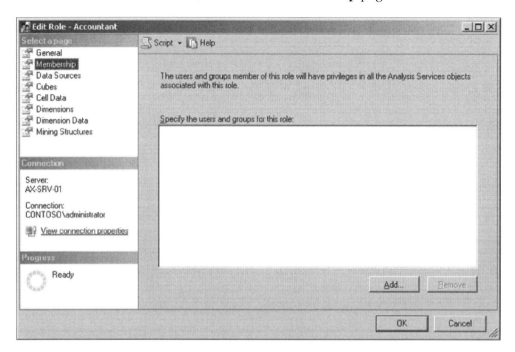

5. On the **Membership** page, click on the **Add** button. This will load the **Select Users or Groups** form. Add which Dynamics AX users from Active Directory should access the Analysis Services cubes. Once completed, click on the **OK** button in the **Edit Role** window.

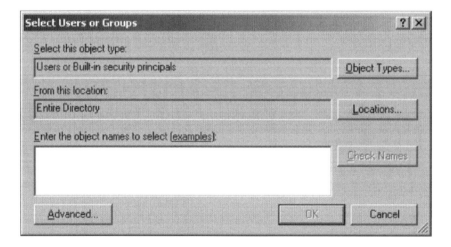

Summary

Setting up Dynamics AX is not just about setting up and configuring the base and extended server components, but includes setting up security as well.

Security is not only important but essential in Dynamics AX. The security model in Dynamics AX is unique compared to the security model of other Microsoft server technologies. As with any other server software, the appropriate setup of security is essential. While licensing files unlock and provide the availability of certain features in Dynamics AX, security and configuration keys allow an administrator to control them.

In order to properly secure Dynamics AX, security must be set up in not only the Application Object Server (AOS) but also in each server component; otherwise, users may or may not have access to the content. When implementing security settings, be sure to start by providing the least security settings. This further ensures that the security is tightened in the system. Configuration keys can be used to activate or deactivate features in Dynamics AX. For example, the useful Fill utility, which provides the useful feature of applying a field value across every row in a form automatically, can be activated or deactivated by a configuration key.

In the next chapter, we will cover the event-based features of Dynamics AX that allow alerts and notifications to be sent. Alerts and notifications can be sent to users through e-mail or while they are logged in to Dynamics AX. Such features increase the productivity of users and streamline their tasks automatically.

10
Alerts and Notifications

With the level of complexity and data that is processed in an ERP system, it can be quite difficult and cumbersome for an individual to monitor specific data manually. More importantly, specific personnel may want to be notified when specific criteria are met on a record or item, so they can act accordingly to make critical, timely decisions. Staying informed real-time is not only a nice benefit but it is critical.

For example, a controller or an accounting manager may need to be notified when a payment is due. A warehouse manager may want to be notified when delivery dates have changed, or a CEO or CFO may want to know when sales targets have decreased below margins. The earlier mentioned are just a few examples of information that is important to be notified as soon as possible. Fortunately, Microsoft Dynamics AX has an alerts feature that addresses these requirements.

The alert system in Dynamics AX is flexible and therefore can be used throughout any module because it can work on any table. A user can be notified of an alert either using e-mail or a non-intrusive pop up similar to that of Outlook's incoming e-mail notification. Alerts can also be used for administrative purposes. For example, an administrator may want to be notified when a batch process fails or completes. In this chapter, we will cover the capabilities of the alert system as well as provide an example of setting up an alert.

In this chapter, we will specifically cover:

- Alerts prerequisites
- Alerts permissions setup
- Creating an alert batch job
- Creating alert rules
- Maintaining alerts
- Setting up user alert options

Alerts prerequisites

By default, the alert system may not be functioning properly or at all. Various setup requirements must be met in order for a user to set up alerts. The following is a list of those requirements:

- Permissions (using security keys)
- Active batch job for processing alerts
- Ensure user options are set up for alerts
- Setup delivery method (e-mail):
  - ○ Valid SMTP e-mail server
  - ○ E-mail templates

Alerts permissions setup

To specify user permissions, in order for a user to be able to benefit from the usage of the alert system, they must be assigned the necessary permissions. Permissions must be set using the **User groups** form in the **Administration** module. For more information on setting permissions, refer to *Chapter 9*, *Security and User Administration*. The following table contains a list of security keys, user group permission locations and what functions they provide, the recommended user group to be created, and which users should be assigned to those groups:

Security key and user group permission location	Functions	Recommended group	Recommended users
BasicMisc (Basic > Miscellaneous) and BasicTables (Basic > Table)	<ul><li>Manage a user's own alerts</li><li>Allow a user to create their own alerts</li><li>Allow a user to view their alerts</li><li>Access detailed business data from alerts</li></ul>	AlertsUser	Users and Administrators

Security key and user group permission location	Functions	Recommended group	Recommended users
BasicSetup (Basic > Setup)	• View and modify all rules from any user • Create rules for any user	AlertsAdm	Administrators
BasicPeriodic (Basic > Periodic)	• Set up and control alerts batch jobs	AlertsSetup	Administrators

The previous list provided the necessary alert permission setup for rich client users. However, additional permissions must be set up for users using the Enterprise Portal. The following table lists the Enterprise Portal security keys and follows the same format as the previous table. Before assigning the permissions, make sure to set the **Viewing** drop-down field in the **User group permissions** form to **Security (incl. Web)**.

Security key and user group permission location	Functions	Recommended group	Recommended users
EPEventRuleList (General > Miscellaneous > "Rule list")	• View user's own alerts • Delete user's own alerts • Access detailed business data from alerts	EPAlertsUser	Users and Administrators
EPEventRuleInfo (General > Miscellaneous > "Rule details")	• Modify alert user's own rules • Delete individual alerts	EPAlertsUser	Users and Administrators
EPEventAlertList (General > Miscellaneous > "Alert list")	• Access alerts listed in user's alerts event inbox • Delete individual alerts	EPAlertsUser	Users and Administrators
EPEventAlertInfo (General > Miscellaneous > "Alert details")	• View user's own alert details • Delete user's own alerts	EPAlertsUser	Users and Administrator

Creating an alerts batch job

In order to process and serve alerts, there must be an active batch process running. In order for a batch process to run, a batch server must be set up on a designated AOS (refer to the *Creating a batch job* section in the *Appendix*).

There are two different types of alert categories that operate in an alert batch job. They are as follows:

- Event-based alerts: Trigger notifications based on changes (modifications, creation, or deletion) on records since previous batch iteration
- Due date triggered alerts: Trigger notifications when rules are honored or not based on a specified due date

It is recommended that a separate batch group be created for each alert category. Event-based alerts should run as frequently as possible to provide the "real-time" effect of receiving notifications. However, as the amount of event-based alerts increases, the performance of the AOS set up as the batch server, proportionally decreases to compensate for this load.

A batch job that processes "due date" based alerts does not need to run as frequently as the event-based alert batch job. In fact, it can run only once a day. Preferably, right after midnight, when the system load is at its lowest and the date has just changed over to a new day. However, there may be a need to run the due date batch job more than once a day to serve notifications based on alerts that were generated the same day of their alert rule due date. In this case, running the batch process during the time of day when server utilization is at its lowest is the best choice (for example, during lunch time). It should also be noted that the batch server will continue to notify an alert that has not been acknowledged for a specified time window interval. It should also be noted that once a batch job processes a due date alert rule, it will not process it again even if the batch job runs more than once during the same day. Not only does this make sense, it also prevents redundant use of computing resources.

As in many typical cases (but not all), the same AOS is set up to provide client access as well as set up as a batch server. Consider the possibility of having a separate AOS to run batch jobs only if performance begins to degrade acceptable user access on the AOS that is mainly used for client access.

Setting up an event alert batch job

In order for event-based alerts to be processed automatically, a batch job must be set up for them to work properly. To set up or modify the event-based alerts, perform the following steps:

1. Open the **Change based alerts** form located in **Basic | Periodic | Alerts | Change based alerts**.

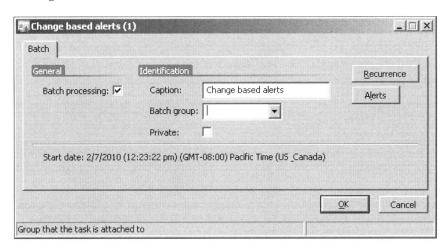

2. On the same form, in the **Batch group** drop-down, select a batch group in which to run the designated event (change-based) alerts batch job.

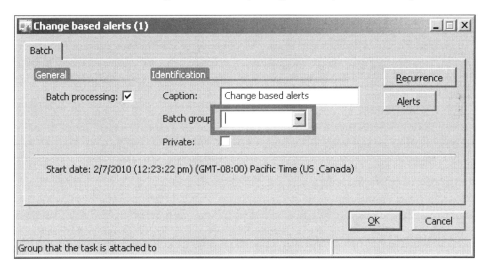

3. To specify the time and frequency that the event alerts will run, click on the **Recurrence** button to open the **Recurrence** form.

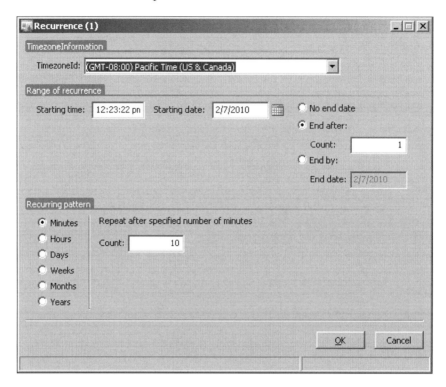

4. In the **Recurrence** form, specify the time that the batch job for alert events should run and how long it should reoccur thereafter. Once the appropriate properties are specified, click on the **OK** button.

5. To be alerted when this batch job ends, fails, or is canceled, click on the **Alerts** button in the **Change based alerts** form.

6. In the **Setup alert for batch job** form, you can also specify to be alerted by pop ups, which will notify you when you are logged into the AOS using a pop up. Once the appropriate options are marked, click on the **OK** button.

7. To complete the set up of the event-based alerts, click on the **OK** button in the **Change based alerts** form.

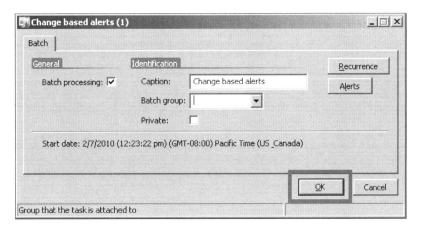

Setting up a due date alert batch job

Setting up the due date alerts is very similar to setting up the event-based alerts. Having said that, setting up a batch job is required to process due date alerts. To set up or modify the due date-based alerts, you will need to perform the following steps:

1. Open the **Due date alerts** form located in **Basic | Periodic | Alerts | Due date alerts**.

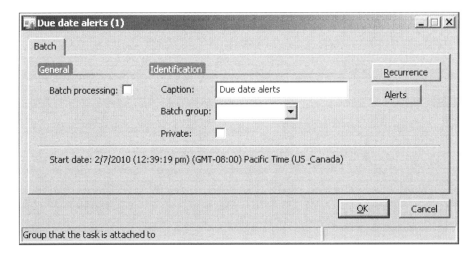

2. In the **Batch group** drop-down, select a batch group in which we run the designated due date alerts batch job.

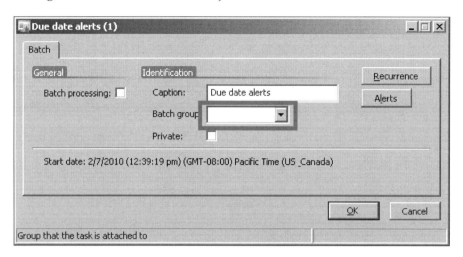

3. To specify the time and frequency that the due date alerts will run with, click on the **Recurrence** button to open the **Recurrence** form.

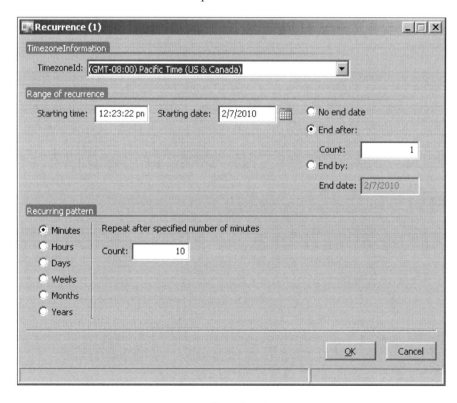

4. In the **Recurrence** form, specify the time that the batch job should run for and how long it should reoccur thereafter. Once the appropriate properties are specified, click on the **OK** button.

5. To be alerted when this batch job ends, fails, or is canceled, click on the **Alerts** button in the **Due date alerts** form.

6. In the **Setup alert for batch job** form, you can also specify to be alerted by pop ups, which will notify you when you are logged in to the AOS using a pop up. Once the appropriate options are marked, click on the **OK** button.

7. To complete the setup of the due date-based alerts, click on the **OK** button in the **Due date alerts** form.

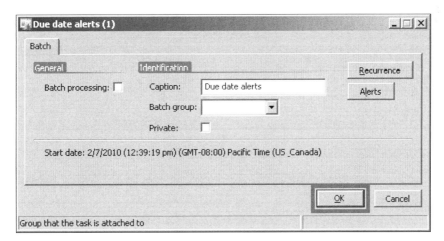

Setting up the Batch Processing Window interval

Unacknowledged due date alerts will continue to be processed for a specified number of days. This number is considered to be the window interval. To specify the window interval, perform the following steps:

1. Open the **Alerts** parameters form in the Basic module by going to **Basic | Setup | Alerts | Alerts parameters**.

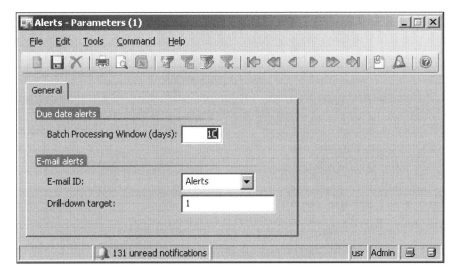

2. In the **Alerts – Parameters** form, specify the number of days for the due date window. The recommended default value is **10**. Ensure that an **E-mail ID** is specified. An e-mail ID is the template that will be used for alert e-mails. To create an e-mail template, go to **Basic | Setup | E-mail templates**. Specify a unique **Drill-down target** value. The **Drill-down target** ensures a unique method of identification, so that when a user wants to "drill down" to an alert's notification, it does not confuse it with multiple databases.

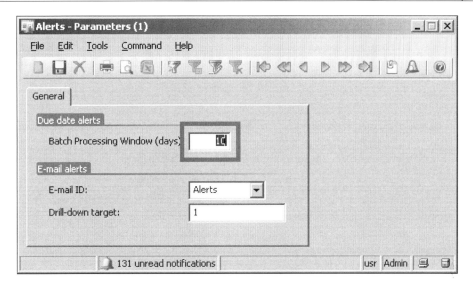

Creating alert rules

Now that the batch jobs are set up and configured to process alerts, users can now create alert rules to receive notifications. Alert rules are the very conditions that alerts run on. Alert rules can be specified in virtually any form. The general process of creating alerts is summarized in the following diagram followed by the basic steps to implement a rule on any record in Dynamics AX:

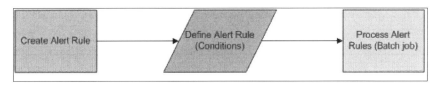

1. Create an alert on a record.
2. Specify an alert rule (conditions):
    a. Event (alert me when).
    b. Condition (alert me for).
    c. Expiration constraint (alert me until).
    d. Alert conditions (alert me with).
    e. Who to notify (alert who).
    f. Alert method (alert me by).
3. Save the alert, which submits it to the alert's batch job.

Alert example: Notification of when a purchase order status has changed

An example of how an alert can be used is to track purchase orders whose statuses have changed to a "Stopped" status. This would be useful for an employee to quickly respond to the purchase order and make any modifications to a purchase order or perform other tasks if necessary.

Since the process for creating alerts is similar no matter what form they are in, the following steps can be adapted for other forms and scenarios as well.

The following steps outline the process for creating an alert on a purchase order to track when the status has changed:

1. Open the **Purchase Order Details** form by going to **Accounts Payable | Common Forms | Purchase Order Details**.

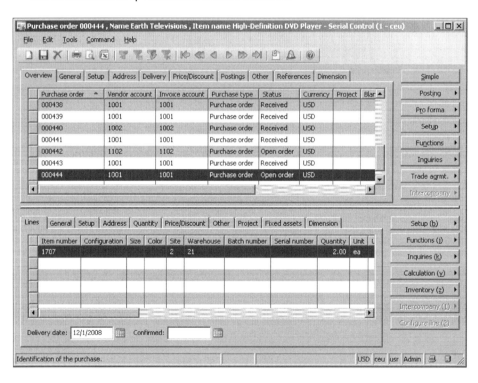

2. Right-click on any field on the header for the current record and click on the **Create alert rule...** option to open the **Create alert rule** form. It is important to click on the header section; otherwise, if you click on the lines section, the system will only refer to the purchase lines table.

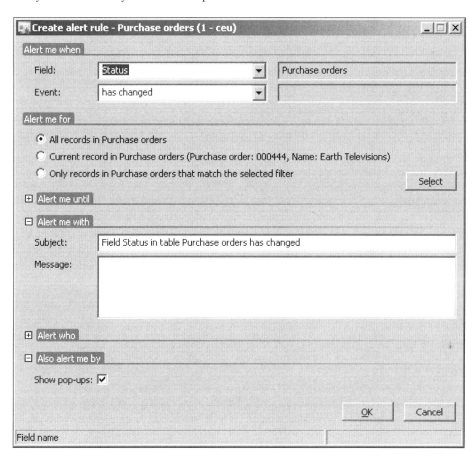

3. In the **Create alert rule** form, you may specify which field to set the alert rule on. In this case, select the **Status** field from the drop-down list. Set the event property to **has changed**. Leave the rest of the parameters defaulted or provide extra options if desired.

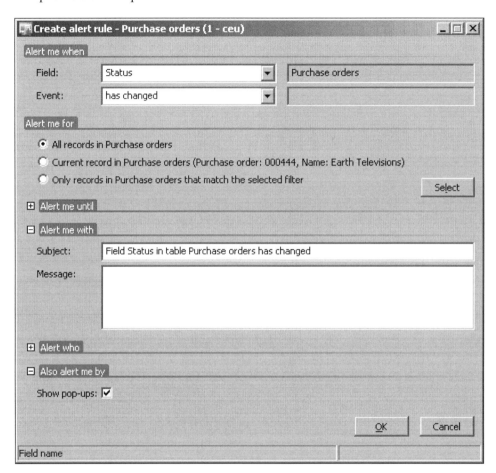

4. When you have completed setting up the alert rule, click on the **OK** button. The newly created alert rule will now be listed in the **Manage alert rules** form.

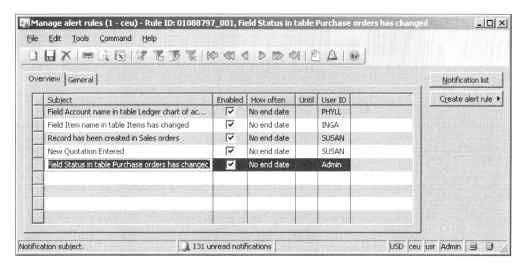

5. A user's alerts can be accessed by simply clicking on the bell icon in the status bar in the Dynamics AX client, on any form or the bell icon in the Dynamics AX toolbar.

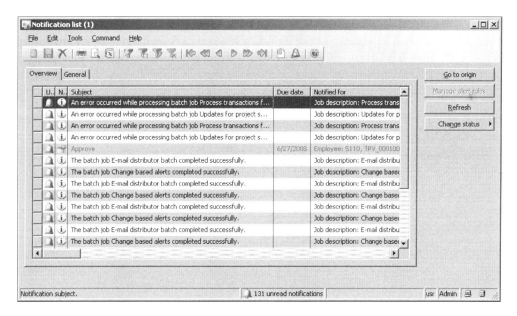

Maintaining alerts

Depending on the setup, the number of notification entries from alerts can increase significantly. The more alerts that exist, the more time it takes to process notifications. Therefore, it is good practice to periodically maintain a pristine notification repository. There are two methods for cleaning up alerts. One method is to run the alert cleanup wizard. The other is to manually delete the events. The following two sections outline both processes.

Cleaning up event queues automatically

Fortunately, in Dynamics AX 2009, there is a form called the **Notification clean-up** form that can be used to clean up notifications automatically. The following steps describe the process:

1. Open the **Notification clean-up** form found in **Administration | Periodic | Notification clean-up**.

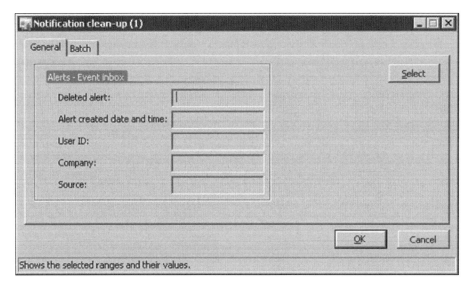

2. Click on the **Select** button to create a Dynamics AX query with appropriate **Criteria** to make filters. Once the appropriate filters have been made, click on the **OK** button to return to the **Notification clean-up** form.

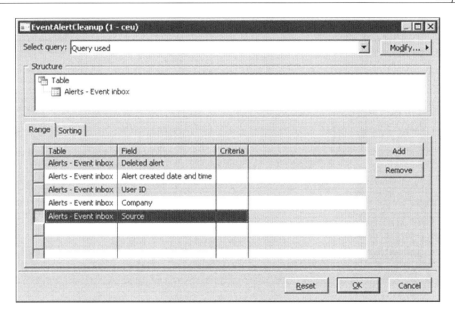

3. Click on the **OK** button to run the clean-up on the notifications based on the query specified.

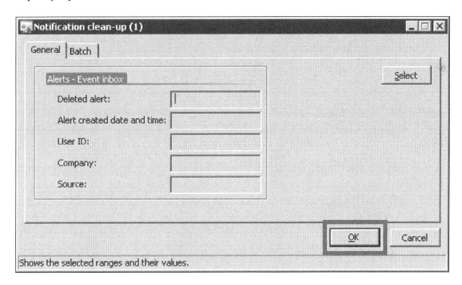

Running the **Notification clean-up** form provides an easy method of cleaning up notifications. The **Notification clean-up** form can also be a batch process that is run periodically to clean-up notifications. To set up the **Notification clean-up** as a batch job, please refer to the batch job example in the *Appendix*. The next section covers a similar process, but manually.

Cleaning up event queues manually

Another option for cleaning up alerts and notifications is to manually delete them. To delete unwanted alerts, you must delete them from the **EventCUD** table. The following steps outline this process:

1. Open the **Application Object Table (AOT)** then go to **Data Dictionary | Tables | EventCUD**.

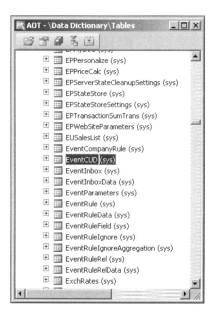

2. Right-click on the **EventCUD** table and click on **Open** from the context menu to browse the table.

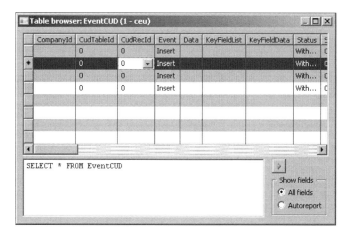

3. Select the appropriate line that you want to delete and simply delete the record. This action will permanently remove the alert from being processed by the alert batch job.

Manually being able to delete notifications provides more control over which events to delete. It is also a method to view the specific details of a notification, which is useful — should the need arise — to troubleshoot alert issues.

Preventing alerts during data import

When importing data into a company account, by default, alerts will be generated if they are contained in the imported company. This may be unnecessary and also spam unwanted notifications to users from alerts they may have already received from another company. Fortunately, there is an easy way to disable (or enable) this option. The steps are as follows:

1. Open the **Import** form that is used during data imports by accessing **Administration | Periodic | Data export/import | Import**. Then click on the **Advanced** tab.

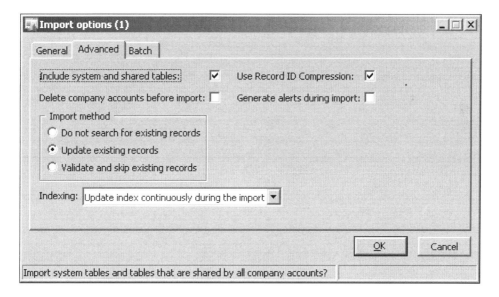

2. Uncheck (or check) the **Generate alerts during import** option then click on the **OK** button to save the parameters and to have them applied during an import.

Setting up user alert options

Alerts can be controlled and customized not only on the server level, but on the user level as well. For example, various settings such as a user's e-mail or if they would like to receive alerts, can all be specified in the user's options. Since alerts can also be controlled at the user level, they will only be specific to the user. The following section provides steps on how to specify alert settings in a user's options:

1. Go to **Administration | Common Forms | Users**. In the **User** form, select a user and click on the **User options** button to view the user's personal options. Similarly, a user can also view their own options by going to the **Dynamics AX menu | Tools | Options**.

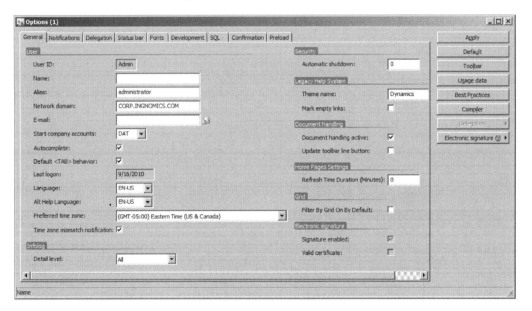

2. In the **General** tab, ensure that the **E-mail** field is specified.

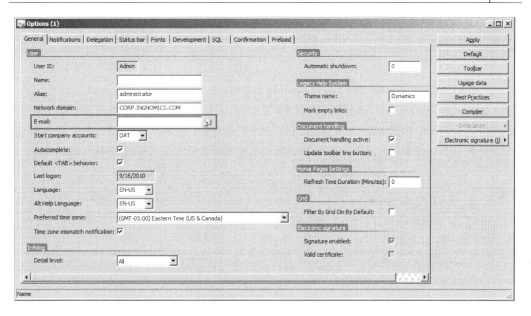

3. To specify more specific options on how alerts are notified, click on the **Notification** tab. To specify the interval, in which notifications should be delivered to the user, enter a value specifying the number of minutes. To specify whether a user should either go to an alert setup or the form in which an alert was set up, when clicking on an alert, specify its **Pop-up link destination**. You can also control the delivery and display of alerts by changing the **Send alert as e-mail message** setting or **Show pop-ups** setting respectively.

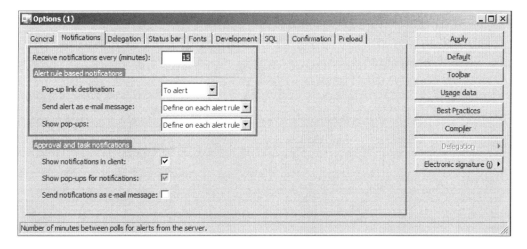

4. **Approval and task notifications** are the notifications that pertain to Workflow. Such notifications may appear during a workflow process. For example, if the user is assigned to approve a purchase order, they will be immediately notified. Notifications may be displayed as a user is logged into Dynamics AX. To suppress this, simply unmark the **Show notifications in client** checkbox. To send e-mail notifications of workflow tasks, simply mark the **Send notifications as e-mail message** checkbox.

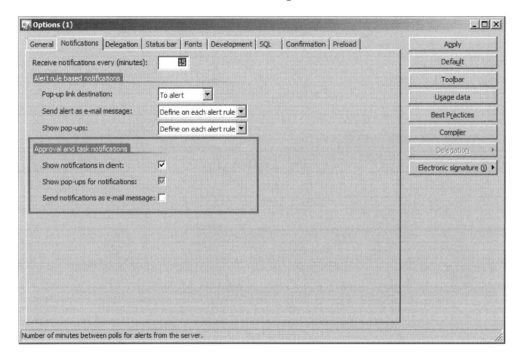

5. When appropriate settings have been specified, click on the **Apply** button to save the changes.

Summary

Not only having access to information, but to be notified in real time as information changes, is becoming increasingly important as a business requirement. It is no longer efficient for a user to always check for updates on information that is important to them. Alerts in Dynamics AX are a powerful way to bring information to a user, which they may have once manually had to go out of their way to keep track of.

The alert system in Dynamics AX is also a handy way for an administrator to keep track of system functionality. For example, many batch jobs may run during after hours. Such batch jobs may be critical for business processes that need to occur the following day. If a batch job fails, it is not only beneficial for an administrator to know but also critical. Therefore, being notified using e-mail about the status of a batch job can certainly assist the function of a system administrator.

In the next chapter, we will look at how to tweak the Dynamics AX setup to ensure that your Dynamics AX environment is working as efficiently and robustly as possible.

11
Tuning Your Setup

Once Dynamics AX is operational with the appropriate setup and customizations, it is beneficial to optimize its performance. Performance can be tweaked either by upgrading hardware or by tweaking software to utilize its resources efficiently. Furthermore, you can scale-up or scale-out hardware or software as described in the section *Phases of a Dynamics AX Implementation* of Chapter 1, *System Planning and Hardware Sizing*. For example, to increase performance at the hardware level, you can add additional memory or processors to an AOS server. Or, you can increase performance at the software level by adding an additional AOS instance. Additionally, you can make tweaks within the operating system to improve performance. For example, increasing the processing priority level of the AOS service process may also increase the AOS performance.

Since Dynamics AX is extremely flexible, there is not a single setup for all deployment scenarios. It is also a very efficient and stable system due to its code base, which has matured over the years. However, with the addition of customizations, third-party modules or an increase in capacity levels, performance may degrade. Typically, a developer can tweak code or an administrator can tweak settings in the AOS, database, or extended server components. In some cases, simple modifications can alleviate large headaches in the future. Fortunately, there are tools available to ease this process.

In this chapter, we will cover the specific configuration settings that can be done on both the client and server components as well as go over various methods, tweaks, techniques, and tools that all assist you in tuning your setup to perform at its optimal level. Performance may also vary along different hardware configurations and no matter how many software configuration setting tweaks are made in Dynamics AX or the database; network and hardware will still be a limitation. Henceforth, also consider possible hardware or network limitations.

In this chapter, we will specifically look at the following:

- Accessing the Application Object Server (AOS) configuration
- Tuning an AOS for best performance
- Accessing the client configuration

Accessing the Application Object Server (AOS) configuration

By default, the setup program performs all the labor necessary to get a fully functional Application Object Server (AOS) up and running. However, to actually provide specific parameters, configuration settings, or simply modifications for an AOS, this must be done in the Microsoft Dynamics AX 2009 Server Configuration application, which is automatically installed when you install an AOS. If you installed more than one AOS, as is the case in typically all implementations, one server configuration application is used for all AOSes. To access the server configuration application, follow these steps:

1. To run the Microsoft Dynamics AX 2009 Server Configuration application, simply go to **Start | Administrative Tools | Microsoft Dynamics AX 2009 Server Configuration**. Otherwise, access it by going to **Start | Control Panel | Administrative Tools | Microsoft Dynamics AX 2009 Server Configuration**.

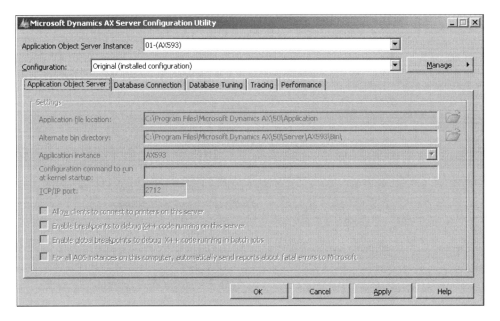

2. Select the AOS that you want to modify the settings for from the **Application Object Server Instance** drop-down. As you may have noticed, you cannot make any modifications to the configuration settings for any AOS.

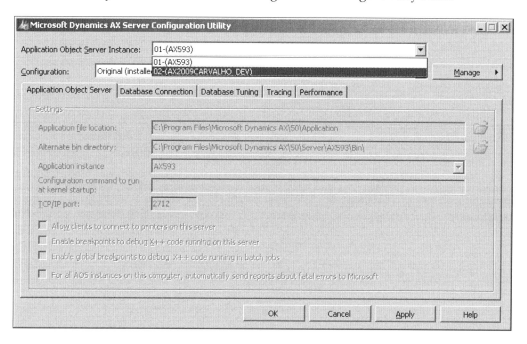

3. Once you have selected the AOS, you would like to make configuration modifications on, click on the **Manage** button and then click on the **Create configuration...** menu item to create a configuration for the selected AOS.

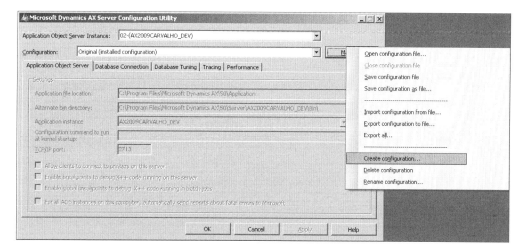

4. After clicking on the menu item, you will be prompted to provide a name for the configuration. Name it based on what the configuration settings will be for. For example, if you want to provide debugging tweaks, a good name for the configuration would be "Development". If you want to make a high-performance setup for a Production AOS, a good name would be "Production". If you wanted to speed the process of creating additional configuration files, you may base a new configuration file based on another configuration file. If that is the case, simply make sure **Active configuration** is selected. This will simply copy the current selected configuration file settings and duplicate them. If this is your first configuration file, selecting either **Active configuration** or **Original configuration** will make no difference. The **Original configuration** is synonymous to the default configurations, which are the default, out-of-the-box, settings.

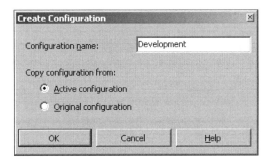

5. Once you have created the configuration, you will notice that the fields are no longer read only and you can now modify the configuration settings. You should also notice that the **Configuration** drop-down now has the newly created configuration's name called **Development**.

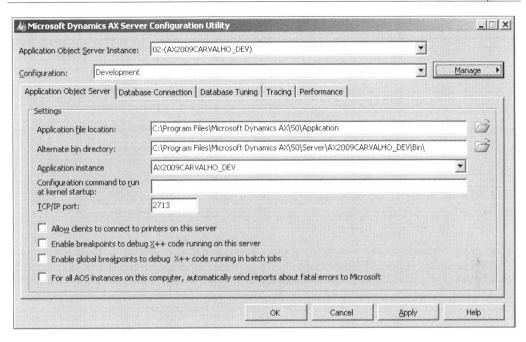

The earlier mentioned steps provide the method for creating custom configurations for the Application Object Server (AOS). This is necessary if you want to modify any parameters or configuration settings shown throughout the rest of the chapter. This chapter provides what parameters and settings are available and recommendations of specific parameters to set for best performance.

AOS configuration settings

The Application Object Server (AOS) configuration settings provide parameters to manipulate and control the AOS's performance, file locations, database location, and so forth. Any modifications performed on the settings should be approached with strict caution and should be well-tested before being set for a live, production environment.

The following table describes what each property in the Microsoft Dynamics AX 2009 Server Configuration application is for. Next to the parameter name, in parenthesis, is the command line parameter that can be used if running the server from the command line.

Application Object Server Tab	
`Application file location (-directory=<spath>)`	The location where all the Application Files and Label files are located. This should not have to be modified by default because the installation program automatically sets the Application File location.
`Alternate bin directory (-bindir=<path>)`	The directory where the AOS server can access kernel text data (`.ktd`) files. Kernel text data files are normally stored in the application file location. Specifying this allows you the option to store a copy of the kernel text data files in a separate location.
`Application instance (-application=<applicat ionname>)`	The name of the Application instance to run as. This list is generated based on the file location specified for the Application File Directory setting above.
Configuration command to run at kernel start up	The command line parameters settings that can be used to run the AOS.
`TCP/IP port (-port=<portnumber>)`	The port in which the AOS will listen on, for clients to connect. The default is 2712 and each AOS that is installed thereafter will increment by one from this number.
`Allow clients to connect to printers on the server (-exposeserverprinters)`	This option allows clients to access the printers that the AOS server has access to.
`Enable breakpoints to debug X++ code running on the server (-xppdebug=<0,1>)`	For an AOS that a developer will be developing on, enable this option, so that a developer can set break points in X++ code for debugging purposes.
Enable global breakpoints to debug X++ code running in batch jobs	For an AOS that a developer will be developing on, enable this option, so that a developer can set break points in X++ code in batch jobs for debugging purposes.
For all AOS instances running on this computer, automatically send reports about fatal errors to Microsoft.	A global option, when marked, it will provide feedback on fatal errors that are sent through the Internet directly to Microsoft, so that they can assess the error and come up with fixes to prevent the error in the near future more quickly.

Database Connection Tab	
`Microsoft SQL Server` `(-database=<databasename>)`	If using a Microsoft SQL Server database, you will be able to select the server and named instance from the drop-down and then select the database name. By default, when installing the database from the installation wizard, the database is automatically associated with the AOS.
Oracle	If using an Oracle database, simply select this option. For more information on the Oracle parameters, please consult the Oracle database documentation (`http://www.oracle.com/ technology/documentation/index.html`).

Database Tuning Tab	
`Maximum open cursors` `(-opencursors=<number>)`	The default value is 90. This parameter specifies the maximum number of database cursors to keep open, which will also be reused.
`Maximum buffer size` `(-sqlbuffer=<number>)`	The maximum size of the buffer of data that is received from a SQL query. The larger the buffer, the more data that can be received at one time. The default value is 24. If errors occur when Dynamics AX attempts to query SQL or Role Center web parts fail, in some cases, increasing the buffer size may alleviate the problem. It is recommended to only increment by 2 (2,000 bytes) each until the errors go away. As the value increases, the performance between the AOS and SQL Server decreases. Therefore, be very cautious and only change when necessary.
`Transaction retry interval` `(-retry=<time>)`	The default value is 5 seconds. This parameter controls the time, a re-execution on a transaction should occur after it has experienced a deadlock.
`Array fetch ahead` `(-fetchahead=<number>)`	The default value is 100. This parameter controls the number of records that the AOS fetches at the same time.
Local ODBC log file location	The location on the local drive of the AOS server computer in which errors, warnings, or important notifications from the ODBC connection can be stored.

Database Tuning Tab

Allow INDEX hints in queries (-hint=<0,1>)	The option, when marked, allows queries in X++ with custom specified index hints to override the default assigned by Database Management Systems (DBMS).
Number of connection retries (-newconnectionretrycount=<number>)	The number of times to retry connecting to a database before determining a connection failure.
Connection retry interval (-newconnectionretrydelayms=<time>)	The time interval (in milliseconds) in which to retry connection attempts to the database.
Limit the number of inactive connections	This allows or disallows concurrent inactive connections to the database to remain open.
Maximum number of inactive connections	This specifies the number of concurrent inactive connections to the database that should remain open.
Use literals in join queries from forms and reports (-sqlformliterals=<0, 1>)	If enabled, the AOS will use literals instead of parameters for complex joins to increase performance. Enable this if reports or forms take a long time to query data.
Use literals in complex joins from X++ (-sqlcomplexliterals=<0,1>)	If enabled, the AOS will use literals instead of parameters in complex joins, which can increase performance.
Generate ORDER BY clauses from WHERE clauses (-ignoredatasourceindex=<0, 1>)	If enabled, the AOS will automatically generate ORDER BY clauses from WHERE clauses, which may improve query performance.
Include LTRIM in all SELECT statements to remove leading space from right-aligned columns (-hint=<0, 2>)	When enabled, the AOS will use LTRIM on all queries to the database. The benefit of using LTRIM is that it automatically performs a table scan to ensure data consistency and integrity. However, this will cause a performance decrease.

Tracing Tab

Log directory location	The location where logs are stored from tracing.
RPC round trips on server (-TraceEventsEnabled=1)	The Trace Remote Procedure Call (RPC) between the server and any client.
X++ method calls (-TraceEventsEnabled=100)	This traces all calls of X++ methods on the AOS.
Number of nested calls (-TraceXppMethodCallDepth=<number>)	The default is 3. This parameter controls the depth in X++ method calls.

Tracing Tab

Function calls (-TraceEventsEnabled=101)	This traces any function call in X++ on the AOS.
Start trace (-TraceStart=1)	This activates the trace.
Stop trace (-TraceStart=0)	This deactivates the trace.
SQL Statements (-TraceEventsEnabled=202)	These trace all SQL statements that are sent to the database from the AOS.
Bind variables (-TraceEventsEnabled=203)	The Trace columns in SQL that are used as input bind variables—variables that are passed as parameters instead of literal values in SQL statements.
Row fetch (-TraceEventsEnabled=204)	This traces all rows that are returned to the AOS from SQL.
Row fetch summary (-TraceEventsEnabled=205)	This traces the time it takes for the AOS to have a result set to return from SQL and the number of records contained in that result set. This is an excellent feature for determining, which queries are causing bottlenecks.
Connect and disconnect (-TraceEventsEnabled=200)	This traces the connections and disconnections between the AOS and database.
Transactions: TTSBegin, TTSCommit, TTSAbort (-TraceEventsEnabled=201)	This traces queries in the AOS that use the TTS statements.
Allow client tracing on Application Object Server instance (-TraceAllowClient)	When enabled, this allows Microsoft Dynamics AX 2009 to control tracing information. For more information, review the Client Configuration sections in this chapter.

Performance Tab

Minimum packet size to compress (-compressionminsize=<number>)	The smaller the packet size chosen, the greater the performance increases. Tweak this option to specify the smallest packet size that can be compressed. Compression will increase performance in slower networks.
Processor Affinity	When the default is selected, the AOS server operating system will determine how to balance load across CPUs. Otherwise, you can manually override this and specify which CPU will process the AOS functions on. Depending on your setup, this may improve server performance.

Advanced AOS configuration settings

Although the Microsoft Dynamics AX 2009 Server configuration application provides the most common parameters in which to manipulate the functions, performance, settings, and configuration of an AOS instance, there are additional parameters that have been left out and can only be accessed through the command line or configuration file interface. The following table lists the advanced AOS parameters:

Advanced AOS Parameters	
Compression disabled (-compressiondisabled)	When present, this will disable packet compression. It is recommended that you do not disable packet compression, as it will degrade the client and server performance communication.
Code Access Security level (-caslevel=<enable/ disable/trace>)	By default, this is enabled. Code Access Security (CAS) in Dynamics AX controls access to specific APIs.
Maximum concurrent sessions (-MaxConcurrent UISessions=<value>)	The minimum value is 0 and the maximum value is 65535. Using this, you can control the number of users that can access the AOS. This is useful when an AOS is load balanced. For example, each AOS in a load-balanced cluster should allow roughly 60 users.
Maximum concurrent guest sessions (-MaxConcurrent GuestSessions=<value>)	The minimum value is 0 and the maximum value is 65535. Using this, you can control the number of anonymous users that can access the AOS.
Maximum concurrent web sessions (-MaxConcurrent WebSessions=<value>)	The minimum value is 0 and the maximum value is 65535. Using this, you can control the number of Enterprise Portal users that can access the AOS.
Maximum concurrent Business Connector users (-MaxConcurrentBCSession s=<value>)	The minimum value is 0 and the maximum value is 65535. Using this, you can control the number of Business Connector users (from Snap Ins or third-party integration software) that can access the AOS.
Maximum memory load (-MaxMemLoad=<value>)	The default is 0. When modified, this parameter determines the maximum percentage of physical memory that is allocated for the AOS to utilize.

Advanced Database Parameters	

`Create DSN`
`(createdsn=<microsoftsqlserver,`
`oracle>)`
	Creates a data source in the ODBC manager in the Windows.

`DSN (-dsn=<portnumber>)`	Connects to a specific DSN port.
`ODBC or OCI mode (-dbcli=<ODBC,` `OCI>)`	Runs Dynamics AX in either ODBC or Oracle's OCI mode.
`Database server` `(-dbserver=<servername>)`	Specifies the database server name.

Advanced Tracing Parameters	

`Trace file size`
`(-TraceMaxFileSize=`
`<number>)`
	The default is 10MB. Specifies the maximum size a trace file can be.

`Trace buffer size`
`(-TraceBufferSize=`
`<0:64>)`
	The default is 20KB. Specifies the buffer size of the trace log. Maximum possible value is 64KB.

Creating an AOS Configuration: An example

Now that you are able to modify the server configuration, you may be wondering which settings it would make sense to modify? In the following process, we will modify the settings appropriate for a development environment. If we continued from the previous example, we should already have a Developer configuration file created without having the necessary configuration settings. By default, debugging is not enabled.

To set up a "developer friendly" AOS make sure you have the following parameters set:

- Enable breakpoints to debug X++ running on this server
- Enable global breakpoints to debug X++ code running in batch jobs

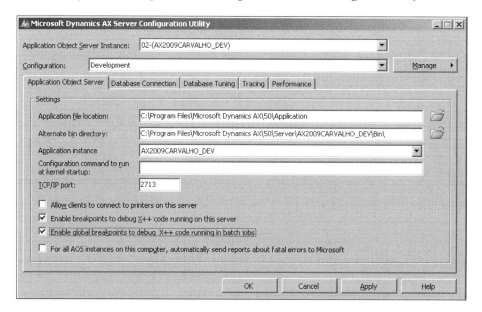

Tuning an AOS for best performance

Optimizing an AOS depends on what the AOS is used for. For example, an AOS that is load balanced should only allocate a certain number of resources on the server it is running on. Similarly, an AOS that is only used for the Enterprise Portal may not want to allow access to rich client users. Therefore, before taking any steps to optimize the performance of an AOS, make sure you have properly defined a role that the AOS has.

There are two ways to distribute load in a Dynamics AX environment. They are the following:

- Non-load-balanced cluster
- Load-balanced cluster

A cluster of AOSes are simply a group of AOSes. It doesn't necessarily mean that they are load balanced. However, a load-balanced cluster does indeed mean that a group of AOSes in a cluster are load balanced. The following sections will describe in more detail what a non-load-balanced cluster and a load-balanced cluster are.

Don't set up an AOS for load balancing if you are using third-party software or hardware to load balance an AOS. Consult the setup documentation of the third-party software or hardware.

Non-load-balanced cluster

A non-load-balanced cluster does not have a main AOS that is dedicated to delegating client connections to the appropriate AOS. Instead, each AOS in the cluster acts independently. Each AOS has to be provided in the client configuration file for the client to connect. Based on a list of provided AOS servers in the client configuration file, the client will attempt to access each server in the order listed to find an available server. If a server's workload has reached its maximum level, then the client will simply attempt to connect to the next AOS.

Load-balanced cluster

Microsoft Dynamics AX provides the option to load balance two or more AOS's together. This is similar to how a web farm works for a SharePoint site. Alternatively, you may opt to use hardware or another software solution to load balance AOS access. It is recommended to have one AOS for no more than 50-60 users. In a load-balanced cluster, one AOS is a dedicated load balancer, delegating client connections to the appropriate AOS. It is not directly used either for interactive purposes or for processing application code. Once a client is connected to the load balancer AOS, it will then determine which AOS it should connect to. If an AOS goes down, the load balancer AOS will automatically re-route clients to an active and available AOS without having to make any modifications to client configurations. Also, as a company grows and more users are needed, it is as simple as installing a new AOS and connecting it to the load balancer.

If a load balancer AOS goes down, clients will connect to other AOS's listed in the client configuration in a round-robin fashion. This scenario is similar to a non-load-balanced cluster.

As previously mentioned, to set up load balancing, we must set up one AOS as the load balancer. Afterwards, each additional AOS in the load-balanced cluster will automatically listen for client connection requests from the Load Balancer AOS. However, in order for an AOS to be a load balancer, it must first satisfy the following criteria:

- Cannot be a Batch Server
- Must be an AOS that is active

The following steps describe the process of setting up load balancing in Microsoft Dynamics AX 2009:

1. Open the **Cluster configuration** form by going to **Administration | Setup | Cluster configuration**.

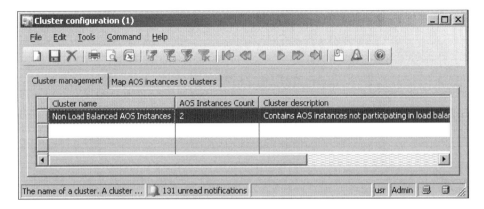

2. Once in the **Cluster configuration** form, click on the **Map AOS instances to clusters** tab.

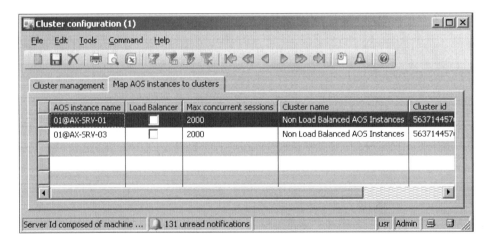

3. In the **Map AOS instances to clusters** tab, select the AOS instance in which to act as the load balancer and mark the **Load Balancer** field.

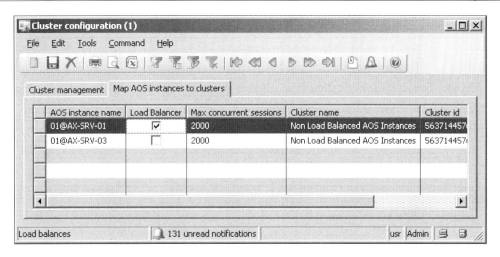

As you can see, setting up a load-balanced cluster in Dynamics AX is quite simple and requires very little configuration or tweaking of settings. When load tends to increase and performance degrades, adding a new AOS into a load-balanced cluster greatly improves performance and is quite simple to do. You can add as many AOS's as desired to a cluster. The process is the same for every additional AOS that is added.

To summarize, a non-load-balanced cluster requires more administrative work to update the client configuration files with the available AOS's. However, with a load-balanced cluster, the AOS that acts as the load balancer, once setup with all the available AOS's will automatically delegate clients to an AOS in a cluster with the most available resources.

Certainly, having a load-balanced cluster may seem like a desired setup to go with, as it requires less administrative maintenance. It also provides a method for consolidating specific business functions. For example, one cluster of AOS's may be specifically dedicated to batch processing. Similarly, another cluster may be dedicated to an external Enterprise Portal site that can experience a significant load of external user access while a cluster for internal users may not experience as much load. Also consider that in a load-balanced cluster, at least three AOSes are required while in a similar non-load-balanced cluster, only two are required—to provide load distribution.

Accessing the client configuration

When installing a development environment, which includes installing all the client, base server components, and extended components on the same system, you can simply run the client and access the AOS without modifying any settings. However, when there is more than one AOS installed, typically in every implementation, there will at least be a Development (DEV), Testing (TEST), Staging (STAGE), and Production (PROD) environment. In this instance, configuration modifications will be necessary to access each AOS. If connecting to a Load Balanced Cluster, you will only have to connect to the Load Balancer AOS. The main AOS will take care of delegating the client access between the other environments.

Not only will there be a need to have configuration modifications done to access each individual AOS but also each individual application code layer (for example, CUS). Otherwise, by default, the layer is the User layer (USR). To do all the necessary modifications as well as provide start up parameters, client performance tweaks, and so forth, it will have to be done in the Microsoft Dynamics AX 2009 Client configuration form, which is installed along with the Microsoft Dynamics AX 2009 Client.

The following steps describe an example of the process for accessing and modifying the Dynamics AX 2009 Client configuration application for creating a development configuration, so that developers can perform modifications on a designated application layer:

1. To run the Microsoft Dynamics AX 2009 Client configuration application, simply go to **Start | Administrative Tools | Microsoft Dynamics AX 2009 Configuration**. Otherwise, access it by going to **Start | Control Panel | Administrative Tools | Microsoft Dynamics AX 2009 Configuration**.

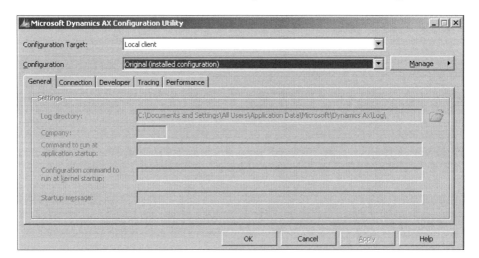

2. Select which configuration to modify. For example, if you want to modify the configuration for the rich client, select **Local client** in the **Configuration Target** drop-down. If you want to modify the Business Connector configuration, select **Business Connector** from the **Configuration Target** drop-down.

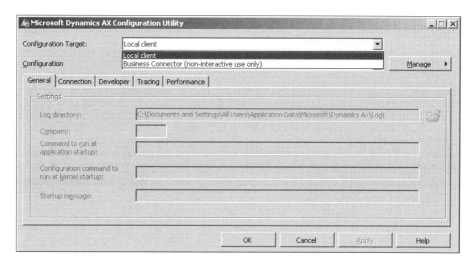

3. Click on **Manage | Create Configuration** to create a new configuration.

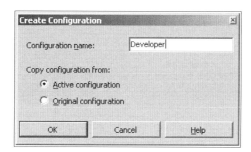

4. Now that you have created a new configuration, you can edit the parameters.

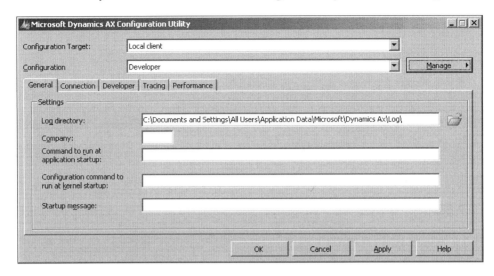

5. Specify the following parameters, such as the default company account to open a custom message or any additional parameters when the client starts in the **General** tab.

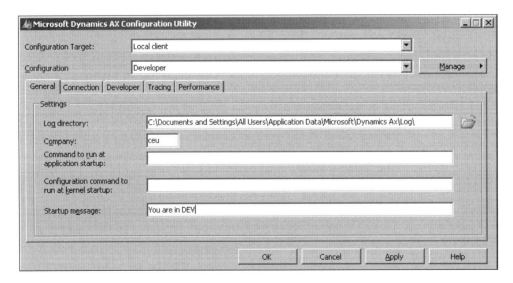

6. Specify the Development AOS in the **Available Application Object Server instances** section.

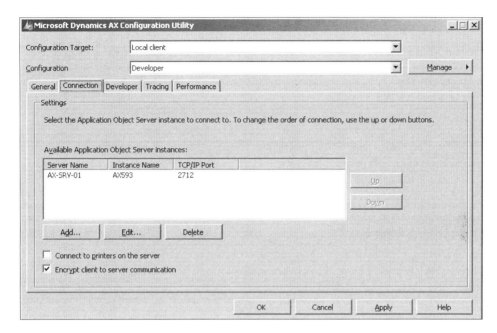

When setting up a client configuration for a non-load-balanced cluster, add all the available AOS's in the **Available Application Object Server instances** section; otherwise, users will only connect to the AOS listed. In a load-balanced cluster setup, the load balancer AOS should be added. For additional redundancy, it would also be beneficial to have all the AOS's in the load-balanced cluster listed, so that clients will still be able to connect to Dynamics AX, even if the load balancer AOS is unavailable.

7. In order to access specific layers and enable debugging options, specify the desired parameters listed in the **Developer** tab. The succeeding section lists the available parameter settings and their purposes. Make sure you specify which layer to develop on as well as provide the appropriate license code to access the layer.

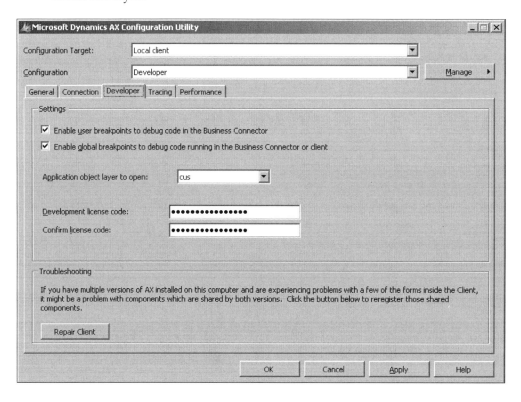

Now you should have a solid grasp of how to create custom client configurations. Client configurations, in essence, are the doorway to access Dynamics AX either as a developer or basic user. In the following section, you will be provided with details on each available parameter and its capabilities.

Client configuration settings

The following table describes the fields in each tab of the Microsoft Dynamics AX 2009 Client configuration form. As stated earlier, this form is automatically installed into the Windows Server Administrative Tools when the Dynamics AX client is installed. Typically, during an implementation, administrators will want to create several configuration files. These configuration files should provide different levels of user access.

General Tab

Log directory (-log=<path>)	The directory in which errors, warnings, and important notifications are logged to.
Company (-company=<string>)	This specifies a company in which to connect to once logging into Dynamics AX.
Command to run at application startup (-startupCmd=<command>)	This provides commands to run when the Dynamics AX rich client starts up.
Configuration command run at kernel startup (-extracmd=<command>)	This provides additional commands for the kernel to run when it starts up.
Startup message (-startupmsg=<string>)	This displays a message that prompts the user once he/she logs into Dynamics AX.

Connection Tab

Add (-aos2=host:port)	This adds an AOS to connect to. Specify the AOS server name, instance (optional), and port in which the AOS instance is running on.
Edit	This edits the selected AOS connection information.
Delete	This deletes the selected AOS connection.
Connect to printers on the server (-useserverprinters)	If enabled on the connected AOS, this allows the client to access printers on the AOS server.
Encrypt client to server communication (-aosencryption=<0,1>)	This encrypts data that is sent from the client to the AOS.

Developer Tab

Enable user breakpoints to debug code in the Business Connector (-xppdebug=<0,1>)	When enabled, developers can debug X++ code that is accessed by the Business Connector.
Enable global breakpoints to debug code running in the Business Connector or client (-globalbreakpoints)	When enabled, developers can debug X++ code that is accessed by the Business Connector and client.
Application object layer to open (-aol=<string>)	Layer in which to access when logging in to the AOS.

Developer Tab

`Developer license code (-aolcode=<string>)`	Provides the license code in which to access the layer.
Confirm license code	Confirms the provided license code.
Repair Client	Fixes rich client if its files or setup has been corrupted.

Tracing Tab

`Start trace (-TraceStart=1)`	This starts the trace.
`Stop trace (-TraceStart=0)`	This stops the trace.
`RPC round trips to server (-TraceEventsEnabled=1)`	The Trace Remote Procedures Calls (RPC) from client to the server.
`X++ method calls (-TraceEventsEnabled=100)`	The Trace X++ code that is invoked on the AOS.
`Number of nested calls (-TraceXppMethodCallDepth=<number>)`	This is the maximum depth in which to trace X++ method calls.
`Function calls (-TraceEventsEnabled=101)`	This traces all functions that are called on the AOS.
`SQL Statements (-TraceEventsEnabled=202)`	This traces SQL server statements on the AOS server.
`Bind variables (-TraceEventsEnabled=203)`	This traces columns that are used as bind variables.
`Row fetch (-TraceEventsEnabled=204)`	This traces rows that are returned from the SQL server.
`Row fetch summary (-TraceEventsEnabled=205)`	This traces the number of rows and time elapsed during fetching those rows from the SQL server.
`Connect and disconnect (-TraceEventsEnabled=200)`	This traces the connection and disconnection between the AOS and the database.
`Transactions: TTSBegin, TTSCommit, TTSAbort (-TraceEventsEnabled=201)`	This traces all TTS commands called by the AOS.

Performance Tab

Select the appropriate setting that tweaks the best cache performance setting for the client.

Advanced client configuration settings

Although the Microsoft Dynamics AX 2009 configuration application provides the most common parameters in which to manipulate the functions, performance, settings, and configuration of a client, and AOS instance, there are additional parameters that have been left out and can only be accessed through the command line or configuration file interface. The following table lists the advanced additional configuration parameters:

Advanced client parameters	
`Help directory (-helpDir=<path>)`	Specifies the directory in which help files are stored.
`Language (-language=<string>)`	Specifies the language.
`AOT import file (-aotimportfile=<File.xpo>)`	Imports an XPO file and compiles once the client starts. This is handy for quickly promoting code modifications across multiple environments.
`Trace file size (-TraceMaxFileSize=<number>)`	The default is 10MB. This specifies the maximum size a trace file can be.
`Trace buffer size (-TraceBufferSize=<0:64>)`	The default is 20KB. This specifies the buffer size of the trace log. The maximum possible value is 64KB.

Summary

After reading this chapter, you should have a better understanding of how the AOS can be configured. Different configuration settings help to optimize an AOS for greater performance. You should also realize that optimization of the AOS is in fact based on the purpose in which the AOS is optimized for. For example, an AOS that will be used by one or more developers will need to have debugging enabled. However, having debugging enabled is not suitable for a Production AOS since, debugging hampers performance considerably.

When determining the performance for an AOS, the key is to define the role it will play. For example, a production AOS should always perform at peak performance. Therefore, it is important to take the time to ensure that the hardware, network, and AOS parameters are setup and optimized for a Production AOS to provide the best performance possible. However, the same may not be necessary for a Development and Testing environment, which may need to have debugging, logging, or tracing enabled. All three put a strain on the performance. Repetitive testing, for bench marking purposes, will help determine if a production AOS is suitable for production use. The earlier mentioned parameters for the AOS configuration, in this chapter, will be a handy reference to tweak the performance of an AOS.

In the next chapter, we will cover the process of not only the proper recommendations for backing up a Dynamics AX environment, but also how to maintain a Dynamics AX environment once it is up and running.

12

Backup and Maintenance

The previous chapters covered the process of setting up and running Dynamics AX and its components. This chapter focuses on maintaining the integrity of Dynamics AX throughout its life cycle.

Performing the relevant maintenance tasks ensures that Dynamics AX will function at its best and minimizes potential issues that may occur with data inconsistencies. Data errors become more difficult to resolve as data inconsistencies go unnoticed. The best way to prevent data inconsistencies is to perform regular maintenance tasks such as consistency checks and synchronizations. However, in worst case scenarios, when such methods do not prevail, a database restoration may be the most appropriate solution. In this chapter, we will cover the most common maintenance tasks that should be performed on a regular basis, specifically the following:

- Backing up a Dynamics AX database, the application files, Role Centers, and Enterprise Portal
- Re-indexing
- Performing data consistency checks
- Synchronizing a Dynamics AX database

Backup

The simplest and quickest solution for many issues that may occur is recovery. Therefore, having a backup and recovery plan for Dynamics AX is not only helpful but necessary, as it is with any other system that houses critical data.

Since Dynamics AX consists of multiple base and extended server components, different components have specific backup requirements. The following sections will cover the necessary components that must be backed up for best recovery. What the following sections do not cover are the operating system recovery procedures. For specific operating system backup and recovery procedures, please consult Windows Server 2003 or 2008 documentation (`http://technet.microsoft.com/en-us/library/cc770266(WS.10).aspx`).

> The following sections are only basic examples. More advanced procedures, third-party applications, or hardware may be required, depending on your setup and implementation.

SQL Server backup

Since all the data in Dynamics AX is stored in a database, it is essential to back up the data on a regular basis. Perhaps you already have other databases that are backed up during a SQL Server maintenance job. If so, you can easily add your Dynamics AX database to your existing job. Otherwise, you can use the following process to create a new SQL Server maintenance job that will automatically back up your Dynamics AX database:

1. To back up the database, log in to the SQL Server that contains the Dynamics AX database and go to **Management | Maintenance Plans**.

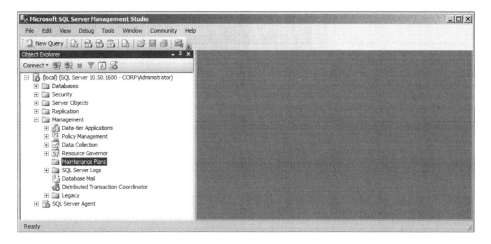

2. Right-click on **Maintenance Plans** and click on **Maintenance Plan Wizard** to create a new backup routine. (If you want to add a new database to the backup plan, right-click on an existing maintenance plan (for example, DB Backups) and click on **Modify**.)

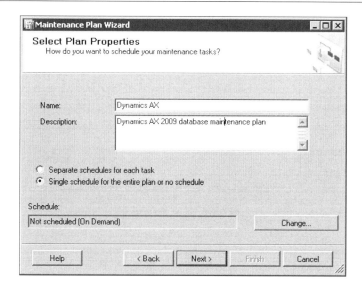

3. For the backup to automatically run during specific dates and times, you will need to create a schedule. To create a schedule, click on the **Change...** button in the **Maintenance Plan Wizard** to load the **Job Schedule Properties** window. In the **Job Schedule Properties** window, specify the desired date and time parameters for the job to occur automatically, and then click on **OK**.

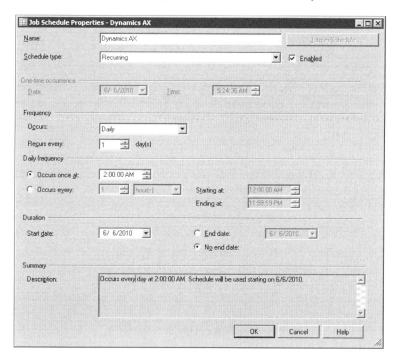

4. To proceed to the next step of the wizard, click on the **Next** button. In the following step, select the appropriate maintenance tasks. There are several tasks to select. For example, database integrity for checking if there are any data or log errors, shrinking a database for when the log file gets too big, or even rebuilding and updating the index to ensure optimal performance. All are useful tasks; however, this example has **Back Up Database (Full)** checked. Click on **Next** when completed.

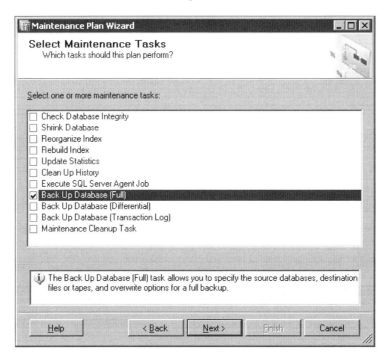

5. The next step is to specify the order for maintenance tasks to execute. In this example, there is only one task; therefore, the order does not matter. If there was more than one task to select, then the order of the tasks could be rearranged as desired.

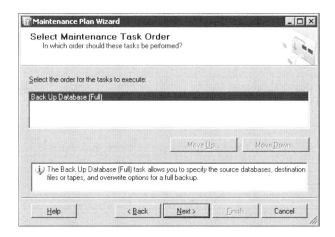

6. The next step is the configuration of the maintenance task. In this example, in the **Define Back Up Database (Full) Task** screen, select the database in which you want to fully back up as well as specify additional parameters such as backup medium, location, expiration, and schedule. Once all the desired parameters are set, click on **Next**.

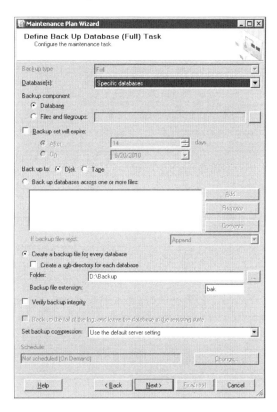

7. In the following step, specify the output method for the maintenance plan
    results and then click on the **Next** button for the final step.

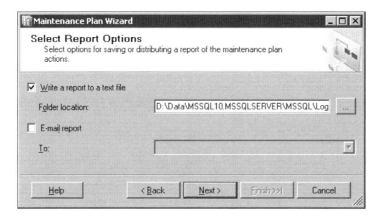

8. In the final step, review the entire maintenance plan for approval, and once
    you are satisfied, click on the **Finish** button.

There are more advanced methods that can be used as well as additional settings
that can also be tweaked, such as doing a full or differential backup to save space.
Nonetheless, the earlier mentioned steps are a simple and straightforward way to
ensure that your Dynamics AX database will be backed up automatically. Keep in
mind that backup processes may be different using third-party backup software or
hardware. In that case, you must consult the normal process of backing up
a database.

Application file backup

Since the application file directory contains critical application code such as object customizations and the label files, it must be periodically backed up. Therefore, a backup plan should be in place. Because there are many methods and applications for file backup, this section will not cover the specific methods or applications. Instead, we will back up the application files for each appropriate AOS. For example, `%Program Files%\Microsoft Dynamics AX\50\Application\Appl\AX593`, is the directory for the application files of the `AX593` AOS. The application file directory location is stored in the **Application file location** setting in the **Microsoft Dynamics AX Server Configuration Utility**. To access the setting, perform the following steps:

1. In Windows, go to **Administrative Tools** and open the **Microsoft Dynamics AX Server Configuration Utility**.

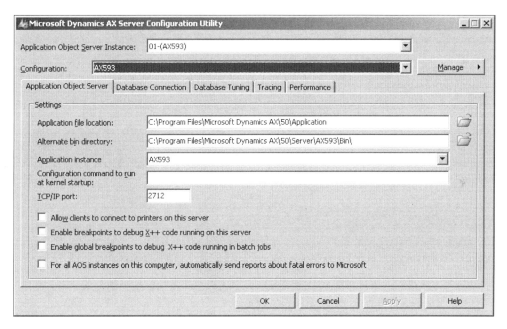

2. Select the appropriate **Application Object Server Instance** as well as the **Configuration** from the drop-down menu.

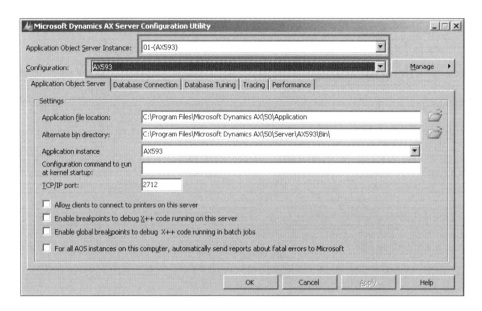

3. Verify that the **Application instance** setting is correct. If not, select the appropriate instance from the drop-down menu. Typically, the **Application Object Server Instance** setting should match with the **Application instance** setting.

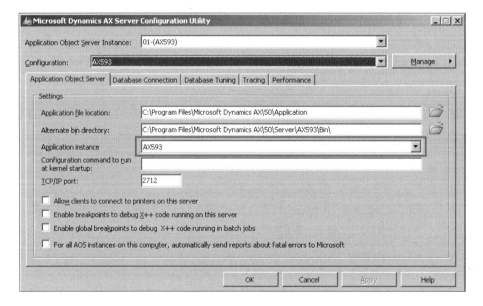

4. The application file base location is C:\Program Files\Microsoft Dynamics AX\50\Application. Yet the actual application file directory for the AX593 AOS is a combination of both the Application file location setting and the Application instance setting. Thus, the location is C:\Program Files\Microsoft Dynamics AX\50\Application\AX593. If you navigate to this directory in Windows Explorer, you will see all the application files and label files.

The earlier mentioned steps provided the method of locating the correct location to back up an application file directory for a specific environment. You can simply back up the application file base location and thus back up all the encompassing sub directories, without discriminating which environments would be backed up. However, consider that each environment may have different backup requirements or the requirements may change through an implementation. Therefore, backing up each directory individually would make sense.

Role Centers and Enterprise Portal backup

The content files for Role Centers and the Enterprise Portal should also be backed up. Typically, these files are ASP.NET files; however, depending on customizations, these files may also be JavaScript files. There is really no specific limitation as to what files should be backed up for the Role Centers and Enterprise Portal, therefore, the entire content directory should be backed up. The content directory for Enterprise Portal specific pages are stored in %Program Files%\Common Files\Microsoft Shared\Web Server Extensions\12\TEMPLATE\LAYOUTS\ep. Therefore, this directory should be part of a file backup routine.

Since the Enterprise Portal relies on SharePoint Server, it is also important to back up the SharePoint data and application files. For information regarding how to back up SharePoint, refer to the following documentation: http://office.microsoft.com/en-us/sharepoint-designer-help/back-up-restore-or-move-a-sharepoint-site-HA010069939.aspx.

The Enterprise Portal content files are contained in Dynamics AX as Managed Content web objects. However, if recovering the complete Role Center and Enterprise Portal installation, the Enterprise Portal content files will be overwritten by default, unless otherwise specified during the installation. To prevent the overwrite of the content files, uncheck the **Create Web Site** option during the installation.

Re-indexing

As tables increase in size, the time to traverse the data also increases. In a properly indexed table, the performance impact is proportional to the amount of data. However, if a table is not indexed or has not been indexed for some time, performance can be significantly hampered. Now we will cover the process of re-indexing tables in Dynamics AX:

1. In Dynamics AX, go to **Administration | Periodic | SQL Administration | Re-index**.

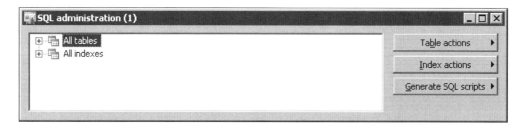

2. Select a table in the **All tables** node or an index in the **All indexes** node to re-index. If you want to re-index all tables, then select the **All tables** node. If you want to re-index all indexes, then select the **All indexes** node. When selected, click on the button **Index actions | Reindex**.

Re-indexing every table or index in Dynamics AX can take a while and consumes a lot of processing resources, thus making a system incapable of performing normal business tasks. Therefore, it is recommended that you perform this during off-peak hours. It is also beneficial to routinely re-index tables throughout the year or whenever table record counts significantly increase. This will help to ensure that Dynamics AX will operate at its best performance, especially when retrieving and viewing records.

Consistency check

Now that the process of backing up data and other critical files in Dynamics AX has been covered, the next approach is to ensure that the data is set up and operating at optimal efficiency. A consistency check can be run to ensure that data is consistent, valid, and structured correctly with the data model. For example, the consistency check tool will determine instances such as, when field data is incorrect or if field data does not exist in supported tables. If possible, the consistency check tool may also automatically fix errors; however, it is recommended that errors are fixed manually to ensure that the proper fix is applied. The consistency check tool can run across all modules or on individual modules. The following steps outline the process of running a consistency check in a Dynamics AX environment:

1. Open the **Consistency check** form in **Basic | Periodic | Consistency check**.

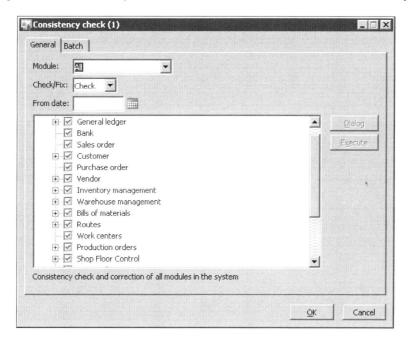

2. Select the module and specify any additional parameters, such as the date on which errors should be checked from as well as, specifying the consistency check tool to only check or fix the errors. Additionally, a query can be specified when applying the consistency check on a table by clicking on the **Dialog** button. Click on the **OK** button to run the consistency check. Once completed, the infolog will load with results of the consistency check.

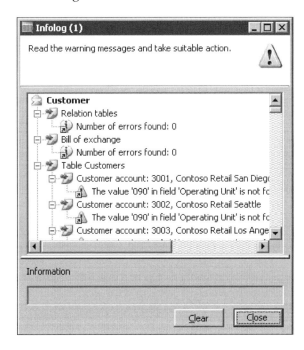

Performing a consistency check is an excellent method to validate data within Dynamics AX. This is useful to run during the initial stages of an implementation, especially after data imports, as data may not always be formatted correctly when imported into Dynamics AX.

Database synchronization

Whenever the object data model in Dynamics AX is modified, database synchronization is required. In Dynamics AX, this typically occurs automatically. However, at times it does not and at times there may be a need to manually synchronize the data model from Dynamics AX tables, fields, base enums, and extended data types, with the database. For example, if extended data types, base enumerators, tables, or field information is changed in Dynamics AX, the SQL database tables must be updated to be in sync. This may occur when the licensing schema changes in an environment or a modification is made. It is recommended to run this tool often to ensure that the data model in Dynamics AX is in sync with SQL. The following steps describe this process:

1. To synchronize Dynamics AX against SQL tables, run the **SQL administration tool in Administration | Periodic | SQL administration.**

2. Click on the **Table actions** button and click on **Check/Synchronize** to check if the Dynamics AX data model is in sync with SQL tables.

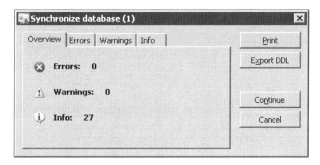

3. Then, pay special attention to any errors and warnings as they can signify data inconsistency and possible data loss. Information messages are not a concern since they do not affect data integrity or structure. If errors or warnings do exist, they must be fixed. Typically, running the synchronization fixes these issues. Since synchronization may delete fields in SQL tables, data may also be lost. Therefore, before performing synchronization, back up the Dynamics AX database in SQL. Once the database is backed up, click on the **Continue** button to synchronize the database.

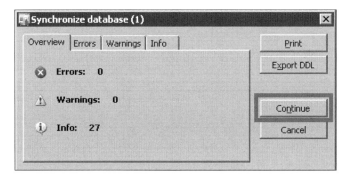

 In some instances, manual intervention may be required. For example, in common cases when tables need to be re-indexed, you would browse the tables in SQL Management Studio and delete the deprecated indexes. Once complete, run the synchronization utility again.

4. If you are successful, there will be no message. However, if the synchronization fails or encounters errors, an **Infolog** window will appear with the errors. This may require manual intervention such as going into SQL Server and modifying the data manually.

Performing a synchronization is a straightforward approach to ensuring that the underlying database is in sync with the data model in Dynamics AX. It should be noted that the synchronization is one way. Any differences in the database that do not exist in Dynamics AX, will be overwritten by the data model in Dynamics AX. Having said this, it is also a good idea to back up a database before performing a synchronization.

Summary

This chapter focused on the common processes of backing up and maintaining Dynamics AX on a regular basis. However, depending on the hardware setup, more advanced techniques may be utilized.

Regular maintenance of a system allows many benefits and should be adopted as a common practice for a Dynamics AX implementation. This will ensure that not only is the system working as efficiently as possible, but will also validate data during a consistency check. The best method of prevention is early detection. Therefore, detecting errors before they turn into issues will save time and money.

In the Appendix, we will cover additional topics on Dynamics AX administration and configuration that did not fit in other chapters, yet are still relevant to know and understand for a Dynamics AX implementation.

Appendix

Appendix A contains a combination of miscellaneous topics regarding the base server components of Dynamics AX that are beneficial for you to know for an implementation. Appendix A may also contain additional settings, configuration options, or troubleshooting techniques that extend content already explained in the previous chapters. We will cover topics such as:

- Setting up Global Search
- Creating a batch job
- Managing batch jobs
- Common troubleshooting techniques

Setting up Global Search

Global Search is a feature in Dynamics AX that allows the search capabilities across any specified table and field with the simplicity that resembles Internet search engines. Global Search not only works within Dynamics AX but in the Enterprise Portal as well, with no extra setup required. When you search for item names, customers, or any other field, the search query will return one or more links to forms or pages (if in the Enterprise Portal) that display the record for easy and quick editing.

Additionally, as with the most common internet search engines, you can search using quotes for literal matches or use Boolean operators such as AND or OR to further manipulate search queries.

To set up the Global Search feature in Dynamics AX 2009 we must set up the **Data Crawler** using the following steps:

1. Go to **Basic | Setup | Data Crawler** and open the **Table setup** form.

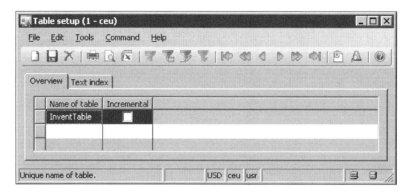

2. Select the table in which to modify which fields to search as well as additional options. To add a table to the data crawler for search capabilities, simply create a new record. Checking the **Incremental** field allows the indexing to be incremental, which is faster than recreating the search index. However, the table must have a modified data field available. If **Incremental** is selected, you cannot unselect it; rather, you must delete the line and set up the table for search from scratch. Once a table is selected, click on the **Text index** tab.

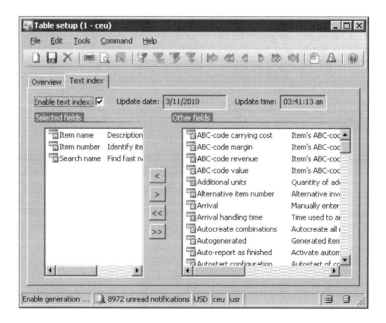

3. Select one or more fields from the right side that you want to be searchable by bringing them over to the left side.

4. Now that the fields to be searched have been selected, the next step is to imitate the data crawler to activate the global search capabilities. To do this, go to **Basic | Data Crawler | Data Crawler**.

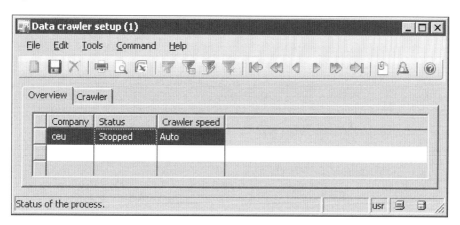

5. If steps 1 through 3 were performed correctly, a data crawler will automatically be set up but not activated for the company account that the table setup was performed in. To modify the default settings and start the data crawler, select the data crawler for the current company account and go to the **Crawler** tab.

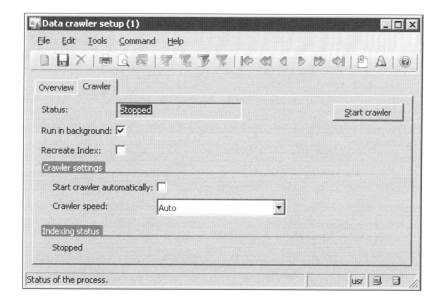

6. In the **Crawler** tab, various settings are available. If **Recreate Index** is marked, then the entire index for the table fields in the **Table setup** form will be recreated. Additionally, the **Crawler speed** may be modified. The faster the crawler speed, the more processing resources are consumed. If **Auto** is selected, only an acceptable amount of resources will be used depending on the user load. To start the data crawler automatically once the first user logs into the environment, mark the **Start crawler automatically** checkbox.

7. Once the appropriate settings are set, you can go ahead and start the data crawler. To start the data crawler, simply click on the **Start crawler** button. The effect may not be instantaneous and may take several minutes to initiate.

Creating a batch job

Automated batch jobs can be created and set up for virtually every Periodic form. Before creating a batch job, verify that the batch server is setup and running. As an example of setting up a batch job, we will create one for the **Notification clean-up** form in the **Administration** module.

The event inbox is where alerts are stored. In some instances, this table can be full of unnecessary and old alerts, which can cause issues on the Unified Work list Web part on the Enterprise Portal. This form will delete notifications from alerts based on filters specified in a Dynamics AX query.

The following steps outline the process of setting up a batch job for the Notification clean-up form, which can be adapted to any form capable of running as a batch (a form with a Batch tab):

1. Open the **Notification clean-up** form found in **Administration | Periodic | Notification clean-up**.

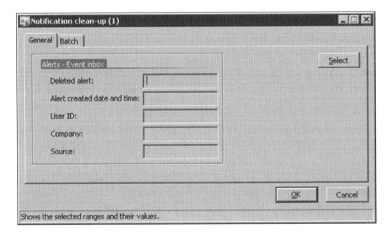

2. Click on the **Select** button to create a Dynamics AX query with appropriate filters.

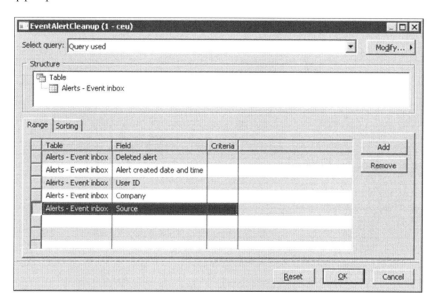

3. If necessary, you can add additional filters by clicking on the **Add** button. If nothing is specified, every record will be selected since there is no filter. In this example, we will be deleting all Workflow events. Select the **Source** line and click on the **Criteria** cell, a lookup button will appear in which you can select **Workflow**. Click on the **OK** button to apply the changes.

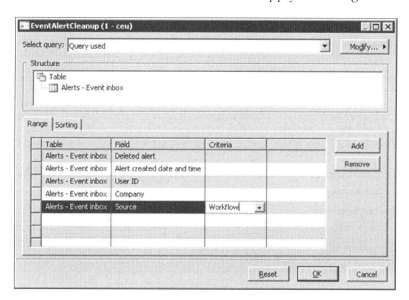

4. Now we are back in the **General** tab of the **Notification clean-up** form. **Workflow** is now listed as the source. Click on the **Batch** tab to create an automated batch job to reoccur on a specific date and time.

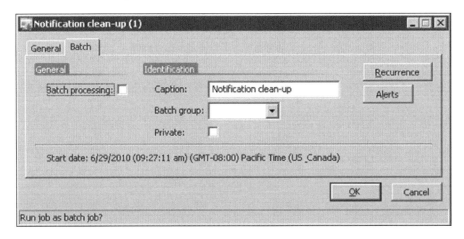

5. Select a **Batch group** from the drop-down list. To create a new batch group, simply create one in the **Administration | Setup | Batch group** form. In the **Identification** group, if the **Private** checkbox is marked, that means only the current user can run the batch job. Mark the **Batch processing** checkbox to enable batch processing. The **Recurrence** button is where you can specify when the batch job should run automatically and how many times. The **Alerts** button is where you can specify the method of alerting based on the batch job's events. Once the settings have been updated, click on the **OK** button to submit the batch job.

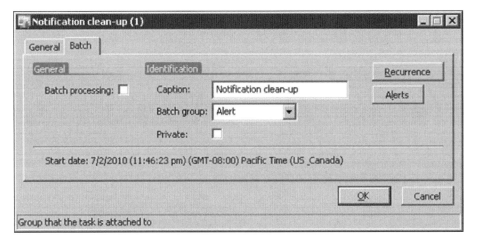

Managing batch jobs

Whether you desire to delete, modify, or troubleshoot a batch job, it all comes down to using the batch job management forms. The following section describes each form and their common uses. The forms to manage batch jobs are all located in the **Basic** module. Although the **Administration** module contains batch job forms, they are only related to the setup and not the actual management of individual jobs.

View current batch jobs

The **Batch** job form, found in **Basic | Inquiries | Batch job**, allows you to view the current status of a batch job. This form also allows you to view specific details such as the current task that the batch job is running or to modify the current state of a batch job.

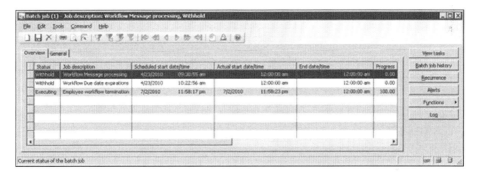

You will also notice that the **Recurrence** and **Alerts** buttons are available, similar to forms that are enabled for batch job processing. This is where you can modify and override the recurrence and alert settings that were originally specified when the batch jobs were created.

Additionally, the **Log** button provides a detailed log of the batch job in the **Infolog**; however, this feature does not provide the best view of the batch job history. Therefore, to view a detail of a batch job's history, select a batch job and click on the **Batch job history** instead. This form can also be loaded from **Basic | Inquiries | Batch job history**.

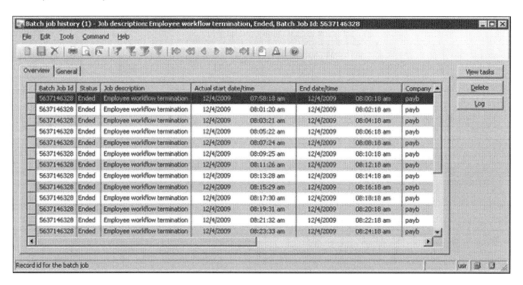

Depending on the batch job, the history of a batch job can accumulate relatively quickly and generate a large amount of log data. Perhaps, it is only necessary to log errors. To modify a batch job's log verbose level, simply select a batch job from the **Batch job** form and click on the **General** tab.

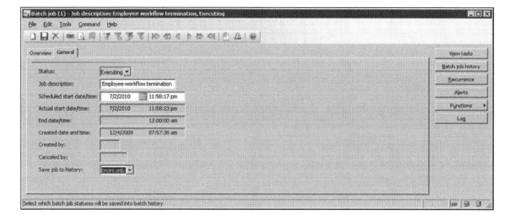

Common troubleshooting techniques

The following section contains common techniques for troubleshooting issues in Dynamics AX. These techniques are beneficial to know and may come in handy during or after the implementation of Dynamics AX. Such techniques that will be covered are as follows:

- When application modifications are not appearing
- How to troubleshoot AOS starting issues

When application modifications are not appearing

At times, the application modifications may not appear. The most common reason is that modifications were recently imported while users were logged into Dynamics AX. Typically, this happens if a user's session was open when modifications were imported. Every time a user is logged into Dynamics AX, objects will come from the Application Object Dictionary (AOD). Objects such as forms that are opened, are cached to the AOD for more rapid access. Because of this, any updates to these forms will not be updated until a user logs out and then back into their Dynamics AX session. Fortunately, there is a method to force the update of the application objects. The following steps outline this process:

1. Go to the Microsoft Dynamics AX menu found in the top-left corner of Microsoft Dynamics AX 2009 client.

2. Go to **Microsoft Dynamics AX menu | Tools | Application Objects | Refresh AOD**. Depending on the permission levels, this interface may or may not be available.

3. Allow the refresh process to run. The time may vary; however, this is typically a quick process. The following **Infolog** message will be displayed once successfully completed:

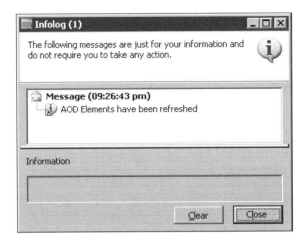

Another method for refreshing application objects is to force the rebuilding of the Application Object Index (axapd.aoi) file. This file is used by the kernel to index every object in Dynamics AX. It is automatically generated by the AOS, especially when an AOS is started for the very first time. To force the rebuild of the axapd.aoi file, follow these steps:

1. Shutdown the AOS.
2. In the AOS's Application File directory, delete the axapd.aoi file.
3. Start the AOS.

How to troubleshoot AOS starting issues

If an AOS does not start, verify that the server settings are properly setup. The best way to diagnose why an AOS does not start is to view the event log for any suspicious errors. The following troubleshooting steps will help you to determine why an AOS is not starting.

- Open the Windows Event Log and check if there are any suspicious errors. Any errors may indicate the precise issue.
- Verify that the server settings are properly set up, especially the following:
  - Application File location
  - Database server
  - Dedicated port number

B
Appendix

Appendix B contains a combination of miscellaneous topics regarding the extended server components of Dynamics AX that are beneficial for you to know for an implementation. Appendix B may also contain additional settings, configuration options, or troubleshooting techniques that extend content already explained in the previous chapters. We will cover topics such as:

- Enterprise Portal tips
- Common troubleshooting techniques
- Modifying Component Services Properties in Windows Server 2008 R2
- How to install Analysis Extensions on SQL Server Analysis Services 2008 and 2008 R2
- How to automatically process SQL Server Analysis Services Cubes
- Setting up the Enterprise Portal in SharePoint 2010

Enterprise Portal tips

The following section contains additional methods and techniques for setting up and configuring the Enterprise Portal.

Multiple instances of an Enterprise Portal in a web server

When there are multiple Dynamics AX environments set up, it would be convenient and sensible to also have a separate Enterprise Portal site for each environment. By default, this is not possible. Fortunately, with some minor modifications, you can achieve this. Prior knowledge on how to install and setup a single Enterprise Portal site is required. The following steps provide the process for setting up multiple Enterprise Portal environments on the same server. Each step must be repeated for each individual Enterprise Portal site.

1. Open the `web.config` file for the Enterprise Portal site in a text editor, such as Notepad. This is found in the root folder of the Enterprise Portal site.

2. After the `<configSections>` tag, add the following text:

```
<sectionGroup name="Microsoft.Dynamics">
      <section name="Session" type="System.Configuration.
SingleTagSectionHandler, System, Version=1.0.5000.0, Culture=neutr
al,PublicKeyToken=b77a5c561934e089" />
</sectionGroup>
```

3. After the `</system.web>` tag, add the following text and replace the **Configuration** tag's location to point to the appropriate AOS client configuration file location. This configuration file will be used to determine what AOS to connect to:

```
<Microsoft.Dynamics>
    <Session Timeout="15" Configuration="C:\ConfigFiles\DEV_AOS_
Config.axc" />
</Microsoft.Dynamics>
```

4. Restart the Internet Information Services (IIS) web server by running **iisreset** in the Windows Command Prompt to apply the changes.

Common troubleshooting techniques

The following section contains common techniques for troubleshooting issues in Dynamics AX. These techniques are beneficial to know and may come in handy during or after an implementation of Dynamics AX. Such techniques that will be covered are as follows:

- Unable to install components when there are multiple environments
- Troubleshooting techniques for Enterprise Portal issues

Unable to install components when there are multiple environments

If you are trying to install multiple Dynamics AX server bases or extended components (for example, for multiple AOSes or Enterprise Portal websites) and are unable to install the components to the desired server, simply verify that the Business Connector is pointing to the correct AOS for the components to be installed in the **Microsoft Dynamics AX 2009 Client Configuration** utility.

Troubleshooting techniques for Enterprise Portal issues

If the Enterprise Portal is installed but does not start, try restarting IIS by running **iisreset** in the Windows Command Prompt. Although simple, restarting the IIS web server service typically resolves most issues. Otherwise, you can try the following instead:

- On the web server, verify that the business connector configuration is pointing to the correct AOS in either the **Microsoft Dynamics AX 2009 Client Configuration** or in the `web.config` file.
- Verify that an Enterprise Portal site exists for the Dynamics AX environment in the **Administration | Setup | Internet | Enterprise Portal | Web sites** form.
  - ° If the site exists but is not listed in the form, manually add it.
  - ° If the site does not exist at all, proceed to follow the appropriate setup process for installing the Enterprise Portal.

Modifying Component Services properties in Windows Server 2008 R2

In Windows Server 2003 and Windows Server 2008, changing the properties of objects, such as DCOM Config objects, is a very straightforward process for an Administrator to accomplish. However, in Windows Server 2008 R2, even an Administrator cannot modify these settings. Fields remain read-only, as shown in the following example of the IIS WAMREG admin Service Properties:

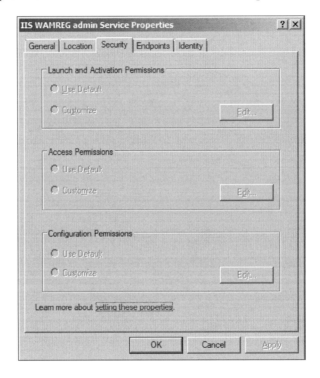

This can be confusing when performing the setup and configuration of Kerberos Authentication for IIS on a Windows Server 2008 R2 environment, as explained in *Chapter 5, Setting Up Kerberos Authentication*. Fortunately, there is a method to restore the same functionality that existed in the previous versions of Windows Server. This method is explained in the following steps for the **IIS WAMREG admin Service** whose GUID is **{61738644-F196-11D0-9953-00C04FD919C1}**:

Modifying the Windows Registry is risky and can damage your server. Be sure to make a backup of your Windows Registry before performing any modifications.

1. Open the Windows Registry editor by going to **Start | Run** and running **regedit**.

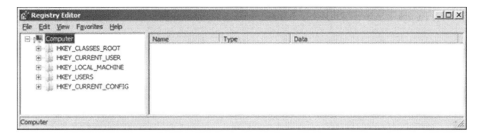

2. Navigate to **HKEY_CLASSES_ROOT\AppID\{61738644-F196-11D0-9953-00C04FD919C1}**.

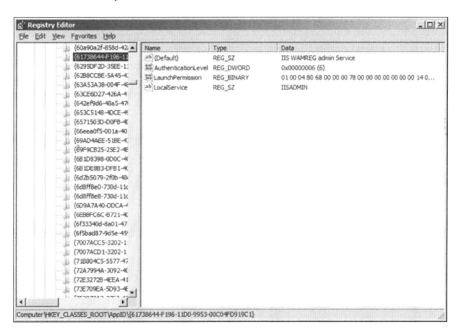

3. Right click on **{61738644-F196-11D0-9953-00C04FD919C1}** and click on
   Permissions….

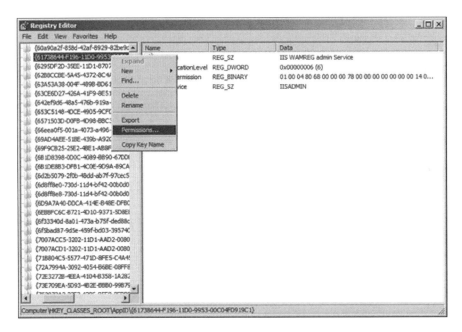

4. In the **Permissions** window for **{61738644-F196-11D0-9953-00C04FD919C1}**,
   select the **Administrators** group and click on the **Advanced** button.

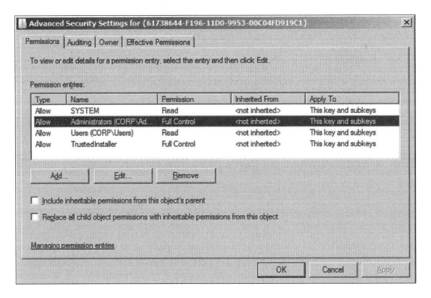

5. In the **Advanced Security Settings** window, select the **Administrators** group permission and go to the **Owner** tab.

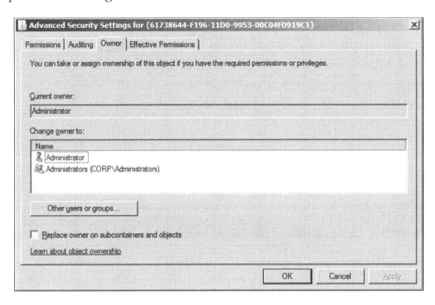

6. Select each owner listed in the **Change owner to** section, and click on the **Apply** button. This ensures that the security settings are appropriately set for the Administrator to perform administrative functions. When complete, click on the **OK** button to return to the original **Permissions** window for **{61738644-F196-11D0-9953-00C04FD919C1}**.

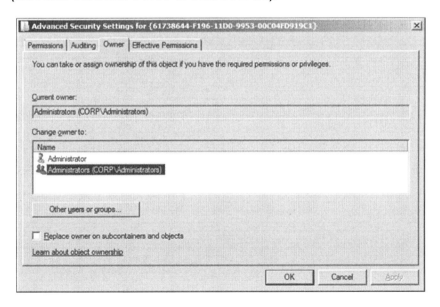

7. In the **Permission for {61738644-F196-11D0-9953-00C04FD919C1}** window, select the **Administrators** group and mark **Allow** for **Full Control** permissions and then click on **OK**.

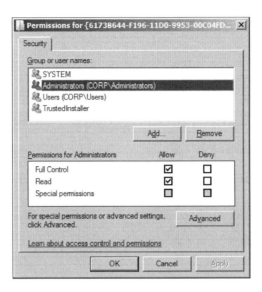

8. After performing these steps, reopen **DCOM Config** and go to the **Security** tab of the **IIS WAMREG admin Service** to modify the security settings.

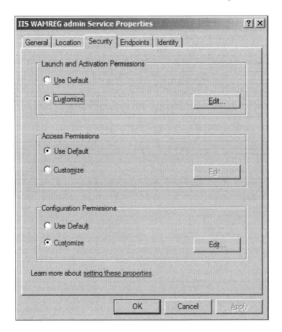

How to install Analysis Extensions on SQL Server Analysis Services 2008 and 2008 R2

The Dynamics AX 2009 installation program was designed to only install Analysis Extensions if SQL Server Analysis Services 2005 with SP2 is installed despite the fact that Analysis Extensions can work on SQL Server 2008 or SQL Server 2008 R2. To install Analysis Extensions on SQL Analysis Services 2008 or 2008 R2, you must first install it on SQL Analysis Services 2005. For example, you can temporarily install SQL Server Analysis Services 2005 on a test system. The entire process is outlined as follows:

1. Open **SQL Server Management Studio**.

2. Log in to an **Analysis Services** 2005 database that already has Analysis Extensions installed.

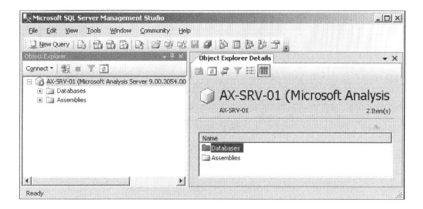

3. Select the Analysis Extensions database to copy to Analysis Services 2008/2008 R2. By default, this database is named Dynamics AX. Right-click and go to **Script Database as | CREATE To | New Query Editor Window**. You can also click on **File**—to automatically output contents to a file, or **Clipboard**—to automatically copy contents to the clipboard. This will create the XMLA definition of the Analysis Extensions database.

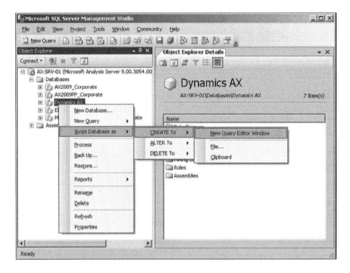

4. In the newly created query window of the XMLA definition for the Analysis Extensions database, select all the text and copy it or save it to a file. The goal is to save this definition, so that we may create the Analysis Extensions on Analysis Services 2008/2008 R2.

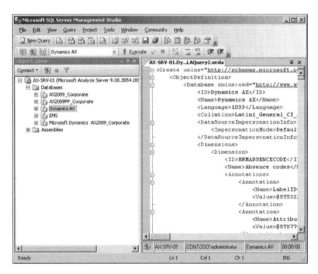

5. Now that the XMLA definition for Analysis Extensions database is saved, we can now log in to the Analysis Services 2008/2008 R2 database in the Management Studio.

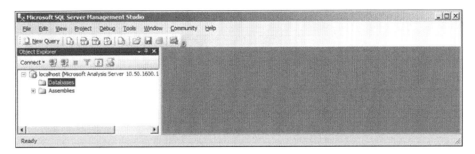

6. In Analysis Services 2008/2008 R2, create a new database by right-clicking on the database folder and clicking on **New Database...**.

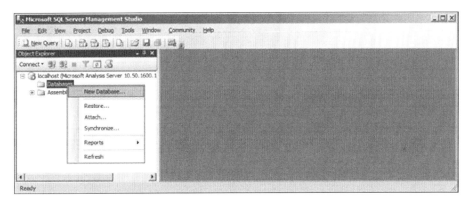

7. In the **New Database** window, specify the appropriate parameters. It is recommended that **Impersonation** remain set to **Default**. When the required settings have been specified, click on the **OK** button to create the OLAP database.

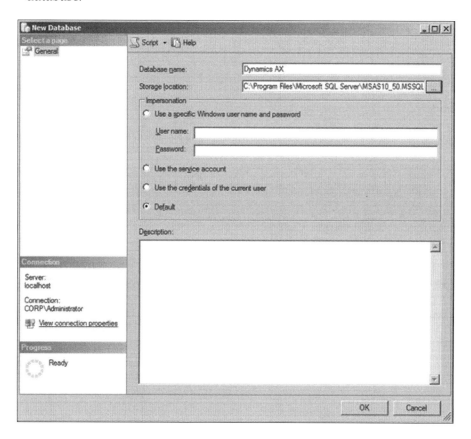

8. Now that you have created a new OLAP database on the 2008/2008 R2 version of Analysis Services, create a new XMLA query.

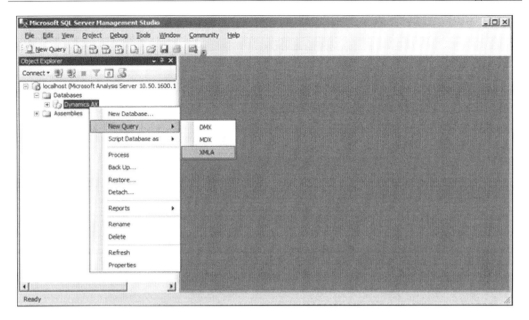

9. In the query window, open or paste the XMLA definition, generated from step 4.

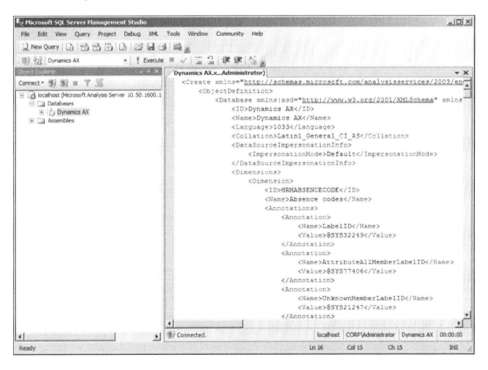

10. Execute the XMLA query by clicking on the **Execute** button or by pressing *F5*. The execution will create the Analysis Extension database. This process may take several minutes to complete.

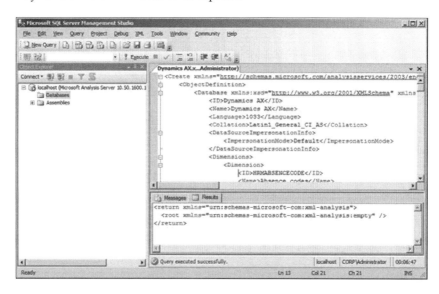

11. Now, Analysis Extensions can work with Analysis Services 2008/2008 R2. The process may also be handy for migrating and backing up OLAP databases because the entire definition of an OLAP database can be defined as XMLA.

How to automatically process SQL Server Analysis Services Cubes

In order to have the latest data presented in the Dynamics AX 2009 OLAP Reports, such as the ones contained in Role Centers, the SQL Server Analysis Services cubes must be processed regularly. Typically, processing the cubes once a day is sufficient for most basic business needs. However, for companies that utilize business intelligence more than average, this may not be sufficient. The more frequently cubes are processed, the more up-to-date that data in the OLAP reports is.

Many common automated procedures for SQL Server, such as backing up a database, can be performed by using SQL Maintenance Jobs. Unfortunately, you cannot automatically process SQL Server Analysis Cubes the same way. In order to automatically process cubes, a SQL Server Integration Services package must be created and scheduled to run as an SQL job. The following steps outline the process of automating the cubes:

1. Load **SQL Server Business Intelligence Developer Studio** (BIDS).

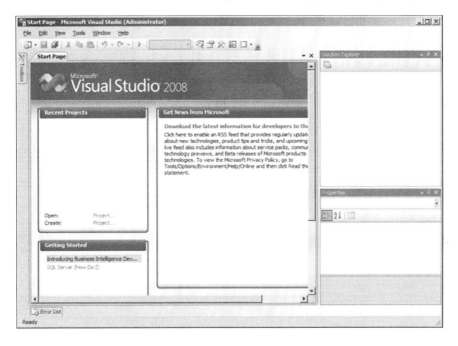

2. Create a new **Integration Services Project**.

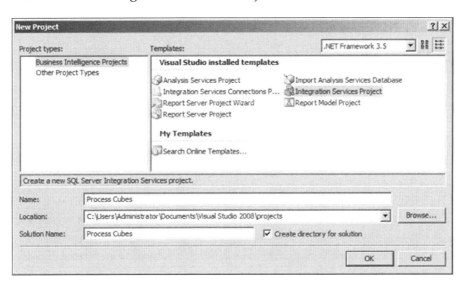

3. Add a new connection to the Integration Services Project by right-clicking on the **Control Flow** tab and click on **New Connection…** and select **MSOLAP100** for an Analysis Services connection.

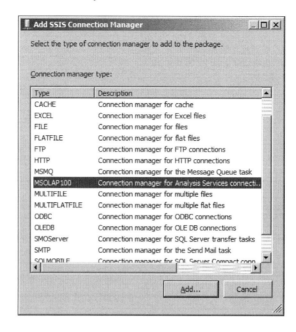

4. Provide the appropriate connection information. If the Analysis Server is on a separate server than the Database Engine and Kerberos Authentication are setup, append ;SSPI=Kerberos to the end of the connection string. To specify additional connection options and to test the connection, click on the **Edit** button.

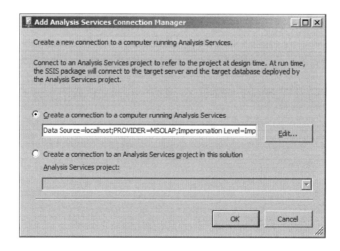

5. In the **Connection Manager** window, specify the **Initial Catalog** to the Analysis Extension's OLAP database. Test the connection to verify that it works. Once complete, click on the **OK** button to save. Then, click on **OK** in the **Add Analysis Services Connection Manager** window to finally save and create the connection manager.

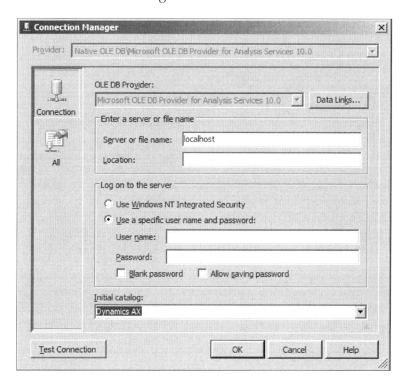

6. Now that the connection is set up, drag over an **Analysis Services Processing Task** from the **Toolbox**.

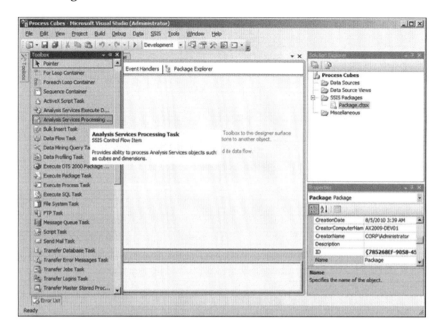

7. Right-click on the task and **Edit** the task.

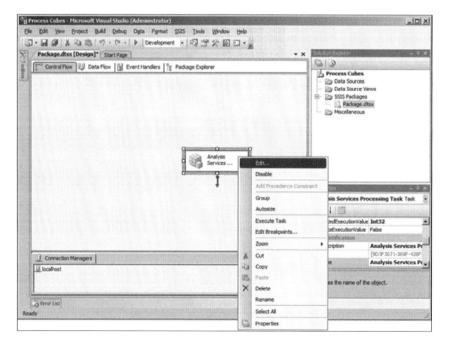

8. In the **Analysis Services Processing Task Editor**, select **Processing Settings** and click on the **Add** button to select which cubes you want to have processed.

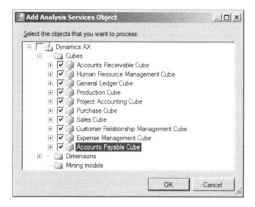

9. After you have selected the appropriate cubes to be processed and they are added to the **Analysis Services Processing Task Editor**, click on **OK** to save.

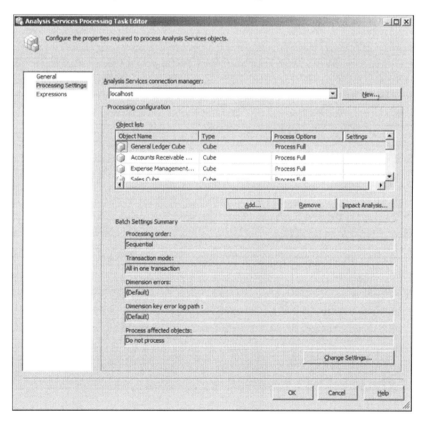

10. In **Visual Studio**, build the project by going to **Build | Build Process Cubes**.

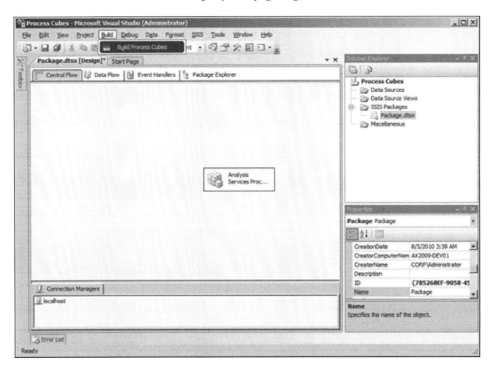

11. Once the project builds successfully, the next step would be to create a SQL job that runs the SSIS package on a specific schedule. To create a job, open the **SQL Server Management Studio** and log in to the **Database Engine** server and select the **SQL Server Agent** node.

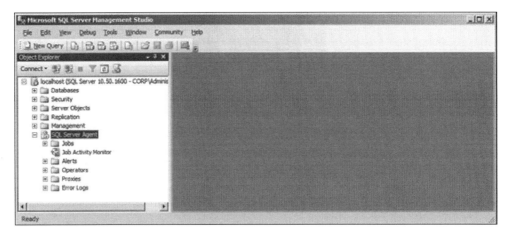

1. In the **SQL Server Agent**, right-click on the **Jobs** folder and click on **New Job...** to create a new job that will automatically process the cubes.

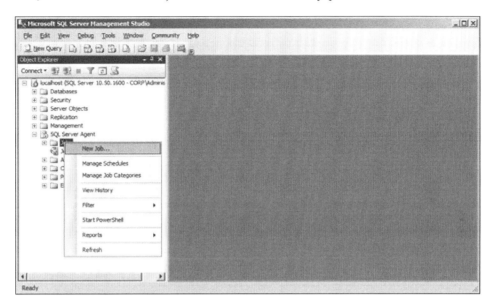

2. In the **New Job** window, in the **General** page, provide a **Name** for the job.

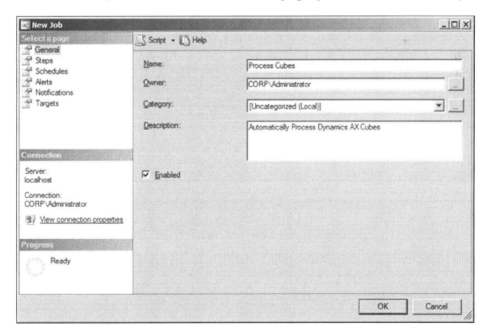

3. Select the **Steps** page and click on the **New** button to create a new job step that will run the SSIS package to process the cubes.

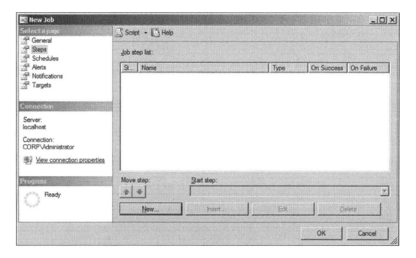

4. In the **New Job Step** window, specify a name for the step, change the type to **SQL Server Integration Services Package**, select **Package source** to be **File system,** and browse for the dtsx file that was built in Visual Studio from step. When the appropriate fields are specified, click on the **OK** button to create the step.

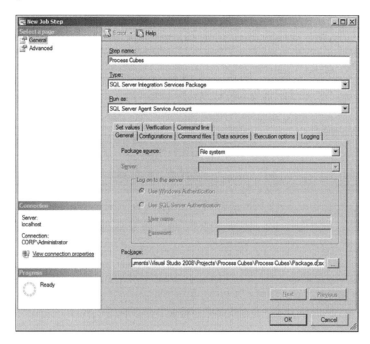

5. Now that we are back in the **New Job** screen, go to the **Schedules** page and click on the **New** button to specify a recurring date and time to process the cubes.

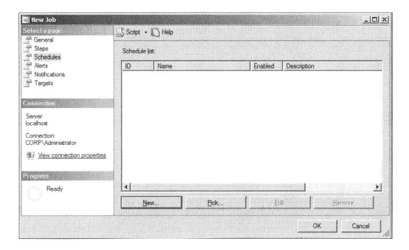

6. In the **New Job Schedule** window, provide a name, date, and time information which the job should run automatically on. Click on the **OK** button when complete to create the schedule.

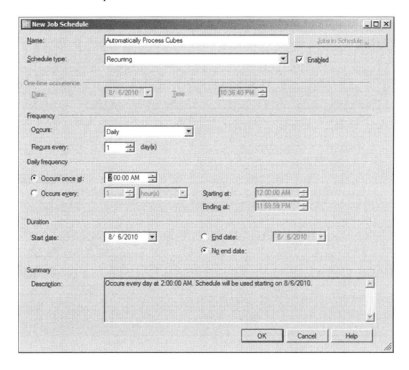

7. There are additional pages in the **New Job** window, such as providing an e-mail to contact, which can be used when a job errors or completes. To finally create the job, click on the **OK** button.

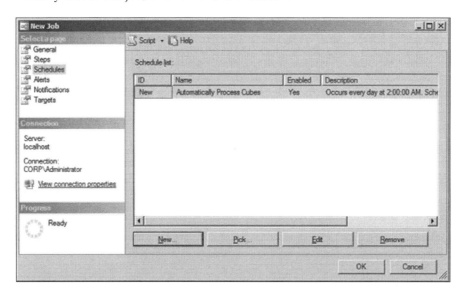

Now that the SQL Job has been created, to process cubes, the job will run the SSIS package that was created to process cubes automatically at the specified date and time.

Setting up the Enterprise Portal in SharePoint 2010

The Enterprise Portal was originally designed to work with SharePoint 2007 or Windows SharePoint Services 3.0. With appropriate configuration steps and hotfixes, the Enterprise Portal can work in SharePoint 2010 as well. It will not be until the next release of Dynamics AX where the Enterprise Portal will take full advantage of new features of SharePoint 2010, yet this does not mean you cannot benefit such as an updated user interface and better overall performance.

There are specific prerequisites that must be in place when setting up the Enterprise Portal for SharePoint 2010. The following list of prerequisites for setting up the Enterprise Portal on SharePoint 2010 are as follows:

- .NET Framework 3.5 (x64 version only)
- Windows Server 2008 SP2 or R2 Standard or Enterprise Editions
- SQL Server 2005 SP3, 2008 or 2008 R2

- SharePoint 2007 or Windows SharePoint Service 3.0 with SP2

- Hotfix Rollup 5 and Hotfix 2278963 for Dynamics AX 2009 SP1

After the earlier mentioned hotfixes have been applied, if you want to upgrade an existing deployment of the Enterprise Portal that is on SharePoint 2007 or Windows SharePoint Services 3.0 to SharePoint 2010, simply run the SharePoint 2010 installation wizard to upgrade. Otherwise, you can install the Enterprise Portal on an existing SharePoint 2010 installation.

In the following sections, we will cover the process of installing and setting up the Enterprise Portal on a new installation of SharePoint 2010:

- Creating a SharePoint Web Application

- Installing the Enterprise Portal content

Before performing the following steps, ensure that your SharePoint 2010 deployment has been fully configured.

Creating a SharePoint Web Application

1. In Windows, open the **SharePoint 2010 Central Administration** by going to **Start | All Programs | Microsoft SharePoint 2010 Products | SharePoint 2010 Central Administration**.

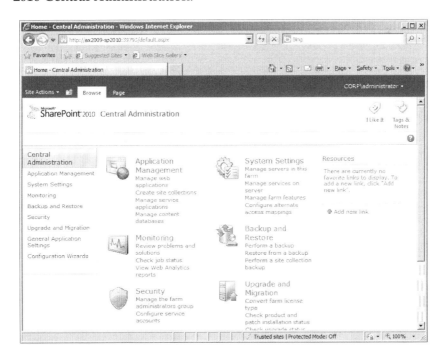

2. Under **Application Management**, click on the **Manage web applications** link to open the **Web Applications Management** page.

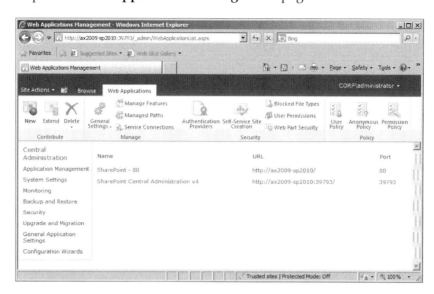

3. In the ribbon, click on the **New** button to begin the process of creating a new SharePoint application to install the Enterprise Portal on.

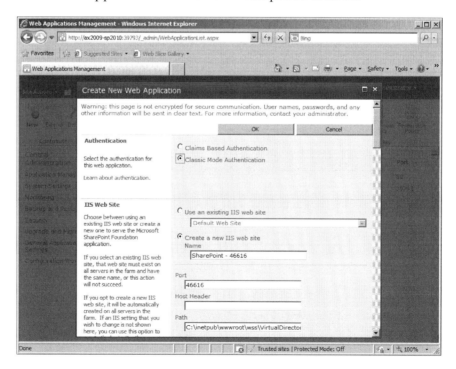

4. To easily identify the application, provide a recognizable name. In this example, the name of the AOS that the Enterprise Portal will be associated prefixes the default site name.

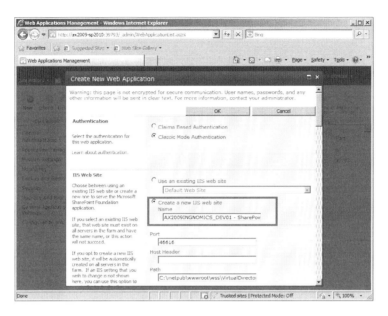

5. Under the **Security Configuration** group, ensure that **Negotiate (Kerberos)** is marked.

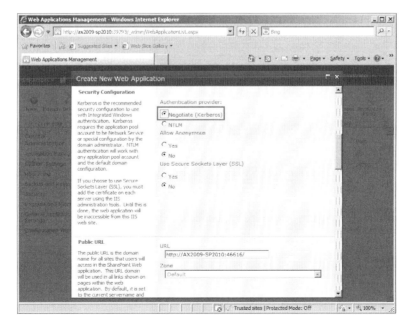

6. In the **Application Pool** section, provide a recognizable name for the site's application pool. In this example, the Enterprise Portal's AOS name has been prefixed. Also, for the **Database Name and Authentication** section, rename the **Database Name** to an easily identifiable name. For example, **WSS_ Content_<AOS Name>**.

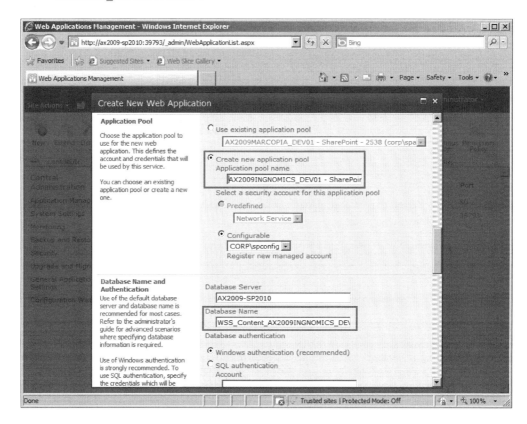

7. Under the **Application Pool** section, click on the **Regisiter new managed account** link under the Configurable drop-down. This will load the **Register Managed Account** view.

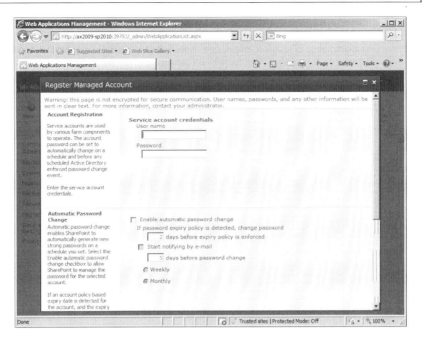

8. In the Register Managed Account view, provide the Business Connector Proxy Account username and password. When complete, scroll to the bottom and click on the **OK** button.

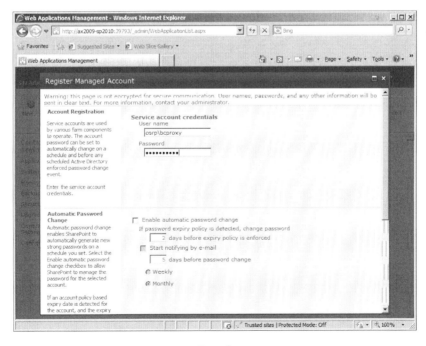

Due to a bug in the **Create New Web Application** setup process, after you click on the **OK** button in the **Register Managed Account** view, your previous settings will not be saved. Ensure that you provide the appropriate settings in the **Create New Web Application** view again before proceeding further.

9. The Application Pool security account should now be set to Business Connector Proxy Account.

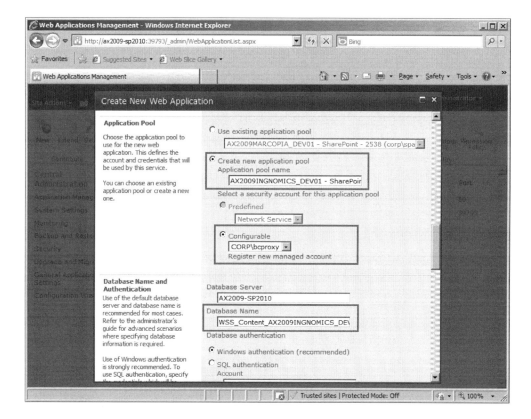

10. When complete, scroll to the bottom and click on the **OK** button to finally create the SharePoint application.

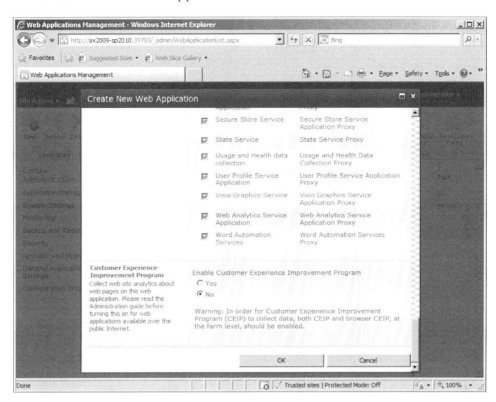

11. Now that we have created the SharePoint application, we can proceed to install the Enterprise Portal content.

Installing the Enterprise Portal content

The process of installing the Enterprise Portal content into a SharePoint 2010 application is identical to the process of installing the Enterprise Portal content into a SharePoint 2007 or Windows SharePoint Services 3.0 application. The following steps will cover the process of installing the Enterprise Portal content in SharePoint 2010:

1. Run the Dynamics AX 2009 Setup Wizard and mark the **Role Centers and Enterprise Portal** checkbox, then click on the **Next** button.

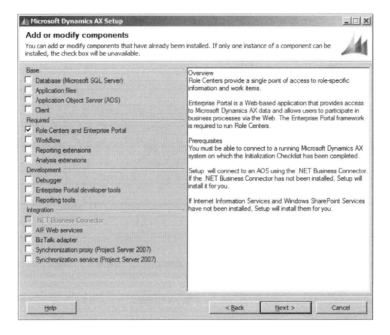

2. In the **.NET Business Connector proxy account information** step, provide the password for the Business Connector proxy account.

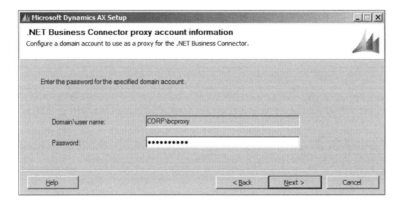

3. In the **Role Centers and Enterprise Portal framework: Configure IIS** step of the wizard, select the SharePoint application that was created in the previous section from the **Web site** drop-down list. Ensure that all the checkboxes are marked and click on the **Next** button to continue.

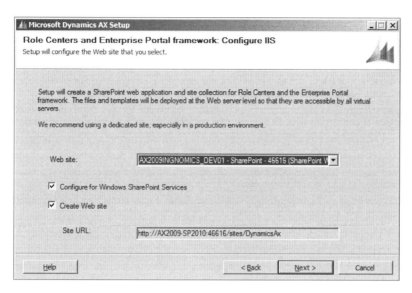

4. In the **Ready to install** step of the wizard, ensure that the **Restart IIS after installation is completed** checkbox is marked and then click on the **Install** button to finally install the Enterprise Portal content.

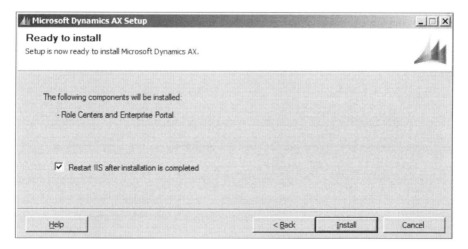

5. Ensure that the installation was successful.

If the installation was unsuccessful, mark **Open the log file when the Setup closes**. This will open the log file to further identify the reason the installation failed. If there was an error with the **SysEPDeployment** object, log into Dynamics AX and compile the **SysEPDeployment** class and re-run the Enterprise Portal setup process again.

5. Verify that the Enterprise Portal site is running by going to the Enterprise Portal site as defined in **Administration | Setup | Internet | Enterprise Portal | Web sites**.

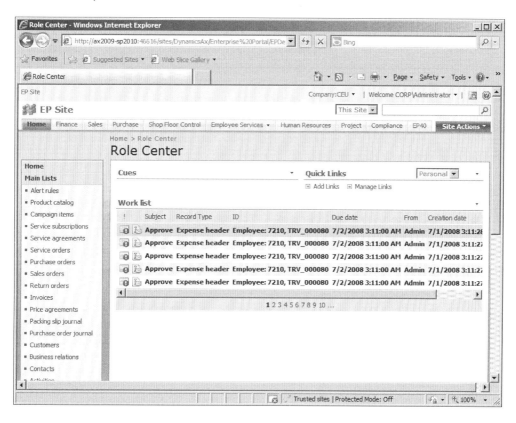

Index

B

backup
  about 307, 308
  application file backup 313-315
  SQL server backup 308-312
batch job
  additional filters, adding 327
  Alerts button 329
  creating 326
  creating, steps 328
  managing 329
  Recurrence button 329
  viewing 329
batch processing window interval
  setting up 268
Business Connector 219
Business Data Lookups (BDL) 253
businesses (B2B) 159

C

Central Administration page 109
channels, filesystem adapter
  specifying 163-168
client configuration
  accessing 298, 299
  advanced client parameters 305
  advanced settings 305
  Connection Tab 303
  Developer Tab 303, 304
  Development (DEV) 298
  General Tab 303
  modifying 300, 301, 302
  Performance Tab 304
  Production (PROD) 298
  settings 302
  Staging (STAGE) 298
  Testing (TEST) 298
  Tracing Tab 304
Code Access Security level
    (-caslevel=<enable/disable/trace>)
    292
Component Services
  setting up 121, 122
Component Services properties
  in Windows Server 2008, modifying 336-
    340

Compression disabled
    (-compressiondisabled) 292
configuration keys, Dynamics AX security
    model 220
Connect and disconnect
    (-TraceEventsEnabled=200) 291
Connection retry interval (-newconnectionre
    trydelayms=<time>) 290
Connection Tab, client configuration
  Add (-aos2=host:port) 303
  Connect to printers on the server (-us-
    eserverprinters) 303
  Delete 303
  Edit 303
  Encrypt client to server communication
    (-aosencryption=<0,1>) 303
consistency check 307, 317, 318
CreaDSN (-dsn=<portnumber>) 293
Create DSN (createdsn=<microsoftsqlserver,
    oracle>) 293
Create New Web Application page 61
Create purchase requisition form 154
Custom (comma delimited) 198

D

data
  exporting, from Dynamics AX 198
  importing, from Excel spreadsheet 204-208
Database Connection Tab, Application
    Object Server (AOS)
  Microsoft SQL Server
    (-database=<databasename>) 289
  Oracle 289
Database Server 217
Database server (-dbserver=<servername>)
    293
database synchronization 319, 320
Database Tuning Tab, Application Object
    Server (AOS)
  Allow INDEX hints in queries (-hint=<0,1>)
    290
  Array fetch ahead (-fetchahead=<number>)
    289
  Connection retry interval (-newconnectionr
    etrydelayms=<time>) 290

tips 333
user permissions, setting 246-249
Enterprise Portal backup 315
Enterprise Portal content
installing 364-366
**Enterprise Portal setup, in Load Balanced
web farm**
benefits 72
deploying, in SharePoint NLB web farm 74,
75
diagram 74
prerequisites 73
event alert batch job
setting up 262-265
event queues
automatic clean up 274, 275
manual clean up 276, 277
Excel spreadsheet
about 198
data, importing from 204-208
generating 198-204
Execute button 346
external end points, filesystem adapter
specifying 169-173

F

filesystem adapter
channels. specifying 163-168
external end points, specifying 169-173
used, to set up AIF 162
Framework (AIF) component 159
Fully Qualified Domain Name (FQDN) 99
**Function calls (-TraceEventsEnabled=101)
291**

G

General Tab, client configuration
Command to run at application startup
(-startupCmd=<command>) 303
Company (-company=<string>) 303
Configuration command run at kernel
startup (-extracmd=<command>) 303
Log directory (-log=<path>) 303
Startup message (-startupmsg=<string>)
303
global search

crawler automatically checkbox 326
Crawler tab 325, 326
Data Crawler, setting up 324
Incremental field, checking 324
setting up 323

H

hardware
Application file server, configuration 18
Application file server, requirements 18
hardware planning
AOS, requirements 18
database sizing 16, 17
items, requiring 13, 14
minimum database server requirements 17
setup scenario 17
virtualization 15
Help directory (-helpDir=<path>) 305

I

ICS 48
IIS
about 78
configuring, for Kerberos authentication
124, 126
using 22
Information Services (IIS) 218
Infrastructure Planning and Design. *See*
IPD
installation, Analysis extensions
on SQL Server 79
steps 79-82
installation, AOS
steps 48-52
installation, Dynamics AX Application files
steps 38-47
installation, Dynamics AX Client
steps 53, 54
installation, Dynamics AX database
Add or modify components screen 28
manual process 30-37
Microsoft Dynamics AX Setup installation,
running 28
New Database window 31
Securables page 37
Select Object Types window 35

S

Scaling Up Your Data Warehouse with SQL Server
URL 16
Secure Sockets Layers (SSL) 218
security keys, Dynamics AX security model 220, 221
security profiler tool
using 229-231
security requirements
for base server components 217
for extended server components 217, 218
for integration components 218, 219
security requirements, for base server components
Application File Server 217
Application Object Server (AOS) 217
Database Server 217
security requirements, for extended server components
Application Integration Framework (AIF) 219
Business Connector 219
Role Centers and Enterprise Portal 218
Service Principal Name (SPN)
configuring 99-101
setspn.exe 99
setspn -L AX2009-DEV01$ command 101
SharedLibrary.DynamicsAXOLAP data source 114
SharePoint
configuring, for Kerberos authentication 108-111
SharePoint 2010
Enterprise Portal content, installing 364, 365, 366
Enterprise Portal, setting up 356, 357
SharePoint Web Application, creating 357-363
SharePoint Application, Enterprise Portal
Business Connector proxy user, creating 65, 66
creating 58-65
SharePoint Web Application
creating 357-363

software planning
database software 22
extranet topologies 23
intranet topologies 23
large-scale topology 23
Permission requirements 24, 25
pre-selected 2009 licensing options 21
single server topology 22
small-scale server topology 22
software integration 22
SQL Analysis Services
configuring, for Kerberos authentication 112, 113
SQL Report Services connection string, setting 114, 115
SQL Reporting Services
configuring, for Kerberos authentication 111, 112
SQL Report Services connection string
setting 114, 115
SQL Server Analysis Services 2008
Analysis Extensions, installing 341-346
SQL Server Analysis Services Cubes
processing, automatically 346-356
SQL Server backup 308-312
SQL Server Database requirements
URL 16
SQL Server Reporting Services. *See* SSRS
SQL Server Reporting Services setup, Dynamics AX
steps 90-92
SQL Statements (-TraceEventsEnabled=202) 291
SSRS 82, 250
Staging (STAGE) 298
Standard (data file) 198
Start trace (-TraceStart=1) 291
Stop trace (-TraceStart=0) 291

T

TCP/IP port (-port=<portnumber>) 288
Testing (TEST) 298
Trace buffer size (-TraceBufferSize= <0: 64>) 305
Trace file size (-TraceMaxFileSize= <number>) 293, 305

X

Thank you for buying
Microsoft Dynamics AX 2009 Administration

About Packt Publishing

Packt, pronounced 'packed', published its first book "Mastering phpMyAdmin for Effective MySQL Management" in April 2004 and subsequently continued to specialize in publishing highly focused books on specific technologies and solutions.

Our books and publications share the experiences of your fellow IT professionals in adapting and customizing today's systems, applications, and frameworks. Our solution based books give you the knowledge and power to customize the software and technologies you're using to get the job done. Packt books are more specific and less general than the IT books you have seen in the past. Our unique business model allows us to bring you more focused information, giving you more of what you need to know, and less of what you don't.

Packt is a modern, yet unique publishing company, which focuses on producing quality, cutting-edge books for communities of developers, administrators, and newbies alike. For more information, please visit our website: www.packtpub.com.

About Packt Enterprise

In 2010, Packt launched two new brands, Packt Enterprise and Packt Open Source, in order to continue its focus on specialization. This book is part of the Packt Enterprise brand, home to books published on enterprise software – software created by major vendors, including (but not limited to) IBM, Microsoft and Oracle, often for use in other corporations. Its titles will offer information relevant to a range of users of this software, including administrators, developers, architects, and end users.

Writing for Packt

We welcome all inquiries from people who are interested in authoring. Book proposals should be sent to author@packtpub.com. If your book idea is still at an early stage and you would like to discuss it first before writing a formal book proposal, contact us; one of our commissioning editors will get in touch with you.

We're not just looking for published authors; if you have strong technical skills but no writing experience, our experienced editors can help you develop a writing career, or simply get some additional reward for your expertise.

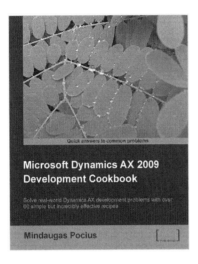

Microsoft Dynamics AX 2009 Development Cookbook

ISBN: 978-1-847199-42-3   Paperback: 352 pages

Solve real-world Dynamics AX development problems with over 60 simple but incredibly effective recipes

1. Develop powerful, successful Dynamics AX projects with efficient X++ code

2. Proven AX recipes that can be implemented in various successful Dynamics AX projects

3. Covers general ledger, accounts payable, accounts receivable, project, CRM modules and general functionality of Dynamics AX

Microsoft Dynamics AX 2009 Programming: Getting Started

ISBN: 978-1-847197-30-6   Paperback: 348 pages

Get to grips with Dynamics AX 2009 development quickly to build reliable and robust business applications

1. Develop and maintain high performance applications with Microsoft Dynamics AX 2009

2. Create comprehensive management solutions to meet your customer's needs

3. Best-practices for customizing and extending your own high-performance solutions

4. Thoroughly covers the new features in AX 2009 and focuses on the most common tasks and issues

Please check **www.PacktPub.com** for information on our titles

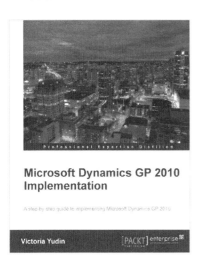

Microsoft Dynamics GP 2010 Implementation

Microsoft Dynamics GP 2010 Implementation

ISBN: 978-1-849680-32-5   Paperback: 376 pages

A step-by-step guide to implementing Microsoft Dynamics GP 2010

1. Master how to implement Microsoft Dynamics GP 2010 with real world examples and guidance from a Microsoft Dynamics GP MVP

2. Understand how to install Microsoft Dynamics GP 2010 and related applications, following detailed, step-by-step instructions

3. Learn how to set-up the core Microsoft Dynamics GP modules effectively

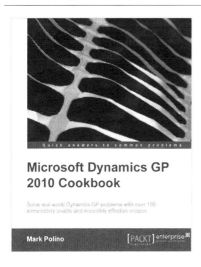

Microsoft Dynamics GP 2010 Cookbook

Microsoft Dynamics GP 2010 Cookbook

ISBN: 978-1-849680-42-4   Paperback: 324 pages

Solve real-world Dynamics GP problems with over 100 immediately usable and incredibly effective recipes

1. Discover how to solve real-world Dynamics GP problems with immediately useable recipes

2. Follow carefully organized sequences of instructions along with screenshots

3. Understand the various tips and tricks to master Dynamics GP, improve your system's stability, and enable you to get work done faster

4. Covers the new features in Dynamics GP 2010

Please check **www.PacktPub.com** for information on our titles